LIVING LANGUAGE RIGHTS

Living Language Rights: Constitutional Pathways to Indigenous Language Education

29 28 27 26 25 1 2 3 4 5

University of Manitoba Press
Winnipeg, Manitoba, Canada
Treaty 1 Territory
uofmpress.ca

For EU product safety concerns please contact Mare Nostrum Group B.V., Mauritskade 21D, 1091 GC Amsterdam, The Netherlands, gpsr@mare-nostrum.co.uk.

Cataloguing data available from Library and Archives Canada
ISBN 978-177284-114-5 (PAPER)
ISBN 978-177284-116-9 (PDF)
ISBN 978-177284-117-6 (EPUB)
ISBN 978-177284-115-2 (BOUND)

Cover Design by OTAMI–
Interior Design by Karen Armstrong

Printed in Canada

The University of Manitoba Press acknowledges the financial support for its publication program provided by the Government of Canada through the Canada Book Fund, the Canada Council for the Arts, the Manitoba Department of Sport, Culture, and Heritage, the Manitoba Arts Council, and the Manitoba Book Publishing Tax Credit.

This book has been published with the help of a grant from the Federation for the Humanities and Social Sciences, through the Awards to Scholarly Publications Program, using funds provided by the Social Sciences and Humanities Research Council of Canada.

CERTIFIED CANADIAN PUBLISHER

LIVING LANGUAGE RIGHTS

Constitutional Pathways to Indigenous Language Education

LORENA SEKWAN FONTAINE

UMP
University of Manitoba Press

CONTENTS

CONTENTS

ILLUSTRATIONS

ACKNOWLEDGEMENTS

This book is dedicated to all residential school survivors who, despite enduring abuse for speaking their ancestral language, were told those experiences could not be addressed in their residential school claims because of the unrecognized status of their language rights in Canada's Constitution. I will never forget the look of shock on their faces when they were informed that their language rights were not recognized. The injustice this experience revealed profoundly influenced my decision to pursue this work.

My research would not have been possible without the love and support of my family, particularly my mother, Doris Young, and her identical twin sister, Esther Sanderson. I am forever grateful for the numerous conversations we had about the importance of our language. They emphasized the significance of honouring relationships as an integral part of our culture and deeply rooted in our language. Many of our discussions revolved around the idea that until our communities speak the language in everyday life, schools will play a crucial role in passing it on to young people. They also asserted that youth have a right to learn their language and to reconnect with the beautiful values and teachings embedded in it. According to them, when the youth learn their language, it will restore healing and cultural pride in many communities.

I am grateful for the assistance I received from Jean Friesen, Gerald Heckman, Mark Abley, and Samara Hand in supporting my research. I would also like to express my profound gratitude to Andrea Bear Nicholas, Amos Key Jr., Karihwakeron Tim Thompson, David Leitch, and Ian Martin for their advocacy and work on language rights for more than a decade. Together, we meet regularly to discuss Indigenous language rights to education.

Special thanks to Verna Kirkness for her encouragement and the insightful exchanges we had in Winnipeg. Her leadership in First Nations Indigenous language education was instrumental in the drafting of the first Indigenous languages legislation in Canada. Her work has paved a strong path for others to follow and has personally inspired me.

I am guided by the foundational work of Violet Okemow, Helen Settee, Pat Ningewance, Helen Cook, and members of the Manitoba Native Education Concerns Group, which formed in the 1980s: Mary Richard, Ruth Norton, Flora Zaharia, Florence Painter, Clarence Nepinak, Caroline Chartrand, Verna McKay, Donna Green, Shirley Fontaine (Malcolm), Audrey Guiboche, and Joe Mercredi. I am also inspired by Aluki Kotierk, who tirelessly advocates for Inuit language rights honouring Inuit Elders' vision for their land claim agreement.

I would like to acknowledge the profound contributions of Murray Sinclair (Miizana Geezhik-Iban), whose work as Chair of the Truth and Reconciliation Commission and as a Senator laid a powerful foundation for the reclamation of Aboriginal languages across Canada. What I want to highlight is his deep commitment to creating a country where Aboriginal children can thrive in being proud of who they are. He wanted every child to grow up without ever doubting that their language and identity matter—that they are not only valid, but vital and powerful. His legacy is a gift to us all: a call to ensure that every Aboriginal child knows the strength of their culture and grows up speaking their ancestral language.

I will forever be grateful for the courageous efforts of my grandparents Elizabeth Jane Young (nee Bignell) and John Young, who risked their freedom during the residential school era to protect the Cree language and culture within our family. During a daunting and restrictive period when the government sought to erase our cultural presence through the forced removal of children, they raised fifteen children (including three sets of twins) who, remarkably, each maintained their Cree language, highlighting the resilience of our family. This taught me that the love my grandparents had for our language and culture overshadows the genocidal policies inflicted upon my family members during their time in residential schools for simply being Cree.

The arrival of my daughter, Sarah (Nimijiien Niibe Ikway), began a transformative period in my life, giving me the necessary courage I required to critically examine Canada's assimilation policy and its impact on our family and our relationship with our language. The courage came from a great sense of responsibility to provide my daughter with a strong foundation in her cultural identity and language. To accomplish this, I had to understand why my family did not pass on the language to me and to confront the silent shame I felt toward my identity and language.

PREFACE

In 2002, while completing my master's degree in law in Arizona, I would often travel to our ceremonies. During one of my trips to Minneapolis, I had a vivid dream that I had travelled to the core of the Earth. Although it was cold and pitch black, I was not scared, but I was deeply curious. I kept wondering to myself: *How did I get here? Where am I? Did I die? Am I buried alive?* Then, as I sat still in the darkness, I heard very old voices. I listened attentively to see if I could understand what they were saying. I realized they were speaking Anishinaabemowin (Ojibway language), the language we speak on my father's side of the family and the language we pray in at ceremonies. Suddenly, the mood of my dream turned serious. For some reason, I knew I had to listen carefully, even if I could not understand the words. I felt as though some part of me, on some level, understood. I closed my eyes tightly so that I could focus on feeling the sounds and the words. The melodic voices continued for some time; I am not sure how long. When I finally awoke, I sprang up feeling as though I had been submerged in water for a very long time. I was gasping for air and my heart was beating fast. I also felt extremely anxious. After I calmed myself down and my breathing resumed a normal pace, I reflected on the possible message of my dream.

Later, at the ceremonies, I approached an Elder with an offering of tobacco to have my dream interpreted. Our conversation led me to recognize that my ancestors were informing me that they continue to hover in our territory, where the spirit of our language originates, and that I remain connected to that spirit, even as a non-fluent speaker. The image of our language rooted in the earth is a powerful symbol, a testament that our language comes from and remains rooted in the soil. Upon reflection, I believed that the voices in the dream spoke of the urgency of reviving our language and that more will come.

Although the dream left me with many questions, I take dreams seriously, as do many Indigenous scholars who recognize dreams as a research methodology.[1] For me, the timing of the dream was particularly significant: it occurred shortly after I offered tobacco to enter our traditional teaching lodge, where I made a commitment to protect First Nations languages. At the time I was not sure how to accomplish this but knew that a solution would eventually present itself.

Shortly after this period and after completing my degree, I travelled back to my maternal community, the Opaskwayak Cree Nation in Canada. I planned to stay for a year to reconnect with my family and learn to speak Cree. During this time, I realized the legal implications and inequalities present in Canada's Constitution regarding the right to language transmission.

A Constitutional Gap: First Nations Rights to Language Transmission in Canada

A few months after my move home, I travelled to Vancouver with my mother. I visited my sister while my mother attended a conference on residential schools. On the last day of the conference, I agreed to pick up my mother. When I arrived at the conference venue, I was surprised by the tension in the room as several First Nations people, government and Church officials, and lawyers hovered around a very large table talking heatedly about the loss of language and culture. Some of the lawyers for the government were adamant that because First Nations language rights were not legally recognized in Canada's Constitution, they would not likely be entitled for compensation. I recognized the injustice that was embedded within this perspective. I had just completed two years of studying international law, which recognizes language transmission as a fundamental human right. International law also recognizes the specific language rights of Indigenous peoples in education. Clearly Canada, as a signatory to international treaties that recognize language rights such as the International Covenant on Civil and Political Rights, could not claim that First Nations people have no legal rights to language transmission.

Shortly after the conference, I had an opportunity to assist with a class action suit on residential schools. It was during a time when thousands of First Nations people were filing lawsuits against the federal government and the churches, seeking compensation for sexual and physical abuses. First Nations people were also seeking reparations for their loss of language and culture. Some of the claimants recommended a global fund to support language revitalization, while others wanted the international community to recognize the Canadian federal government for committing genocide by destroying the cultural identity and language of First Nations children through "education." In most cases, First Nations people wanted their grandchildren and great-grandchildren to be able to learn their ancestral mother tongue, as a form of reparation and, more importantly, as an assurance that their languages would be revitalized. Compensation was seen as one of many necessary steps for First Nations language revitalization. Most importantly, the discussions First Nations people had during this time about loss of language uncovered a gap that exists in Canada's constitutional law.

The federal government's position during the residential school settlement negotiations remained similar to their position identified during the residential school conference in Vancouver: because First Nations languages, at the time, were not recognized under Canada's Constitution, the federal government had no legal obligation to provide redress or support for First Nations language revitalization. No government representatives during this time considered how section 35 of Canada's Constitution Act, 1982, which recognizes Aboriginal rights, might influence this issue.[2] In Canada, there are eleven Aboriginal language families, each contributing to the country's rich linguistic tapestry. This diversity underscores the importance of recognizing and preserving the unique cultural and linguistic identities of each First Nation in Canada. The federal government chose not to respond to these legal implications but instead included compensation for loss of language and culture in the Common Experience Payments provided to all former students of federally recognized schools. This "solution" did not address First Nations' legal rights to language transmission, nor did it provide an adequate remedy to their residential school claims. Unfortunately, the negotiated Residential School Settlement Agreement (Settlement Agreement) resolved many residential school claims without adequately dealing with the loss of language and culture.[3]

The government's position on First Nations language rights during this period reminded me, and still reminds me, of a time not so long ago when Canada refused to recognize First Nations rights to land. It took a Supreme Court of Canada decision to radically change that perspective.[4] Although there are many issues with using the courts to define First Nations rights, history does suggest that a positive court decision on First Nations rights can force government to act. In this case, the government's limited position on First Nations language transmission resulted in very little action on residential school claims of language and cultural abuse.

The Legacy of Residential Schools: A Personal Story

As I pondered the significance of these inequalities, I became curious about the implications it had on my generation, most of whom do not speak their ancestral language(s). I started to recognize that many First Nations families today question the value of language, particularly in the education of their children, fearing that First Nations language programs "will negatively impact their children's ability to succeed in their academic programs which are written and delivered in English (or French)."[5] First Nations communities worry not only about their children's success in postsecondary institutions but also about their future employment opportunities if their education focuses on learning to speak, read, and write in a First Nations language. Consequently, a number of First Nations communities and certain segments of Canadian society more generally question whether there is any value at all in teaching First Nations languages to children. Some First Nations leaders will assert publicly the importance of language to cultural identity and then fail to implement First Nations language education in their home territory. Part of the issue is that many leaders are inundated with meeting basic human needs such as access to housing and safe drinking water. Another challenge arises from the internalized shame that many First Nations people still carry from decades of assimilation policies that suggest First Nations languages and cultures do not matter or have no future in society. In reaction to these attitudes and responses, a First Nations organization in Manitoba working in areas related to First Nations language transmission developed a pamphlet entitled *First Nation Languages: Why We Need Them*.[6] The pamphlet attempted to promote the importance of First Nations languages by claiming they are critical to the cultural identity and well-being of the First Nations people.

Recognizing internalized shame and fear associated with language transmission can often be a first, yet complicated, step toward reviving First Nations languages. At the same time, it is also challenging to create an environment for language use to occur in everyday life again. First Nations families along with the federal and provincial governments and public servants all bear a responsibility in supporting First Nations language use and transmission. It's crucial for society to understand that complacency contributes to the decline of First Nations languages, perpetuating a legacy of shame that impacts both First Nations communities and society as a whole.

For me, addressing shame began with acknowledging its presence within me. I also had to delve into my family history to uncover the factors that had impacted our relationship with language. In the process, I gained several important insights. I immediately recognized startling differences among the generations. I also recognized how the attitudes of my generation came to be so different from those of my grandparents and even my parents, and the effect this has on language transmission today.

My grandparents valued our language immensely, but my parents' generation did not pass on the language to my generation. They were reluctant to speak Cree around us, often hiding it during family gatherings by turning their backs when discussing things they did not want us to hear, or simply switching to English. As a result, my cousins, siblings, and I never learned our language. The silence around our cultural identity created a sense of shame and left us with unanswered questions about our Cree and Ojibway identity, as we did not have an opportunity to learn about it at home or at school.

While I was growing up, my mother and father spoke English to my siblings and me. During family gatherings, Ojibway (or Anishinaabemowin, my father's first language) and Cree (Ininimowin, my mother's first language) were spoken intermittently, and only among the adults. When my maternal grandparents were around, everyone spoke Cree, as my grandmother did not speak English and my grandfather rarely did, although he could. French was introduced into my life in the 1970s, when my parents decided to register me in a French immersion school, where I remained until high school.

In some respects, the multilingual instances at home resembled many immigrant homes where the children speak the dominant languages of the country and the grandparents continue to speak the language of their home country, while the parents form a bridge between the two languages and cultures. Significantly, however, my family is not new to Canada—we are "indigenous" to this country and so are our mother tongues. There was always a veil of shame that was cast over my family when they spoke in Cree or Ojibway, which I internalized.

The language challenges my family has encountered resonate with the experiences of numerous Aboriginal families across Canada. Data from the 2021 Canadian census reveals a concerning and declining trend in traditional language usage among Aboriginal peoples. The census showed a 4.3 percent decline from 2016 in the number of Aboriginal people who can converse in an Aboriginal language, dropping by 10,750 people to 237,420.[7] Additionally, there was a reported 7.1 percent decrease in the number of people learning their ancestral language as their first language at home, falling by 14,120 to 184,170 people.[8] This data highlights the ongoing challenges in the preservation and revitalization of traditional languages within Aboriginal communities in Canada. There are also very few people under the age of forty who are fluent in their ancestral language (there are exceptions in Nunavut and other regions of the country). I never questioned the implications of these types of statistics until I related them to my family.

My maternal grandparents and mother were both from generations whose dominant language was Cree. At that time, our home community had very few individuals who communicated in English when they were young. Although my maternal grandparents are no longer alive, their persistence in keeping the language alive reminds us how much can change in one generation. Many people from my parents' generation (over the age of seventy) continue to speak their ancestral languages but have not passed them on to their children. Both my parents' and grandparents' generations attended residential schools, where they experienced shaming of their Cree and Ojibway cultural identities and physical punishment whenever they spoke these languages. Teachers and administrators used shaming to teach children that First Nations languages and culture were immoral or sinful; they used physical punishment to instil fear and provide an ongoing deterrence. As a result, my parents and their siblings left residential school as young adults feeling ashamed of their cultural identity and afraid to speak their ancestral language. Language transmission of my ancestral languages stopped within this generation.

Consequently, very few people of my generation speak their ancestral language, and even fewer in my daughter's generation. The assault on First Nations language transmission has also harmed the Elder-youth relationship in my family. Regrettably, I was not able to get to know my grandparents very well because they only spoke Cree. I feel enormous loss because I could never tell them that I loved them or that I cherished them. As a child, I never learned about our teachings, our relationship to the land, or our family history on the trapline. My parents and their siblings also had an unhealthy relationship to our language and consequently lost an opportunity to be close to their parents as well as the traditional knowledge they carried. My parents did not share our ancestral language with my siblings and me because they were too afraid and ashamed to speak their mother tongue around children.

As I reflected on my family history, the vision in my dream during ceremonies, and my experiences with residential school claims, I began to understand the deep-seated impact of shame directed toward First Nations languages. This shame, rooted in racist ideologies toward First Nations cultures and peoples, is alarmingly widespread. It has historically hindered both First Nations and non–First Nations people from either supporting or promoting First Nations languages and continues to do so. Motivated by this realization, I embarked on extensive research, going beyond my personal experiences to explore the broader consequences of assimilation policies in education and the persistent shaming that affects the transmission of First Nations languages. I discovered that the impact of this history extends beyond First Nations communities; it also includes broader Canadian society's lack of awareness or recognition of the country's original languages, and general ignorance about the history and significance of these languages.

When European settlers first arrived, they were met with a diverse range of First Nations languages, each embodying laws that upheld and revered their distinct cultural identity. The settlers faced the complex challenge of not only learning these languages but also understanding the unique engagement and communication protocols of First Nations. They needed to grasp varied norms and protocols to effectively establish their presence and prosper in First Nations territories. It's noteworthy that First Nations languages have not been transmitted anywhere beyond the continent (unlike French, Spanish, English). My exploration into this overlooked history revealed a startling lack of comprehensive documentation on language transmission. Moreover, the constitutional history of Canada largely omits the vital role of First Nations languages in the formation of the country.

The primary focus of this book is on the transmission of First Nations languages. "First Nations" is a term used to refer to one of three recognized Indigenous peoples in Canada, alongside Inuit and Métis Peoples, but terms like "Aboriginal people" and "Indians" will be used when discussing constitutional and treaty rights more generally. The term "Indigenous peoples" will be used when referring to international contexts. It is important to recognize that "Aboriginal people," "First Nations," and "Indians" are constitutional terms coined by the Canadian government. These terms were established within a context that overlooked the distinct identities of the First Nations as well as those of Inuit and Métis peoples. This conscious oversight has significant implications for the constitutional status and linguistic sovereignty among these nations.

The personal stories in this book are my own, and I do not claim that they represent the experiences of all First Nations people from my generation or any other. Writing these personal narratives is my attempt to humanize the content and give voice to personal experiences with language loss and harm. It's important to acknowledge that these experiences can be deeply traumatic, and that they significantly impact the identity and relationships of First Nations people. In many cases, the trauma associated with speaking these languages—particularly as a result of the residential school system and other oppressive policies across Canada—has significantly hindered our ability to pass on our languages in our communities.

INTRODUCTION

FOUNDATIONS OF FIRST NATIONS LANGUAGE TRANSMISSION

Mii go gewiin maabam Mnidoo gaa-zhi-miin'goying iihow ji-naadziiying iihow nake mii gaa-zhi-miin'gozying iihow gegoo enweying.

For it was the Creator who gave to us this way of life and blessed us with this way of speaking.

Aapji shpendaagwad maada enweying ge-giinwind ji-kendmang ji-moozhtooying geget gwa nishnaabewiying.

This beautiful language is worth more than anything and is what truly lets us know and feel what it means to be Nishnaabe.[1]

Mii ezhi-yaamgal iihow nishnaabemyin mii go ge-zhi-moozhtooyin iihow eyaawiyin geget gwa.

This is how it is when you are speaking the Nishnaabe language, you can truly feel who you are.[2]

First Nations languages, although as different from each other as the many languages of Europe, are largely languages of relationship. According to customary law it is in speaking their language that people can be certain that their way of thinking reflects the values and teachings that were provided to them at the beginning of time.[3] The languages share common characteristics with languages around the world because they are social creations and involve social interactions. First Nations languages are particularly critical to First Nations cultures because they provide a foundation for social order within communities. They are embedded within value systems that inform kin responsibilities between mother and daughter, father and daughter, grandparent and grandchild, siblings, and extended family through generations.[4]

First Nations languages also shape the relationship and responsibilities of First Nations to the living environment.[5] As the intimate connection of the people to the land has evolved, so have the dialects. Hence, First Nations languages are just as diverse as the Canadian landscape itself, deeply rooted in the soil much like the trees and plants that inhabit the land. Sabrina Williams, an intergenerational survivor of residential schools, so eloquently explains the connection between language, relationships, culture, and identity: "All things that are attached to language: it's family connections; it's oral history; it's traditions; it's ways of being; it's ways of knowing; it's medicine; it's song; it's dance; it's memory; it's everything, including the land. Because when I listen to people speak our language I can hear, start to hear where it might have come from."[6]

For First Nations peoples, language also has a spiritual significance because Creator presented language to people. It therefore embodies a unique relationship to Creator and a profound world view of "attitudes, beliefs, values and the fundamental notion of what is truth."[7] Language scholars generally agree that there are spiritual and sacred aspects of language. Herman M. Batibo, linguist and author of *Language Decline and Death in Africa*, states that "the significance of language in human life is that it is central not only to our social interactions and relationships but also in distinguishing us and enabling others to ascertain our positions in society."[8] Similarly, the late Joshua Fishman, a prominent sociolinguist, asserted that language holds a spirit or soul.[9] Fishman also indicated that language represents a moral order, and for some "the heart of morality itself, morality that one can hear and see and feel, even as one brings it forth from one's self."[10] These scholarly perspectives on language emphasize its spiritual nature and shed light on the vital connection between language transmission and the essence of human experience.

Given this deep spiritual and cultural significance of language, colonial efforts to suppress Aboriginal languages were strategic. Europeans viewed these languages as barriers to their colonial ambitions of land acquisition and control. They believed that, if First Nations peoples retained their distinct languages and cultures, it would be more difficult for settlers to claim the land and its resources. In response, colonial governments implemented deliberate policies to eradicate First Nation languages.[11] These measures were designed to weaken the cultural integrity and dismantle the identities of First Nations peoples, thereby facilitating expansion and European settler control.[12]

Colonial language suppression was not unique to Canada. Genocidal policies and systemic discrimination against Indigenous peoples have occurred globally through legal frameworks as well as through education systems.[13] Across various countries, laws and policies have had profoundly detrimental impacts on Indigenous languages. Rodolfo Stavenhagen, former UN Special Rapporteur on the rights of Indigenous peoples, has pointed out the damaging consequences of assimilationist policies embedded in mainstream education. These issues persist today, with Indigenous children still lacking access to education in their own languages and cultural frameworks, which contributes to the ongoing erosion of their cultural heritage. In the words of Stavenhagen: "It is clear that such [assimilationist] education has been largely successful, since over the years the dominant or hegemonic society succeeded in assimilating large segments of the indigenous population through public or missionary schools. At the same time, such education has served to accelerate the transformation and ultimate disappearance of indigenous cultures, and over time a great many indigenous languages have continued to vanish."[14]

Recent research also demonstrates that denying Indigenous children education in their ancestral language can significantly hinder their development, exacerbate poverty, and contribute to a range of psychological issues. Education policies that overlook or ignore Indigenous languages and cultures have been linked to social disruption, as well as to psychological, cognitive, linguistic, and educational harm.[15] Scholars and advocates have identified these impacts as forms of linguistic and cultural genocide given their role in systematically eroding Indigenous identity.[16]

Understanding the profound impact of these issues, many countries now recognize the need for significant language revitalization efforts. Expert analyses conservatively estimate that over half of the world's languages may become extinct by the year 2100, with Indigenous languages at particular risk.[17] The United Nations Permanent Forum on

Indigenous Issues has highlighted the loss of Indigenous languages and cultures as the most pressing challenge Indigenous peoples face today.[18] In response, UNESCO has declared 2022 to 2032 as the International Decade of Indigenous Languages.[19] This initiative aims to draw attention to the threat to these languages and encourage countries to provide necessary resources and support for language revitalization, particularly in education.

Many Indigenous communities are seeking ways to ensure their children can learn in their ancestral languages and are striving to create culturally supportive environments where their language can be reintegrated into community life. Recognizing the right to language transmission within domestic law is an essential step. While legal rights alone will not ensure the revival of languages, they are crucial in securing the needed resources and support for revitalization, especially in the educational system.

In 2015, the Canadian federal government implemented Aboriginal language legislation. Following months of community engagement sessions with First Nations, Inuit, and Métis leaders for co-developing of the legislation, the federal government implemented Bill C-91, known as An Act Respecting Indigenous Languages (the Indigenous Languages Act) in 2019. Section 6 declares that Aboriginal language rights are recognized and affirmed by section 35(1) of the Constitution Act, 1982, as an Aboriginal and treaty right. However, the legislation does not provide a concrete definition of language rights, posing a challenge in understanding the extent of these rights for First Nations. Furthermore, Bill C-91 lacks any specific obligations for the federal government, such as funding for language education.

Since the 1980s, the way Aboriginal and treaty rights are defined in Canada has mainly been shaped through court rulings. A significant decision by the Supreme Court of Canada in 1996, known as the Van der Peet case, set a standard for defining Aboriginal rights. This case revolved around a Sto:lo woman's right to sell fish. The court established that for an Aboriginal practice to be constitutionally protected under section 35, it must be a practice, custom, or tradition central to the Aboriginal people's culture. The Supreme Court emphasized that these Aboriginal practices should be key elements that distinguish their culture.[20] Additionally, the court acknowledged that Aboriginal people have the right to uphold and evolve the fundamental elements of their ancestral cultures.[21] A critical aspect of the court's definition is that these customs, practices, and traditions need to have historical roots that go back before European contact. In the Van der Peet case, Justice L'Heureux-Dubé further clarified that the evolution of Aboriginal rights also includes activities aimed at preserving Aboriginal societies. She stated that any practices, traditions, and customs closely tied to the identity and survival of Aboriginal societies should be considered for protection under section 35(1).[22] This case and its interpretations have significantly influenced how Aboriginal rights are understood and applied in Canada.

Prior to the implementation of the Indigenous Languages Act, a significant hurdle in promoting Aboriginal language rights was that there was no express right to Aboriginal languages in Canada's Constitution. Presently, section 35(1) of the Constitution Act purports to recognize Aboriginal rights, but it offers minimal direction on what exactly it is intended to protect. The text of sections 35(1) and (2) reads:

> (1) The existing aboriginal and treaty rights of the aboriginal peoples of Canada are hereby recognized and affirmed.
>
> (2) In this Act, "aboriginal peoples of Canada" includes the Indian, Inuit and Métis peoples of Canada.[23]

With Aboriginal languages now recognized as an Aboriginal and treaty right under section 35(1), the critical question arises: What does the constitutional right to Aboriginal languages entail or guarantee?

According to John Borrows, Indigenous legal scholar and member of the Chippewa of the Nawash First Nation in Ontario, the *suis generis* framework of section 35(1) emphasizes that Aboriginal law and common law principles must collaboratively inform the standards of judgement for Aboriginal rights.[24] This stipulation recognizes the history of language transmission that is deeply rooted in Aboriginal legal traditions.[25] Additionally, the inter-customary practices of language transmission developed between European settlers and Aboriginal people serve as an additional interpretative tool.[26] Moreover, in the context of Canada's current period of reconciliation, driven by the acknowledgement of genocidal policies that aimed to eradicate Aboriginal languages, there is a heightened responsibility to rectify this history and address the endangerment of Aboriginal languages.

Brian Slattery, a constitutional scholar, highlights the process of decolonization that Canada is currently undergoing. He encourages us to think about and apply Aboriginal law in the context of

> the diverse roles that Indian, Inuit, and Metis peoples have played in the formation of this country and its Constitution. . . . Aboriginal people should be viewed as active participants in generating the basic norms that govern us—not as people on the fringes, helpless victims, or recipients of constitutional handouts from the government or courts, but as contributors to the evolution of our Constitution and most fundamental laws. In short, aboriginal conceptions of law and rights really count—not as curiosities of another time and place or as the denizens of exotic legal pigeonholes, but as a fundamental part of our living traditions.[27]

This implies that First Nations law provides significant and relevant interpretative principles for both historical and modern constitutional language rights related to language transmission in Canada. Slattery argues that Aboriginal language rights could be considered a "generic right," as they are fundamentally linked to the cultural identity of all Aboriginal people.[28] Additionally, he suggests that the the ability to pass a language on to future generations can be viewed as a right to cultural integrity, in line with a more contemporary understanding of Aboriginal and treaty rights. He goes on to argue that Aboriginal people likely have a constitutional right to use their ancestral languages and to access educational and cultural institutions necessary for maintaining and developing these languages.[29]

Canadian language rights scholars such as Denise Réaume and Leslie Green argue that the foundation of language rights extends beyond safeguarding effective communication—it must also recognize the intrinsic value of language. Réaume emphasizes that far from being merely a tool for communication, language holds inherent value and should be acknowledged as such in the framework of language rights.[30] Green adds that language is not just a means for coexistence; it is a constitutive element of our shared existence—an indispensable aspect of human life.[31] Language serves as a conduit for participating in communal forms of human creativity and is an integral part of human existence.[32] Both Green and Réaume contend that language rights in education play a pivotal role in supporting and perpetuating language transmission, enabling children to actively engage in their cultural traditions and community life.[33]

The recognition of language rights of Indigenous children to educational institutions is recognized in article 14 of the United Nations Declaration on the Rights of Indigenous Peoples (UNDRIP) and includes this statement: "Indigenous peoples have the right to establish and control their educational systems and institutions providing education in their own languages, in a manner appropriate to their cultural methods of teaching and learning."[34]

In a significant development, Canada took the crucial step in 2021 of committing to align all federal laws with UNDRIP through the United Nations Declaration on the Rights of Indigenous Peoples Act. The legislation explicitly states that Canada is committed to ensure that its laws are in harmony with UNDRIP. This commitment implies that the Indigenous Languages Act must conform to the principles outlined in UNDRIP. It's important to note that even before UNDRIP, First Nations laws in Canada had already laid the groundwork for recognizing and safeguarding the right to language transmission. These pre-existing laws form the foundation for First Nations constitutional rights to language transmission in Canada and should guide the understanding and implementation of these rights.

The central thesis of this book asserts that First Nations language rights include the crucial right of transmission from one generation to the next. This constitutional right finds its foundation in two primary sources:

(1) First Nations law: First Nations language rights are grounded in First Nations law, emphasizing the responsibility and intrinsic importance of language transmission.

(2) Constitutional law: The inter-customary practices of language exchange between First Nations and the settler population gave rise to a distinctive inter-customary law, laying the foundation for the right to language transmission. Presently, this right finds recognition under the Indigenous Languages Act, which encompasses the entitlement to uphold First Nations languages in education as both an Aboriginal and a treaty right. It is imperative that this right harmonize with international law and the comprehensive acknowledgement of minority language rights in education across Canada to ensure the prevention of any discriminatory treatment of language rights within the educational context.

Chapter 1 explores First Nations laws that govern language transmission and the principles guiding language use, emphasizing the sacred nature of language within the framework of Canada's unwritten constitutional principles. The chapter also examines the inter-customary practices governing language transmission and exchanges between Europeans and First Nations that resulted in a unique body of law. These principles form the foundation for constitutional rights to language transmission for settlers and First Nations. The chapter focuses specifically on the linguistic customs, practices, and traditions that emerged on the Prairies through interactions involving European traders, missionaries, and First Nations people, all demonstrating a historic precedent for First Nations language transmission.

Chapter 2 traces the historical trajectory of the linguistic genocide resulting from Canada's assimilationist education policies. This history was identified by the Truth and Reconciliation Commission of Canada (TRC) as cultural genocide and has been acknowledged as such by a former Supreme Court justice and successive federal governments.

Chapter 3 positions First Nations language transmission as a contemporary constitutional right in education. The chapter outlines the advocacy efforts by First Nations (as well as Inuit) leaders for language rights in education, emphasizing the importance of using legislation to preserve and promote these rights. Ongoing attempts to secure constitutional recognition and the government's acknowledgement of the pivotal role of First Nations language rights in education are evidenced in constitutional negotiations, national studies, and royal commissions.

Chapter 4 asserts the crucial role of international law in recognizing and supporting the right to Indigenous language transmission. A brief overview of other countries' challenges and successes in advancing Indigenous language rights in education is also included.

Chapter 5 analyzes the evolution of the Indigenous Languages Act in Canada, placing particular emphasis on the negotiations between the federal government and First Nations leaders. The chapter considers the implications of the legislation for language transmission within First Nations education, specifically highlighting the need for immersion education. This examination asks whether Canada's commitment to a "new relationship" with First Nations on a "nation-to-nation" basis extends to First Nations language education rights. It also questions whether the government is committed to providing the support and resources required by First Nations for the kind of language education that is necessary for language revitalization.

CHAPTER 1

INTER-CUSTOMARY LAW:

First Nations Language Transmission on the Prairies

This chapter sets out some of the customs, practices, and traditions that facilitated First Nations language transmission between Europeans and First Nations people in the prairie region, spanning three distinct contexts. The first consisted of language exchanges[1] between personnel of the Hudson's Bay Company (HBC), a quasi-governmental entity, and First Nations individuals. These exchanges were compelled by the necessity for linguistic proficiency, crucial for the conduct of trade.[2] A second context for linguistic practices emerged in the realm of education with the arrival of missionaries. This sheds light on a transitional period when the introduction of Christianity coexisted with the preservation of First Nations languages. A third context was the development of the syllabic writing system as a tool for language preservation and transmission. These contexts of language transmission, along with First Nations law that governed language use, established a framework for inter-customary law. In other words, First Nations language rights are located in a body of law that governs language transmission between First Nations and Canada which contributed to the creation of a distinct body of inter-customary law.[3]

Before presenting this overview of evolving language transmission among First Nations people and Europeans, the chapter will outline the linguistic landscape of First Nations in the prairie region and briefly examine First Nations laws that govern language transmission and the principles guiding language use, emphasizing the sacred nature of language within the framework of Canada's unwritten constitutional principles.

Languages in the Prairie Region

It is estimated that over ninety Aboriginal languages (as identified by UNESCO) exist in what is now recognized as Canada.[4] Each of these languages belongs to one of eleven language families. In the prairie region, the main linguistic family is Algonquian. It is one of the largest family languages in North America, with approximately twenty-three languages.[5] In the Maliseet (Malecite) language, which belongs to this large family, the term corresponding to "Algonquian" is *elakomkwik*, loosely translated as "they are relatives" or "they are allies." This expression implies a sense of close kinship among these languages and their speakers. The traditional territory of Algonquian-speaking peoples is vast, spanning the eastern coast of the country all the way to the Rocky Mountains. Although, people in this territory speak a range of different dialects and languages that are all culturally interrelated. The prairie region is also home to several Dakota languages.[6] The speakers of Dakota historically resided in the plains area of North America, frequently venturing to the northern prairie region for trade with other First Nations.

Language: A Sacred Inalienable Inherent Right

One of the main languages of the Algonquian family is Cree. Harold Cardinal, Cree leader and legal scholar, identifies Cree customary law and language as *iyiniw miyikowisowina* (that which is given to the people) and *iyiniw saweyihtakosiwin* (the people's sacred gifts), which emphasizes their origin in the unique relationship between the people and the Creator.[7] This legal framework regards language as a sacred duty that cannot be abandoned or extinguished because of the inherent responsibility to preserve it for future generations. Language is also seen as playing a central role in a people's identity, and surrendering it would be comparable to forfeiting culture or ancestral land.

Ojibway Elder Dolly Neapetung further emphasizes the significance of language to cultural identity, saying, "The Creator gave us a way of life and a language by which we could speak to one another and speak to Him and give meaning to everything that was around us . . . to help us understand the world and other people, our relatives."[8] According to the Creation story, all these instructions are conveyed in ancestral languages, emphasizing the First Nations teaching that language originates from a place of spirit. Consequently, language is considered a sacred part of life. When the people emerged from the spirit realm, language underwent a transformation through their interactions with the living environment. Daily life involved engaging with plants, four-legged animals, birds, rocks, and water, fostering relationships with these entities and cultivating an understanding of each. Language evolved, intertwining with the landscape and people's existence within their homelands, adapting and enriching the people with its versatility and utility. Over time, as needs and understanding expanded, the original language diversified into distinct languages. Linguistic offshoots emerged in different regions, giving rise to a variety of cultural exchanges and dialects.[9] As a result of these intimate interactions with the land, a deeper understanding of language relationships and responsibilities also evolved when communicating in these languages.

Ojibway Elder Ruth Norton, speaking at a Linguistic Rights Conference in Ottawa in 1993, further elaborated on this point: "Languages [are] spiritual, and because *the* languages [are] spiritual... our rights are entrenched in the law of the land, the way that we see it. As our ancestors tell us, the Creator has given us the land that we live in, and with the land, [Creator] has given us the language" (my emphasis).[10] Norton highlights that language and its connection to the land are crucial not only to the development of relationships among human beings but also to the identity of First Nations people. The intricate relationship between language and land is evident in the diverse First Nations languages and dialects tied to specific areas in North America and found within language families and communities. First Nations languages have evolved according to the peoples' relationship to the living environment. The late Vine Deloria emphasized the significance of historical land knowledge that is embedded in First Nations languages and stories:

> That is to say, every feature of landscape has stories attached to it. If a tribal group is very large or has lived on a particular piece of land for many generations, some natural features will have many stories attached to them. I know some place in the Dakotas about which at least a dozen stories are told. These

> stories related both secular events such as tales of hunting and warfare and sacred events such as personal or tribal religious experiences. Each family within a tribe has its own tradition of stories about tribal ancestral lands. In theory it would be possible to gather from the people of the tribe all the stories that relate to every feature of the landscape. If these stories were then arranged chronologically, the result would be the history of the people.[11]

The narratives of the land, along with the history of First Nations, are embedded in First Nations languages.

In my pursuit of a deeper understanding of the significance of First Nations languages and their relationship to the land, I discovered that language was given to First Nations to communicate from the heart about the land, and that language is an intrinsic part of First Nations identity. In Cree, "mother tongue" is expressed as *miteinane*, a term directly translated as "heart-tongue." A further breakdown of the word *mite* (heart) and *inane* (tongue) provides further insight. The root word *inane* is also intertwined with *ininiw* (people of the land) and *inniwmowin* (Cree language). Weaving together these three terms—*miteinane* (heart-tongue), *ininiw* (people of the land), and *inniwmowin* (Cree language)—creates profound meaning: the mother tongue was given to the Cree people of this land to communicate from the heart about the land, as it is an intrinsic part of Cree identity.

Further elaborated, *miteinane*, or mother tongue, means "your life is through your heart," emphasizing that the words used to communicate originate from the heart. Consequently, spoken words are regarded as sacred expressions, emanating from one's spirit and revealing the interconnectedness between the individual and Creation. Through these teachings, I have gained a deep understanding of the profound connection between language and the identities of First Nations.[12] We are people of the heart, and our language is more than just a mode of communication; it mirrors our spirit. Therefore, in the very act of being human, First Nations people speak from the heart. This realization further deepens the connection between First Nations' cultural identities, and the land from which they originate. The teachings derived from these concepts emphasize that our ancestral language is the original language of our traditional territory, and each First Nations language originating on Turtle Island shares a connection between language and its territory.

Upon the arrival of Europeans in the prairie region, the protocols of engaging with First Nations in their languages became integral to official business practices.[13] The political and legal customs employed during trade and other significant negotiations provided a meaningful context for language exchanges. Slattery notes that these protocols typically encompassed formal exchanges of greetings, presents, ceremonial belts, statements of grievance or intent, and reciprocal oral promises. Treaty negotiations, for instance, often involved multiple languages, requiring interpreters to play crucial roles.[14] Borrows argues that Aboriginal practices, customs, and traditions are sources of Aboriginal law,[15] embedded within historical protocols such as feasting practices,[16] gifting,[17] and pipe ceremonies.[18] Furthermore, within these historical instances emerge examples of language transmission between First Nations people and European settlers.

Language Exchange between Hudson's Bay Company and First Nations

Although New France traders and settlers had already interacted with First Nations cultures in eastern Canada, the first Europeans to engage with First Nations languages in the prairie region were employees of the Hudson's Bay Company (HBC). The HBC, established in England in 1670, existed to make profits from the trade of furs but functioned as a *de jure* and *de facto* government over a vast region that was drained by all the rivers and streams flowing into the Hudson Bay.[19] During the pre-settlement fur-trade period, the HBC governed the territory under a charter from King Charles of England. While nominally controlled by a central body of directors in London, the HBC appointed local governors and officers to manage its affairs throughout the trading area. During the seventeenth and eighteenth centuries, HBC employees observed the common law of master and servant, with little attention to anyone else. Although success of the HBC depended on communication with First Nations, the charter said nothing about the languages of non-European people, and certainly nothing about language rights.

The HBC eventually acknowledged the significance of First Nations languages for trading; however, the company established no consistent language policies for either spoken or written language use. Instead, the HBC tried to navigate many languages and dialects with very little guidance, since none of its employees initially had experience with the regional dialects of the interior prairies. The company also had to interact with communities that were culturally very different from their own and from each other as the traders tried to establish business relationships with people they knew very little about.

In the early stages of the HBC, the success of fur traders from New France and Britain depended on First Nations labour, the First Nations economy, and First Nations interpreters to facilitate access to First Nations territories. Notably, two French fur traders, Pierre Radisson and his nephew Jean Baptiste Chouart, advised the HBC to ensure their employees acquired knowledge of the linguistic customary practices of the First Nations they intended to trade with.[20] Drawing from their experiences in the eastern part of the country, Radisson and Chouart stressed that merely learning vocabulary was insufficient. They urged HBC employees to delve deeper into understanding and actively participating in the regional customary communication protocols. For instance, in the local Cree culture, ceremonial exchanges and gift-giving were integral components.[21] These relational systems eventually laid the foundation for inter-societal linguistic practices in the Canadian prairies. The systematic effort of language transmission became an inherent and vital part of the trading system in the region.[22]

During the late seventeenth and early eighteenth century, HBC employees were completely at the mercy of First Nations. Being neither well acquainted with First Nations languages nor with the customary protocols (not to mention surviving on the land), the newcomers had to rely on the patronage of their hosts to learn about First Nations cultures.[23] Some scholars note that First Nations during this period generally dominated the power relationship with the French and the English.[24] Company directors in distant London had to rely on employees to determine how to overcome cultural and linguistic barriers. The HBC had to find individuals who were willing to enter the interior and then locate those who were able to communicate with First Nations in the regional languages and dialects. Initially, the HBC found it challenging to hire Cree-speaking men who were willing to travel into the interior.

Correspondence between the HBC and the governor of the James Bay area posts from 1683 to 1689 illustrates some of the challenges of this initial period. For example, a letter dated 27 April 1683, from HBC headquarters to Henry Sergeant, emphasized the need for men able to communicate in a First Nations language: "You are to Choose out from amongst our servants such as are best qualified with Strength and Body and the Country Language, to travel and to penetrate into the Country, to draw down the Indians by fair and gentle Means to trade with us."[25] Very few men at the time were skilled in any First Nations language. Sergeant responded in a letter dated 13 September 1683 that the HBC would have to entice men financially to travel into the interior.[26] Further correspondence between Sergeant and the HBC reflects the importance of the ability to communicate in the *lingua franca* and having knowledge of cultural protocols of the territory to the success of their venture. For example, in a letter to Sergeant dated 22 May 1685, the HBC expressed its willingness to increase the wages of employees who could speak an Aboriginal language.[27] But Sergeant reported in a letter dated 24 August 1685 that despite the increased wages, none of the men who were approached were willing to make such a risky journey.[28]

Eventually, the HBC located willing and qualified men, including Henry Kelsey and James Isham, two notable employees who provided detailed accounts of the First Nations languages they encountered. Kelsey is recognized as the first European person to travel into the interior of the region between 1690 and 1692. James Isham is noted for the relationships he developed with First Nations communities some fifty years later, between 1744 and 1749. Both men quickly produced Cree dictionaries to provide HBC fur traders with a vocabulary that could assist them in communicating with First Nations communities during trading activities. In addition to the dictionaries, Kelsey and Isham wrote detailed accounts in their journals of language transmission. Although each may have held different views on the linguistic protocols they witnessed, they both included vocabulary and documentation illustrating transmission of language.

Henry Kelsey

Henry Kelsey began his career with the HBC in 1684 as a cabin boy on supply ships bound for the forts of the Hudson Bay region. After Kelsey worked his way up the company hierarchy, the HBC entrusted him to bring trade inland, and he embarked on a two-year journey from

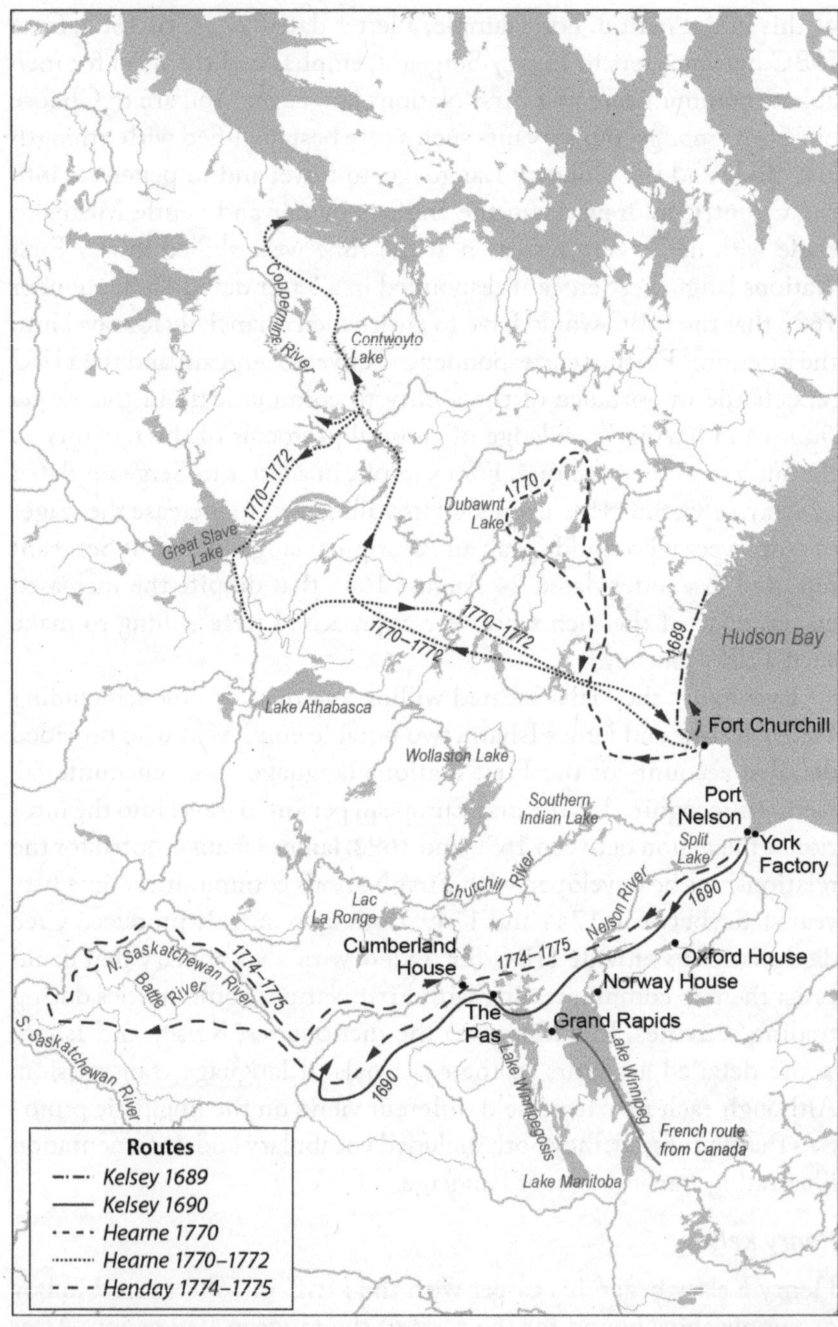

Figure 1. Map of Henry Kelsey's and his contemporaries' routes into the interior. Map by Julie Witmer based on Paul C. Newman's *Empire on the Bay: An Illustrated History of the Hudson's Bay Company* (Toronto: Madison Press Books, 1989) and on the insert map in *The Kelsey Papers* (1929).

York Factory during 1690–1692. His task was to convince First Nations people to trade with the company closer to its posts along the shores of the Hudson Bay. Kelsey travelled into the interior by foot with an unidentified Cree companion in June 1690 and later married a First Nations woman named Eliz. With the assistance of his companion and his wife, Kelsey was able to establish relationships with several First Nations over this two-year period. He was named *Miss-tap-ashish* (Little Giant) by First Nations people after he killed a bear.[29]

As he reported in his journal, one of Kelsey's main objectives for travelling into the interior was to learn First Nations languages: "Through Gods assistance for to understand The native language & to see their land."[30] During his travels, he encountered numerous languages, predominantly from the Algonquian and Dakota families.[31] Although Kelsey writes about several First Nations communities, he would have mainly encountered speakers of Swampy Cree, an Algonquian language, during his travels. The territory of the Swampy Cree people is vast, starting in Northern Manitoba, following the Saskatchewan River in the northeastern part of Saskatchewan, and continuing to the shores of the Hudson and James Bays in Ontario. Today, Swampy Cree are divided into two different groups: the Western Swampy,[32] and the Eastern Swampy or Western James Bay Cree.[33] Several dialects of Cree are spoken in this region, known as "TH," "Y," "N," and "L" dialects.

Kelsey also referred to the Stone Indians in his journal. The HBC also referred to them as Assinae Poets, or sometimes just Poets.[34] They are now commonly recognized as Assiniboine or Stoney Indians. Their traditional territory stretches from southwestern Manitoba to Saskatchewan and into parts of Alberta, northern Montana, and western South Dakota. The next three groups mentioned by Kelsey are not as easily identified. The Mountain Poets were likely part of the Assiniboine people and therefore speakers of the Souian language. Kelsey mentioned them in his journal on 24 August 1690: "This day lay still waiting for a post which came in ye afternoon from ye Capt: of the Mountain Poets Named Washa."[35] Washa was a leader of the Mountain Poets and the only Aboriginal person named in Kelsey's journal. The Eagle Birch Indians were likely Cree-based, since they are not referred to as Poets in Kelsey's journal.[36] The last group, the Naywatame Poets, are the most significant community referred to in Kesley's 1691 journal. There are many theories regarding the identity of the Naywatame Poets. They

[1]

A

DICTIONARY

OF

The *Hudſon's-Bay Indian* Language.

The Perſonal Notes are as follow, *viz.*

I, or Me: Netha
Thee, or Thou: Kethea
He, or Him: Wetha
We: Ne thaun
You: Ke tha woa.

Your Party and ours included: Ke thawn noe
They, or them of a Company: We thaw woa

NOTE, When you wou'd ſpeak of any thing concerning your ſelf, or, That it is mine, obſerve always to put the word Ne, or at leaſt pronounce the N to begin the word with; as for Example, to ſay, it is my awl, Noos ka jick, it is yours, or thine, Koos ka jick. To ſay it is theirs or his, Woos ka jick; and in the plural Caſes you muſt uſe thoſe Words at length, as are inſerted in the perſonal Notes, as for Example, to ſay it belongs to us, Ne thaun Noos ka jick coom. To ſay it belongs to they or them, We thaw woa oos ka jick coom. To ſay it belongs to your Party, Ke tha woa koos ka jick coom, *&c.*

Words beginning Alphabetically.

A

ALL: ca kith tha
awls: oos kau jick
always: keſs cutt
arrive with Canoe, or Ship: Miſh ſha gau
aſhes or Powder: Peh co
ax or hatchet: Chick ka higgen
aſſiſt or help us: Nee ſhoo ca mou wee
arrived by Land: Ta cooſh in
ask a queſtion: Cau quea che ma
ask or deſire, him or them, to give you ſuch a thing: Na tut ta mow
able or ſtrong: Cau thau wiſſue
an able Man: Cau thau wau pai
a Company of able Men: Cau thau wau pai wee uck
above: is ſpim mihk
abandon, to forſake or leave: Na cut taw
arrows: at tuſs
arrow-heads: at tuſs au bisk
angry: This kau tai ſee
air: Ke ſhick
abaſt, or hinder part of a Veſſel: Oo tachk a ta kuk
afore, or the fore-part of a Veſſel: Neeſh taum e ta kuk
aſhamed: Ne pai wiſſue
abhor or loath: Pa qua tau

A advife

Figure 2. Henry Kelsey's Dictionary. *A Dictionary of the Hudson's-Bay Indian Language*, 1710. Courtesy of Internet Archive at https://archive.org/details/bim_eighteenth-century_a-dictionary-of-the-huds_1710.

have been referred to as Mandan,[37] Sioux,[38] Gros Ventre or Atsina,[39] and Blackfoot.[40] However, their exact identity is not certain.

Kelsey's journal does not specify which languages he mastered; he probably knew both the Assiniboine and Cree languages but he referred mostly to Cree in his journal.[41] Kelsey also authored *A Dictionary of the Hudson's-Bay Indian Language*,[42] which contained approximately 600 Cree words and was compiled to assist individuals engaged in the trade. The HBC informed Kelsey of its intention to publish the dictionary for future traders: "You do well to Educate the men in Literature but especially in the Language that in time we may send them to travel If we see it Convenient.... We have sent you your dixonary [*sic*] Printed, that you may the better Instruct the young Ladds with you, in ye Indian Language."[43] For reasons unknown, the dictionary was never published. In fact, Joseph Robson, a former HBC employee, alleged in the mid-1700s that the company had ordered Kelsey's dictionary hidden from the public.[44] For approximately 250 years it was missing until it was "discovered" in the British Library in London in the 1970s.

Kelsey's documentation of both the Cree language and language transmission of the region are particularly remarkable. On 1 September 1691, Kelsey reported in his journal that eight individuals had assisted him with interpretation. One was selected for his knowledge of Cree, and the other seven assisted with translating conduct.[45] Not only did Kelsey acknowledge the men who had assisted him during his travels, he also provided detailed descriptions of ceremonial objects such as shakers (rattles) and pipes, as well as traditional medicines like sweetgrass and tobacco. These sacred cultural objects and medicines are used in various public, social, and cultural gatherings. Kelsey documented the protocols and use of the sacred objects within traditional feasts, pipe ceremonies, songs, and prayers that are linked with language transmission.

Feasting

On 31 August 1691, Kelsey wrote about a community feast prepared for him by First Nations people (in likely what is now recognized as Northern Manitoba) after he accepted the request to travel, recognizing that the feast was a way of communicating their gratitude to him: "This day y Indians made a feast desiring of me to be a post to a parcel of Indians which was to the Northward of us."[46] On 3 September 1690, another feast was held to make the community aware that Kelsey would be speaking on an important issue. During the feast, Kelsey warned the people that their participation in war with other First Nations could prevent the HBC from trading with them in the future.[47]

Ceremonies

Kelsey's journal entries extended beyond mere community reports; he identified language transmission through community feasting practices and pipe ceremonies. He observed that these ceremonies were frequently conducted preceding and following significant deliberations, as well as during times when individuals sought guidance. On 5 September 1691, Kelsey referred to a pipe ceremony held by Elders to celebrate and give thanks for the discovery of their enemies, noting that the men sitting were required to wait quietly for the Elders to come out and smoke their pipes to express their happiness:

> About ten o'clock this morning the young men appearing in sight & carrying out just like a Crane gave a sign that they had discovered their Enemies & as soon as they came within one hundred yards of the tent they sat all down in a Row upon the grass not speaking one word so the old Men lighting their pipes went to them & served them round Crying as if they had been stob'd for Joy that they had found their enemies the young men having brought some of arrows to verifie with thye had been about.[48]

Following this event, on 9 September 1691, Kelsey offered the Stone Indians tobacco to request peaceful relations with the Nayawattame Poets, demonstrating his understanding of the protocols of communication with tobacco offerings: "This morning I went to the Captain of the stone Indians tent carrying with me a piece of tobacco I telling him to make a speech to all his Country men & tell them not to disturbe nor meddle with the Nayawattame poets for I was going back to Invite and incourage them to a peace."[49]

This section of Kelsey's journal reinforces how the protocols of both tobacco and pipe ceremonies are a significant aspect of language transmission. Using the pipe represents the spoken word, and whatever is agreed upon during important discussions is confirmed during the pipe ceremony. Every individual who participates in the ceremony has a responsibility to ensure that instructions are understood, respected, and carried out. Kelsey noted in his description that if a person refuses to smoke the pipe, it means they do not agree with what has been discussed. The following entry reflects his understanding:

> Their second point is Concerning A pipe steam. . . . Now every one of these & all things Else belonging to the steam Afore. Hath speech belongs to every one of them as the makers fancy lead him Now there is but very few Indians/ but we are leading with can get one these pipes & when he hath mind to go to wars or any other way he calls all of them together & tell them his mind so then he Lights the pipe & severth them Round Crying Now their Customs is to take butt four Whiffs of those pipes & if any one hath not a mind to go with him nor answer his request he will Likewise refuse to smoke out of his pipe.[50]

Kelsey's writings on language transmission also refer to the use of the pipe as a way to communicate prayer for travellers about to embark on a dangerous journey: "Likewise they will send these pipes out upon any expedition as when they go for to seek out their Enemies tracks or when they are want of victuals."[51]

Kelsey provided additional details on the protocols of the pipe as a way of communicating prayer or making important decisions. As Kelsey indicated, the pipe was pointed toward the four cardinal directions while being smoked, and songs were sung to express gratitude and thanksgiving:

> *[prayers for everyone]* this being done the master burning a little more sweet grass then taketh a pipe fill'd with tobacco & perfume . . . shall call to the feast so then he goeth out of doors & those which are appointed he call by name two of 3 times over & returning into the tent again lights the pipe which was given to him the pipe being lightened he turneth the end which goeth into the mouth to which place the master of the feast shall direct him which generally first towards our English house & from thence moving round gradually towards the sun rising & so about to**** here the sun is at noon still keeping in motion to where the sun goeth down & then turneth . . . end which goeth into the mouth toward the ground so lighting it the second time handeth it round

> to his companions & as they receive it they give thanks so when they are all gathered together the master will have some victuals & some tobacco ready cut with which they will sing & be merry . . . now they have but two or three Words in a song & they observe to keep time along with him . . . leader of the song for Every man maketh his own songs by virtue of with he dreams of as I have said before & at the Conclusion of every song they give thanks all in general to him with the song belongs to So likewise if any.[52]

Prayer and Song

Kelsey noted several other protocols involving language transmission, including communicating prayer through song when an Elder is called to care for someone in poor health:

> If any of them be sick they use no other means nor know no other help but to sing for which purpose they hire a man & he calls together some men more or less for to accompanie him in his singing so all of them getting a piece of birch Rine & a little stick goes to the sick mans tent then he . . . begins to sing and the Rest Beats upon the Rine the same stroke he uses with his rattle which is made of Birch rine hallow within having some stone or Beads Inclosed in it so when he has sat & sung a while to his patient. . . .[53]

Kelsey's notebook entries also extend to protocols for communicating requests to Elders. Offering tobacco is an important initial step. If the tobacco is accepted, the Elder has communicated his agreement to assist. In the following entry from Kelsey's notebook, the Elder has accepted a tobacco offering and deliberates on what is required to care for the sick person. Kelsey concludes that an offering to the Creator and prayer is important to the individual's healing process: "Contrary Now in such times they will take the best things they have & hang upon Poles as an offering to him which was the cause of his sickness Likewise making a long speech desiring him his health again."[54]

Kelsey also learned about language transmission associated with song and dreaming. He was informed that when the spirit of an animal appears in the dream of an individual and offers the dreamer a song, the spirit and human life are communicating in a sacred way. The song conveys the individual's connection to the spirit of the animal and ultimately provides the community with guidance and direction on important decisions:

> Their sixth point I shall relate is concerning their singing of the songs & from whence they think they have them those they reckon Chiefly for gods are Beast & fowl But of all Beast the Buffalo & of all fowls the voulter & the Eagle which they say they dream in on their sleep & it relates to them when they shall say when they sing & By the means whatsoever they ask or require will be granted or given to them which by often making use of it sometimes happens to fall our Rights as they sat & for the one time it was pass for a truth that he hath a familiar.[55]

Common Regional Language Practices

In another section of his journal, Kelsey acknowledged common regional linguistic practices despite different languages. He noted the similarities between the Stone Indians and the Dakota-speaking Nayaythaway peoples in the following passage: "Now there is a Difference between the Stone Indians & the Nayhaythaways although the principles of their belief is all one & the same."[56]

Kelsey also described language transmission within protocols followed before holding a community feast, as the preparations are considered just as important as the public event itself. First, someone is given the responsibility of making a fire at the centre of a lodge. Someone else has the responsibility of caring for the fire during the ceremony. Smudging the space with traditional medicines such as sweetgrass is another important part of the process. Everything is done to create a sacred space prior to the delivery of important speeches. The preparations are all essential protocols for public speaking:

> Now if they have a mind for to make a feast they will pitch a tent on purpose & after . . . the tent is made & fixt then no woman Kind . . . man must not come within the door of the then . . . (*reference to ceremonial place*) so then the master of the tent & one or two more goeth in & Cutteth out a place for the fire about three foot square in the middle of the tent

> & then the fire being made they take a little sweet grass & lay at every corner (*must be smudged)* of the said square & the putting fire to it they perfume the tent so making along speech wishing all health & happiness both to founders and cofounders.[57]

In spite of the rich detail Kelsey provided in his journals about language transmission, these writings were not shared with the general public until 1926, over two hundred years later. Moreover, his journals subsequently disappeared from public view for a number of years and were eventually retrieved in the Public Records Office in Northern Ireland, mixed in with another collection.[58] Although Kelsey's writings were not used during his lifetime, they provide significant and valuable descriptions of the linguistic history of north central North America of the late 1600s. Kelsey was the first European to write about the language transmission practices, customs, and traditions of First Nations in the Plains and likely one of the first to comment on their social and cultural relevance. Some have noted that Kelsey's "journey to the Plains . . . was only made possible by Kelsey becoming part of the Indian community."[59] It appears unlikely that Kelsey could have completed the initial trek successfully without the aid of First Nations interpreters. Furthermore, his capacity to acquire vocabulary and understand language customs, practices, and traditions was only achievable with the assistance of these translators and interpreters. The reasons behind the prolonged disappearance of these valuable journals remain uncertain.

James Isham

Another important figure from this period is James Isham, who began his career in 1732 with the HBC at York Factory. About nine years later, he was in charge of establishing trade in Churchill. One of his first tasks was to build a fort in the area. During this period, Isham referred to many First Nations he encountered: Nakawawuck, Moquo, Muskekowuck, Keiskachewon, Poetuck, Cawcawquek, Nemau, Wappus, Sinnepoet, (alias) Boskemo, Earchetinues, Missinnepee, Gristeen, pennesewagegwan, Quashe'o, Pechepoethinue, wunnusku, unnahathewunnutitto, Uchepowuck, and the Wechepowuck. These are language groups located north of the Churchill River.[60] Isham indicated that the Wechepowuck language was more of a challenge to learn because one word could have several meanings. The language complexity created a number of communication barriers.[61]

Based on his knowledge of regional languages, Isham authored two dictionaries: the *Vocabulary of English and Indian*, which contains phrases to assist traders; and *A Small account of the Northward Indian language*.[62] Together the two dictionaries contain fifty-eight pages of English and Cree words, with a few words translated into the Assiniboine language.

Among the terms and descriptions contained in the dictionaries are words to assist individuals with small talk, expressions commonly used for greetings and pleasantries during trade. Another section provides traders with language for the business of trading goods, and Isham also translates numbers into a few regional dialects. The following example illustrates a common exchange during hunting: "I shall grieve when you go,"[63] (followed by an Englishman's response): "You'll come again in the Spring."[64]

Isham's dictionaries also present important evidence of the blending of European and Cree world views. Isham uses westernized references to time, such as "seven days in a week" and "twelve months in a year" to describe the year and workdays,[65] while capturing a Cree world view when referring to months. For example, January is referred to as "Little old moon" or "Cold moon," and November is referred to as "the moon the Deer sheds their horns."[66] Several references to seasons also exemplify a Cree world view. For example, spring is referred to as "breaking up of the Rivers."[67] Several more humorous translations also reflect this world view: mustard seeds are referred to as "child's dung" in Cree, and capers are known as "sheep's dung."[68] Evidence of a Cree-European trading system is reflected in phrases such as "This tobacco has a bad taste, I will not trade it," and "Take pitty on me give me good measure with a little over."[69]

Isham's journal not only illuminates the convergence of European and Cree world views but also offers valuable insights into the language transmission protocols observed by First Nations during this period. His depictions of ceremonies mirror the observations recorded by Kelsey. Isham details the customs associated with using the pipe during crucial deliberations. He also points out that a pipe ceremony frequently extends for a significant duration, adhering to a strict protocol of silence that allows for important contemplation. Individuals are also encouraged to carefully consider the words that they use to express their thoughts. Isham describes this period of silence as a time when "the Spirit then puts it in their head to Speak."[70] He also notes that the time of silence prepares people to speak "with a good heart and mind." Isham refers to the four cardinal directions that the pipe is pointed toward during the ceremony.[71] The pipe is frequently smoked as part of a linguistic protocol when visitors enter First Nations territory, often referred to as camps in Isham's journals. Within these pipe ceremonies, speakers typically adhere to a practice wherein chiefs are given the precedence in speaking, and Elders conclude the discussions after the pipe has been smoked.[72] When the ceremony and the deliberations have been completed, the attendees exchange gifts before holding a feast.[73]

Isham's writings were submitted to an HBC committee in London in about 1744. Although the detailed descriptions provide valuable information concerning language transmission in the area at the time, Isham's writings were not published until 1949, two hundred years later. The HBC does not mention them anywhere, and there is no evidence that Isham's work was acted upon.

Kelsey's and Isham's writings made significant contributions to the documentation of language transmission. However, HBC directors residing in England were so thoroughly detached from the necessities of communication with First Nations for trade relationships that they overlooked the value of these records. Nevertheless, Kelsey and Isham played a crucial role in overcoming linguistic barriers and in initiating relationships that other HBC employees would subsequently cultivate. Equally noteworthy is their active participation in the linguistic protocols that they later documented. Additionally, the dictionaries they created serve as important sources of information on the vocabulary employed in trade.

By the mid-1800s, HBC employees had become more involved with First Nations and recognized the value of acquiring both the vocabulary and customary protocols of communication in First Nations languages. HBC Governor George Simpson, a powerful and influential player in company affairs, noted employees who could speak First Nations languages in his Character Book, an indication that the HBC valued knowledge of the region's First Nations languages (see Appendix).

Simpson's Character Book contains a list of chief factors, chief traders, and clerks who joined the HBC anywhere from 1790 to 1821. The list provides details such as the nationality, capacity, length of service, and salary of individuals, in addition to their skills in First Nations languages. Although there was nothing in HBC policy that required employees to learn First Nations languages, it was essential. Many HBC employees were engaged with language transmission in situations associated with ceremonies. They would also become accustomed to them. As result, First Nations language transmission evolved as relationships developed with Europeans.

At the beginning of the nineteenth century, the HBC in Rupert's Land decided to invite missionaries to provide education to First Nations people.[74] The HBC recognized its role in offering education, particularly since there were a number of children born as a result of unions between HBC employees and First Nations women. I now turn to the language transmission that arose in this context.

Missionary Schools

Nineteenth-century missionaries played a significant role in language transmission by providing Christian-based education to First Nations. Schools in the prairie region became part of a larger missionary enterprise that used First Nations languages to convert people to Christianity, but there was never a single coordinated language policy. In some cases, First Nations students were taught to speak, read, and write in English before their conversion, but not at the expense of their ancestral language. In other cases, missionaries had the Bible translated into First Nations languages so that First Nations people could learn to read it in their own language. In any case, quite a few individuals in the early nineteenth century became fluent in both English (and, to a certain extent, French) and First Nations languages, likely because of fur-trade intermarriages. Some missionaries, for their part, would have had to acquire proficiency in the local dialects. Others never learned to speak a First Nations language and worked through an interpreter. Regardless of the tactics used for conversion, the HBC retained a central role in First Nations–European interactions by bringing missionaries into the region.

Indian Mission Schools

In 1820, the HBC hired Reverend John West as the company chaplain. West was an Anglican member of the Church Missionary Society (CMS), an evangelical organization devoted to converting First Nations societies and improving their socio-economic conditions. West subsequently established a mission school in Kildonan (now St. John's, part of Winnipeg, Manitoba) for First Nations children to Christianize them after teaching them to read and write in English.[75] By the fall of 1820, West had recruited his first students: Pemutewithinew (James Hope), the nine-year-old son of Chief Withaweecapo, and Sakachuwescum (Henry Budd), the eight-year-old son of a Métis woman from Norway House.

West continued his recruitment process, approaching a number of First Nation leaders in southern Manitoba, including Chief Peguis. Initially, Peguis was reluctant to send his sons to West's mission school and spent a great deal of time considering his decision. As part of his deliberative process, he conducted a pipe ceremony in which West participated.[76] After the ceremony, Peguis questioned West's intentions for the children after they completed their education. West replied that the children could return home, but in school they "would read the Book that the Great Spirit has given to them . . . and [it] would teach them how to live well and die happy."[77] Eventually, Chief Peguis agreed to support West's mission school but enrolled his nephew instead of his sons.[78]

By 1823, West had recruited ten First Nations children to attend his school. Within two to three years, the students recruited to West's mission school knew a lot about Christianity and could speak and understand English, thanks to "constant drilling, recitation, and daily devotions."[79] Although these children were graduates of "the first 'English as a Second Language program' (ESL) in Western Canada,"[80] they also maintained their fluency in their ancestral language and strong ties to their cultural identity.[81] West's school continued until he returned to England in 1823.

Between 1820 and 1839 West appears to have been the only Anglican missionary who learned to speak Cree.[82] The HBC at that time probably provided interpreters to missionaries who worked in First Nations communities. Missionaries would later rely on the First

Nations graduates from West's mission school to conduct religious work in First Nations communities. The role of these "lay missionaries" became even more important when missionary societies of other church denominations began working in the prairie region.[83] In response to this denominational competition, the Anglican Reverend John Smithurst learned Cree so he could translate communion services for the Elders who did not understand English.[84]

Eventually other missionaries arrived in Rupert's Land. The British Wesleyan Methodist Missionary Society recruited Henry Bird Steinhauer, an Ojibway who had trained as a Methodist minister.[85] Steinhauer could speak Cree as well as Ojibway. In 1842 he helped James Evans to translate the Bible and various hymns into Cree, and later played a central role in the translation of Cree syllabics (discussed later in this chapter). At the same time, a number of Catholic missionaries in the plains area had learned to speak Ojibway. Father George Anthony Belcourt, for example, spent over fifteen years in what is now known as the Archdiocese of St. Boniface. He could read, write, and speak Ojibway,[86] suggesting that his goal of Christianizing Ojibway people would be carried out in their mother tongue. For the Catholic Church, "future apostles were expected to learn the dialects of First Nations and prepare grammars and dictionaries of the same."[87] Belcourt describes the Ojibway language as

> much richer than is commonly thought. It bears great resemblance to the ancient languages. It has, like the Greek, the dual and the two futures. And like that language it has but few radical words, but their manner of forming words for the occasion, by the aid of these radicals, gives a great facility of expression, the same as the Greek.... This language is formed of radical and compound words. The radical words are commonly employed in the familiar style; but in oratorical style, the compound words are used.... This makes the learning of the language rather difficult at first, nearly equal to the acquiring of two languages; but in return for this, one obtains an extra facility in expressing his thoughts with all the force he desires.[88]

The threat of Catholic missionaries entering the region convinced the Anglican Church to hire First Nations graduates from West's mission schools. These individuals would need very little additional training to establish new missions within First Nations communities.[89]

The Christianizing mission in the region radically changed during the mid-nineteenth century. First Nations people were no longer required to learn English in order to become Christians. The Anglicans instead used West's graduates, with their fluency in ancestral languages and kinship ties to First Nations communities, to facilitate conversion in First Nations languages. The church reasoned that these men had a better chance of being accepted in First Nations communities because of their cultural backgrounds. Henry Budd, for example, one of West's earliest graduates, was sent to Cumberland House to work with Swampy Cree. Charles Pratt, another early graduate, was sent to work with Plains Cree and Assiniboine communities.[90]

St. John's College

Between 1850 and 1859, scholarships were awarded to First Nations men who were interested in entering St. John's College, a seminary in the Red River Settlement, to become ordained ministers. The first recorded students were Charles Pratt (1850), Robert McDonald (1850–52), Henry Budd Jr. and John Settee (1850–55), James Settee, John Garrioch, Thomas Cook (1853), and Henry Cockrane (1853–58).[91] These men maintained their First Nations identity through the continued use of their ancestral language while learning to read, write, and speak English.[92] For example, with Henry Budd, the first ordained minister, "using Cree in the church . . . allowed [him] to form a connection with his community membership through language while encouraging them to see language as a unique and important aspect of their group identity."[93] Budd's use of the Cree language enabled him to maintain kinship ties with his culture and community.[94]

During the nineteenth century, First Nations cultural identity endured to some extent, finding preservation through language despite the introduction of a new religion. It's important to note that not all missionaries were intent on eradicating First Nations cultures and languages. First Nations missionaries who embraced a new language and religion managed to sustain a profound connection to their cultural origins and territories through their ancestral language. Consequently, language played a pivotal role in upholding First Nations cultural identity, intricately intertwined with their traditional lands.[95]

Taking an even more supportive stance, the Anglicans extended their efforts through the Native Church Policy crafted by Henry Venn. It's crucial to understand that during this period, the church actively used First Nations men as agents to advance their Christianizing mission, further intertwining the cultural dynamics of language and religion.[96]

Native Church Policy

Henry Venn was the secretary to the Church Missionary Society of the Anglican Church from 1841 to 1872. His views regarding the transformation of First Nations societies while maintaining their ancestral language evolved into the Native Church Policy (NCP) in 1869.[97] The goal of the NCP was to create self-supporting congregations of First Nations Christians. Accordingly, missionaries "were instructed to study the host cultures, learn the languages, and refrain from imposing European habits, tastes, and ideas in order that a distinctly Indigenous institution would develop in an Indigenous setting."[98] The NCP policy was influenced by the failure of the Anglican Church in Ireland to win converts, seemingly a response to the imposition of English on the Gaelic-speaking people of Ireland. Not only did the Irish reject the English language, they also rejected Anglican efforts to convert them. Guided by this history, Venn believed it was necessary to develop an Aboriginal church where First Nations were Christianized through their ancestral languages.[99] Venn therefore ensured that First Nations men had educational opportunities for clerical training, even if they were unable to communicate in English. Correspondence in 1865 between Henry Venn, the General Secretary of the Church Missionary Society, and the Diocese of Moosonee reveals that the Diocese wanted to raise funds to house, train, and remunerate First Nations men interested in pursuing a clerical path. This proposal also included a provision to fund the families who were willing to join these men, and support for teachers who were fluent in Cree and English. In Venn's words:

> Besides those fourteen pure Indian clergymen, speaking no other language than their own should as soon as possible be appointed, who should have under their care the various members of their own tribes during the winter seasons for there would be little difficulty in selecting such agents as most of the tribes have already teachers placed over them several

> being men of *intelligence and . . . considerable influence* [my emphasis]. Those men with their wives and families I would bring to Moose keeping them under instruction for the two winters employing them in the summer as Evangelists, they should then receive ordination as deacons and return of them . . . following their occupation as hunters at the same time [tend to] the spiritual over sight of their tribes. They say of each of those families at Moose would involve a cost of fifty and sixty pounds per annum on their return to their hunting grounds I propose that each of ordained Indians should receive 20 pounds per annum with 5 pounds for traveling expenses to remunerate more highly would I fear be injurious as raising them too high above their relatives and associates and tending to foster pride and self conceit. The five at the principal posts should receive from 120–200 pounds per annum according to nationality, and time of service with a house and allowance for traveling expenses.[100]

Reverend James Settee, a First Nations convert who spoke Swampy Cree, seized the educational opportunities at St. John's, emerging as the second ordained Anglican First Nations minister. Beyond conducting services in First Nations languages, he welcomed members of the settler Icelandic community into his congregation. To facilitate communication, an Icelandic interpreter, proficient in Cree, translated Settee's sermons into the Icelandic language.[101]

Throughout this period, the preservation of First Nations cultures found some support through the continued use of their languages. However, the primary objective of the church was the conversion of First Nations people to Christianity, often at the expense of their own spiritual and cultural practices. Missionaries strategically used First Nations men educated in Indian mission schools, capitalizing on their language skills and cultural knowledge to introduce Christianity into their communities. These schools hinted at the potential for an educational system that could have fostered the preservation of First Nations languages.

Syllabics

Another notable aspect of First Nations language transmission during this period was the use of a writing system known as syllabics in the prairie region, a practice that extended to the area now known as Nunavut. There are, however, two different explanations of the importance and reasons for its creation. One version holds that Westerners developed syllabics to introduce Christianity through literacy and attributes the origins of syllabics to the work of missionary James Evans in the early 1800s. The other version comes from First Nations oral history, which dates the syllabic system back to the 1700s and attributes its origin to two individuals, Mistanaskowew from western Canada and Machiminahtik from eastern Canada, who developed syllabics for language preservation and transmission.[102]

First Nations and the Origins of Syllabics

Nancy Smith (Ak a chah), George Chiefstick, and Jerry Saddleback from Hobbema, Alberta, identify the origin of syllabics for language transmission according to Cree customary law. Its development is associated with ceremonial customs, practices, and traditions. Even today, anyone requesting syllabics teachings must follow protocols that include an offering of tobacco and cloth to the Elder who can provide the oral history and a pipe ceremony (a crucial component of providing the teaching is ceremony).[103]

In 2013, Elder Saddleback provided a detailed account of the oral history of syllabics in Edmonton, Alberta. The workshop was significant because the history has not been published and is rarely taught in a public setting. According to Saddleback, syllabics began in the late 1700s with Mistanaskowew (Badger Call or Badger Voice),[104] a holy man who followed the ways of the Midewiwin (Grand Medicine) society. Although today Midewiwin teachings are commonly associated with Ojibway and Cree communities, historically, membership extended to various Algonquian speaking communities. The connection between Mistanaskowew and the Midewiwin demonstrates the significance of syllabics in the transmission of language. A prophecy during Mistanaskowew's lifetime foretold that the Algonquian peoples would eventually face difficulties in retaining their language, prompting the creation of the syllabic system as a tool for linguistic preservation.[105] The shapes used in the syllabics chart resemble those found in ceremonial lodges. In addition, these symbols are closely associated with Algonquian speaking communities' ceremonial practices and the four directions. As stated by Saddleback, the symbols also incorporate

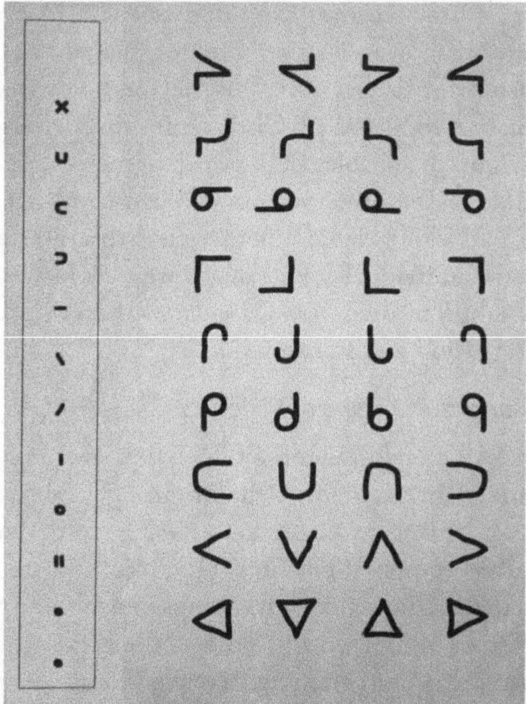

Figure 3. Original Cree syllabics. Drawing by Jerry Saddleback, 2008. Photograph courtesy of Lorena Fontaine.

various components of the universe (Eh Wihkweahkik Kisik).[106] The description of original Cree syllabics is represented in the drawing shown in Figure 3.

The syllabics developed by Mistanaskowew differ slightly from the version later promoted by missionaries. Saddleback indicated that the Elders from his community were unaware of the missionaries' reasons for the changes. In any event, syllabics became a tool of linguistic preservation, created in anticipation of a time when language endangerment would occur. In contrast to Cree oral history, some scholars attribute the birth of syllabics to James Evans, who created the system as a means for introducing Christianity.[107]

James Evans and the Origin of Syllabics

Beginning in 1828, English Methodist missionary James Evans spent approximately six years learning to speak and read Ojibway in the

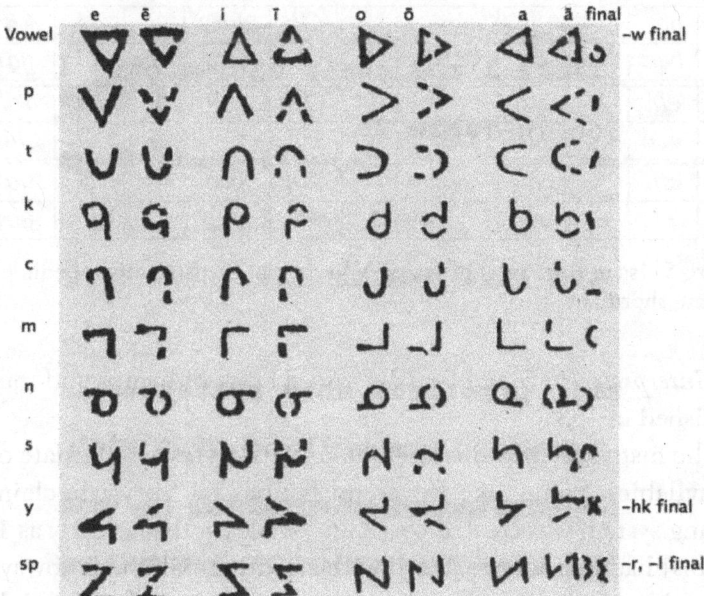

Figure 4. Syllabics used by James Evans, 1841. From John D. Nichols, "The Composition Sequence of the First Cree Hymnal," in *Essays in Algonquian Bibliography in Honour of V.M. Dechene,* edited by H.C. Wolfart (Winnipeg: University of Manitoba, 1984).

community of Rice Lake. After ordination as a Wesleyan minister in 1833, Evans served several other Ojibway communities until 1837. With the language skills he developed, he translated Bible passages from English into Ojibway using Roman orthography following the example of Peter Jones, an Ojibway Methodist minister, who had previously translated portions of the Bible. As Evans studied the language further, he concluded that the Roman alphabet was not always suitable for writing Ojibway.[108] As a solution, certain scholars suggest, Evans developed a better way to represent Ojibway through various phonetic sounds.[109] Others suggest that around 1836, Evans was encouraged by Methodist minister William Case to create a simple writing system for Ojibway using Roman orthography.[110] Although syllabics did not surface immediately, a number of publications by Evans appeared shortly after he was tasked to create the system. For example, *The Speller*

P	*pee*	\	*T*	*tee*	│	*Ch*	*chay*	/	*K*	*kay*	—
B	*bee*	\	*D*	*dee*	│	*J*	*jay*	/	*G*	*gay*	—
F	*eff*	◟	*Th*	*ith*	(	*S*	*ess*	)	*Sh*	*ish*	◞
V	*vee*	◟	*Dh*	*thee*	(	*Z*	*zee*	)	*Zh*	*zhee*	◞
M	*em*	⌒	*N*	*en*	‿	*Ng*	*ing*	‿	*H*	*hay*	◊
L	*el*	◜	*R*	*ray, ar*	/⌒	*W*	*way*	◡/	*Y*	*yay*	(

Figure 5. Isaac Pitman shorthand. Wikipedia, https://en.wikipedia.org/wiki/Pitman_shorthand.

and Interpreter, in Indian and English, a book of hymns and music, was published in 1837.[111]

The historical record is ambiguous with respect to the date of origin for syllabics. Some, like Reverend Nathanael Burwash, claimed the writing system was created by 1836: "We learn that as early as 1836, he [Evans] had not only analyzed with scientific skill the Ojibway branch of the Algonquian family of languages and reduced it to an alphabet of eight consonants and four vowels, but also discovered the secret of its simple syllabic character, and the possibility of writing it by syllabic rather than by alphabetic character."[112]

John Murdoch is sceptical of Burwash's theory because it is based solely on a briefing note written by the Reverend Joseph Stinson in 1841 and lacks corroborating evidence.[113] Murdoch suggests that syllabics originated in an Ojibway syllabic system that was submitted to the Wesleyan Board of Missions in 1836. Following this submission, a committee of five individuals was appointed in 1837 to meet during the Wesleyan Methodist Conference to adopt a uniform orthographical system for the Ojibway language.[114] In the same year, Isaac Pitman published a phonetic shorthand system. Some suggest that Evans was influenced by the Pitman shorthand system since a copy of it was found in his possession.[115]

Shortly after the introduction of the Pitman system, Evans was appointed as the General Superintendent of Norway House, Manitoba. The first recorded Cree syllabic writing system surfaced in this community during this period. One important goal for Evans in his new post was to distribute as widely as possible the Cree syllabic translations of the Bible he had made in previous years. To carry out this task, Evans required a printing press, which he requested from the HBC. However, the company refused to permit anyone to bring a press into the territory, so Evans created his own in the fall of 1840 and released the first plate on 15 October.[116] The following month, hundreds of copies of the hymn "Jesus My All to Heaven Is Gone" were printed in Cree syllabics and distributed widely, and "by mid-June, 1841 [Evans] had printed approximately 5,000 pages of material."[117]

Evans's translating team was largely responsible for the success of this independent printing. Team members were primarily of First Nations ancestry and were either bilingual or multilingual. For example, Thomas Hassell (Chippewyan) had learned fluent Cree, French, and English; Henry Bird Steinhauer (Ojibway) had attended a mission school in Upper Canada and knew Greek, Hebrew, and English in addition to Cree; and John Sinclair, who, as the son of an HBC officer and a Cree mother, was fluent in Cree. Thanks to his multilingual upbringing, Sinclair was an excellent translator and interpreter. Another important member of the team was William Mason, who supervised the mission during Evans's absence. Although Mason was not from a First Nation, his wife, Sophia Mason, was the daughter of a Cree mother and an HBC officer.[118] Sophia would have greatly assisted Mason in his translation work since she was raised speaking Cree.

Cree syllabics were widely circulated through the successful translation work of this dynamic, multilingual team. Several First Nations communities became proficient in this writing system and took the initiative to teach others interested in learning it. Burwash describes the teaching process: "Every man who acquired the new art imparted his knowledge to others, and in a short period of time we hear of men who could read and write as far north as Fort Churchill and as far west as the Rockies."[119] By 1842, knowledge of syllabics was widespread, in places such as York Factory, Fort Severn, and Moose Factory. Evans attributes the rapid rate of syllabics transmission to the close Cree kinship systems of the time.[120] As the knowledge of syllabics grew, however, missionaries began to question whether printing religious texts in syllabics should continue,[121] or whether, according to one suggestion, printed texts should return to the Roman alphabet. William Mason addressed this question in a letter from York Factory on 12 September 1854:

> Before I conclude it will perhaps be advisable for me to say a few words regarding the printing of books in the syllabic characters having studied the system for some years.... I do

think that for grammatical and philological purposes the Roman characters are decidedly the best, I have been confirmed in this opinion since reading the Church missionary intelligence for March 1853. The roots of the Cree words are closed and not open syllables and many words require double consonants to pronounce them correctly. In writing or printing with the syllable of a consonant [you need to] join it to the following vowel to which it does not belong. And it is utterly impossible to spell proper names by them, my translation of the New Testament is intertwined with Roman letters to assist me in making out what the characters were intended to express. What difficulty there may be in some of the languages of this immense country there exists now in expressing clearly and correctly every sound of the Cree by the means of the Roman Characters. When in fact Archdeacon Hunter's translation of St. Matthew's Gospel. . . . and of the young men who had been taught English at the Mission School they read it at once both correctly and fluently and in a week any of the school children could read it. The Reverend Thomas Hurlburt whose extensive knowledge of Indians deserves notice, regrets that the syllabic systems [were] ever adopted, thinks they are very defective and inefficient and should be permitted to fall into disuse. I cannot go so far as this, for the sake of those Indians who have not the opportunity of being taught at the mission stations. Many adults in different parts of the country acquired a knowledge of the syllabic characters themselves, and can both read and write in them. Yet my conviction is that they will be ultimately given place to the Roman Character. I should therefore recommend the immediate adoption of the archdeacon's improved orthography and the printing of his manuscript. Could he remain in English to complete the translation of the entire new testament as well as the prayer book, it would be conferring the greatest of blessing upon our mission. . . . I still think that elementary books and portions of gods [God's] holy word should be circulated amongst our converted Indians in the syllabic character until the roman characters become general.[122]

In his letter, Mason explained the dilemma of using syllabics. It had its virtues, since Roman orthography seemed unable to correctly express every sound in the Cree language. In one example, Mason indicated that double consonants are necessary to pronounce certain words correctly and recommended against the use of syllabics to aid in pronunciation when reading. Mason also noted how easily the Cree language could be taught with syllabics and that many First Nations people were able to learn to read and write Cree fairly quickly. However, despite the success of Cree syllabics, Mason foresaw its demise and recommended the use of syllabics only until more First Nations people could become acquainted with Roman orthography.

Regardless of origin and use, syllabics became the cornerstone for converting First Nations people to Christianity using First Nations languages. These two accounts of its origins require more research to resolve. However, they are complementary in the sense that both First Nations and the missionaries saw value in the writing system as an aid for language transmission, Christianization, and, to a certain extent, language preservation.

Inuktitut Syllabics

Syllabics found another application in the mid-1800s for transmission and literacy in Inuktitut.[123] Carrying out the mandate of the CMS, Anglican missionaries John Horden and Edwin Arthur Watkins learned Cree syllabics before publishing a number of religious texts for Inuit speakers in the 1850s. Horden, initially appointed as Moose Factory schoolmaster in 1851 by the HBC, studied Cree for several months, mastering Cree syllabics and becoming a good interpreter. Eventually he was able to preach to the Cree community on his own. The undated letter in Figure 6 provides an example of Horden's skill with syllabics.

Using Roman orthography, Horden translated the letter handwritten in syllabics by an unnamed Aboriginal person into English. Horden's expertise is also apparent in publications such as a *Collection of Psalms and Hymns, in the language of the Cree Indians of North West America, 1874*, as well as a translation of the New Testament in 1876, both of which were published in syllabics.

Similarly, Edwin Arthur Watkins learned Cree and became interested in translating the Bible into First Nations languages. He travelled to

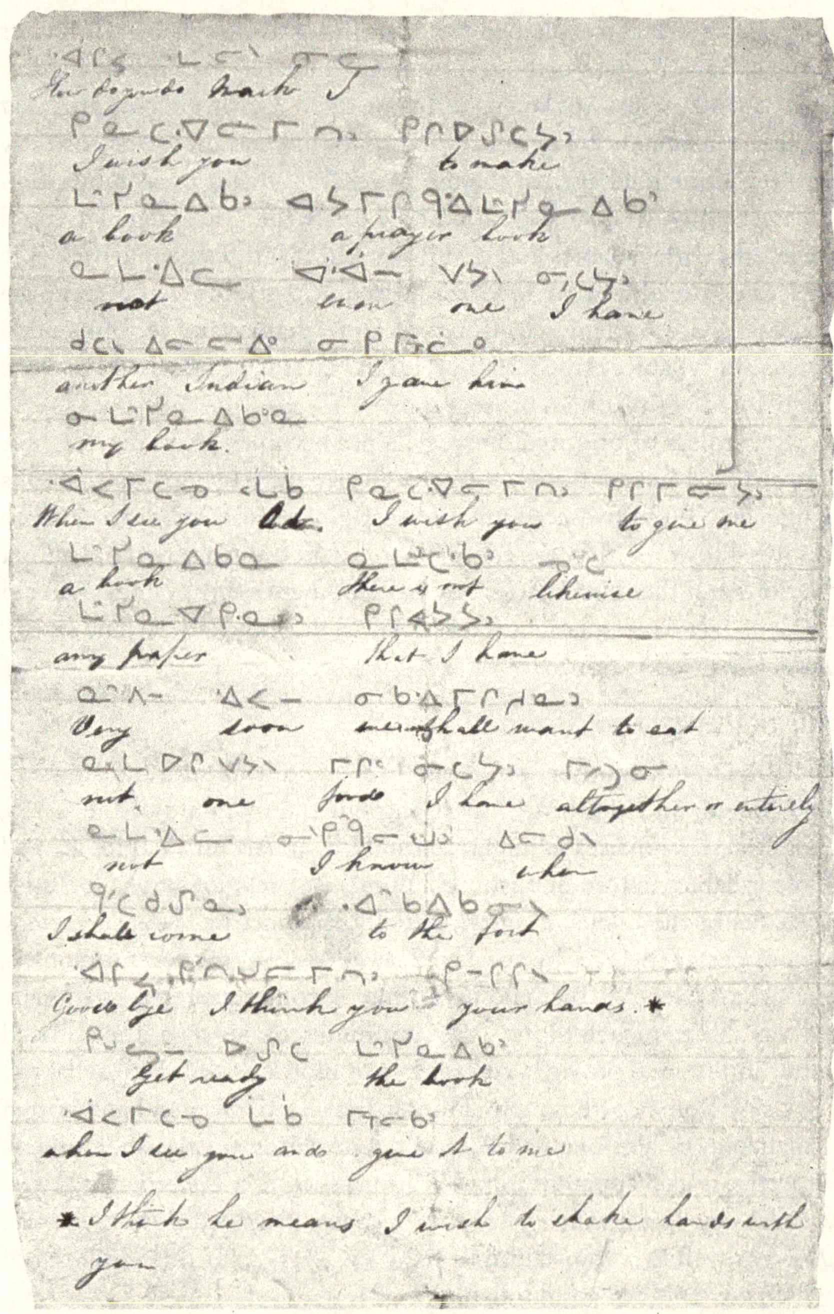

How do you do Mark I
I wish you to make
a book a prayer book
not know one I have
another Indian I gave him
my book.
When I see you [illegible] I wish you to give me
a book there is not likewise
any paper that I have
Very soon we shall want to eat
not one food I have altogether or entirely
not I know when
I shall come to the fort
Good bye I think you your hands.*
Get ready the book
when I see you and do give it to me

* I think he means I wish to shake hands with you

Figure 6. Translated letter from Cree Syllabics to English. Church Missionary Society, Church Missionary Society Records, C1/0 33/117, 1851. Cadbury Research Library: Special Collections, University of Birmingham.

Canada in 1852, living in Fort George on James Bay until 1856, in Red River from 1856 to 1860, in Cumberland House from 1860 to 1863, and then in Portage La Prairie until 1866. As a missionary, he soon learned to communicate in Cree.[124] By 1855, Watkins had translated the Gospels of John and Luke from English into Cree, and in 1865 he gained notice for publishing a Cree dictionary. Watkins intended the dictionary to preserve the Cree language and to provide a resource for traders and others interested in learning Cree.[125] He described the process of learning Cree in terms of "investigating the structure of a beautiful language and seeing its Native rich expressions."[126]

In 1865, Watkins and Horden met with the CMS in England to discuss creating an Inuit writing system.[127] Minutes from the meeting on 24 November 1865 reveal a discussion concerning the possibility of adapting the Cree writing syllabic system to the Inuit language:

> (1) It appears to us very undesirable that any changes, except such as are absolutely necessary, should be made in the Syllabrium as now used; though we quite agree that the system is not so scientifically accurate as could be wished. We consider that in dealing with the uncultivated tribes of North America, *utility* and *simplicity* are more important than philological precision.
>
> (2) In reducing the *Esquimaux* language into syllabic writing, we think that a change may be advantageously made in the *final* symbols. Instead of the arbitrary signs now in use for the Cree, we would propose the adoption of the *half-size* characters of the *same forms* as those employed for the consonants in combination with the vowel *a*. This change might be introduced into the *Cree* language at a future period; but as there is in existence a large supply of Bibles and other publications printed according to the original methods, we would not advocate for any alterations at present.
>
> (3) The additional consonants, *b* and *d*, found in the Esquimaux, may, we think, be represented with sufficient accuracy by the characters for *p* and *t* respectively without the introduction of new forms; especially as the natives frequently pronounce these letters so indistinctly that is difficult to ascertain their true sound.

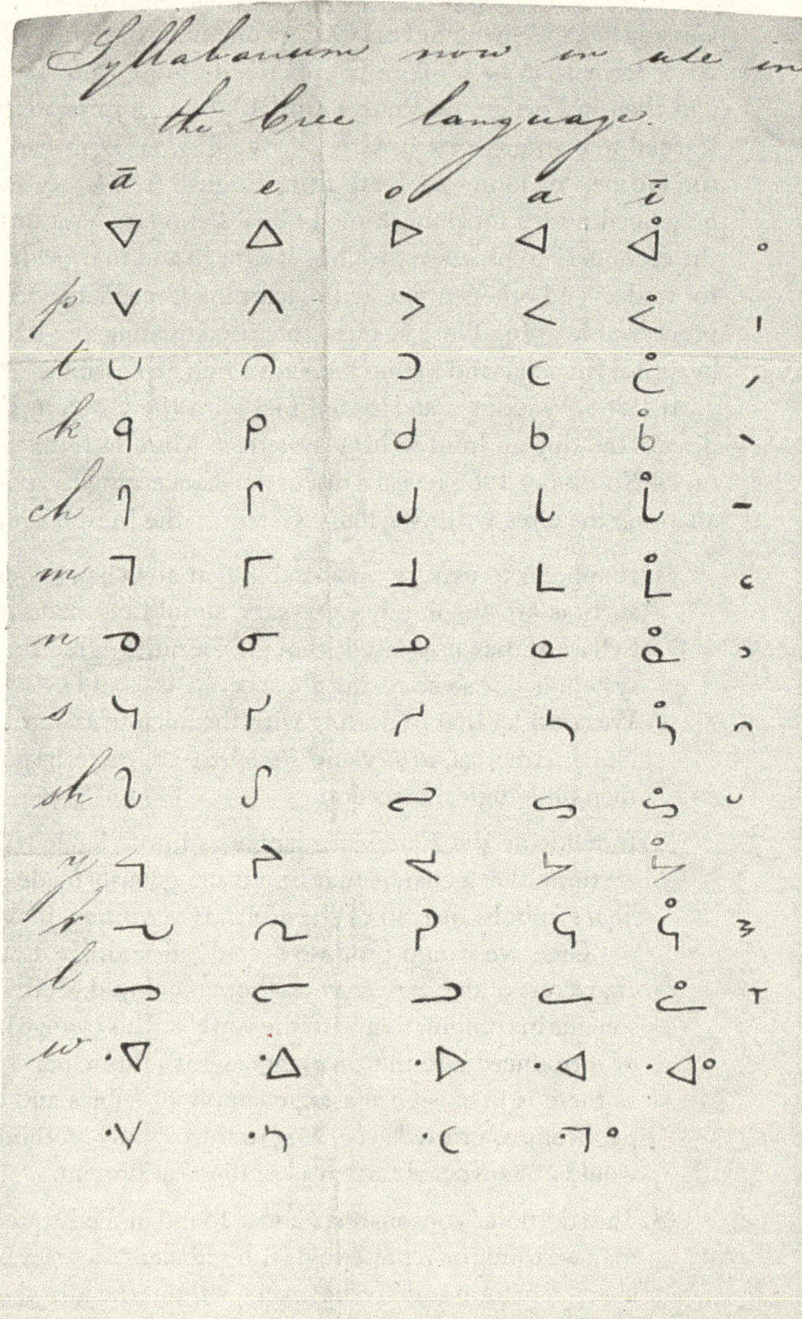

Figure 7. Syllabrium for the Cree language and Syllabrium prepared for the Esquimaux language. Church Missionary Society, CMS G Y C1 F1 1, 1865. Cadbury Research Library: Special Collections, University of Birmingham.

Syllabarium proposed for the Esquimaux language

ā e o a ī

p
t
k
h
m
n
s
sh
r
l
w

double consonants nk
rk

(4) In the Esquimaux language there are some consonants which will need to be represented. For these we have adopted signs which combine as nearly as possible the two separate consonants.[128]

Three months after these deliberations, a letter from Watkins dated 10 February 1866 indicated they would need to find a way to standardize the Inuktitut.[129] A year later, Horden and Watkins created an Inuit syllabics chart. Figure 7 and 8 show Cree syllabics on the left and Inuit syllabics on the right.

After the publication of these charts, Edmund James Peck, a Church of England missionary and founder of the first mission on Baffin Island, would go on to promote the use of Inuit syllabics across the Arctic, meeting with considerable success. A century later, in 1976, the Language Commission of the Inuit Culture Institute approved Inuit syllabics as a standard writing system (Figure 9).

From the eighteenth and nineteenth centuries on, syllabics played a significant role in the transmission of Cree, Ojibway, and Inuktitut.

Concluding Remarks

The initial significant interaction between Europeans and the transmission of First Nations languages in the prairie region took place in the seventeenth century through HBC employees. Cree continued to be the *lingua franca* in the region throughout the HBC fur trade era.[130] Support for the transmission of First Nations languages is also evident in dictionaries created to assist fur traders in learning local dialects. James Isham's dictionary, in particular, stands out as a noteworthy example of the effort to bridge diverse world views by incorporating terminology related to time and other trade-relevant terms.

Moreover, as an employee of the HBC, Henry Kelsey actively engaged in language transmission through communicative protocols such as feasting practices, gift exchange, pipe ceremonies, and the offering of tobacco. These practices highlighted HBC's dedication to promoting communication and understanding between European traders and First Nations, exemplifying a multifaceted approach to supporting the transmission of First Nations languages.

With the arrival of missionaries in the 1820s, language transmission in the prairie region underwent a distinct shift marked by the introduction of a religious-based educational system. While the changes

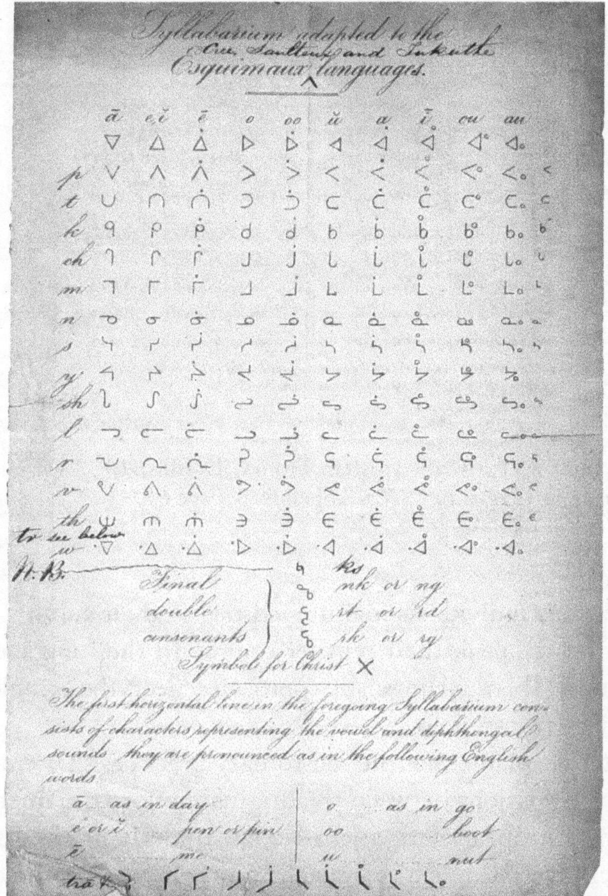

Figure 8. Syllabrium adapted to the Cree, Saulteaux, and to the Esquimaux Language. Church Missionary Society, G Y C1 F1 1, 1865. Cadbury Research Library: Special Collections, University of Birmingham.

brought about by this system influenced First Nations religious and spiritual practices, missionaries did not implement policies to eradicate First Nations languages. Instead, English and other languages such as Latin and French were taught to First Nations students at mission schools. Simultaneously, some missionaries learned to communicate in First Nations languages and even used a new writing system based on syllabics.

Despite ongoing controversy regarding the origins of syllabics, this system emerged as a method of First Nations language transmission amidst significant cultural and political changes. Remarkably, some

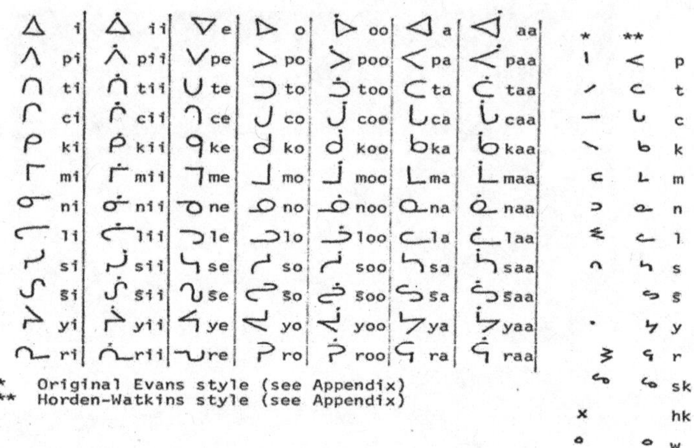

Figure 9. Inuit syllabic writing system. From C.D. Ellis, *A proposed Standard Roman Orthography for Cree* (n.p., 1970). Appendix 5, page 65.

First Nations individuals maintained ties to their cultural identity by continuing to speak their mother tongue in their engagement with Christianity. This dual linguistic approach reflects the complex interplay of language transmission.

Slattery explains that the "customary practices that emerged [regulated] the relations between the original nations of America and the incoming European nation."[131] The law underlying these practices is "not exclusively English or French in origin, nor, on the other hand, purely aboriginal. Both aboriginal and settler groups contributed to its formation; in doing so, they produced something genuinely new and distinctively Canadian."[132] This implies that the right to language transmission is rooted in historical customary practices between First Nations and Europeans, and these practices that supported language transmission are part of Canada's Constitution as unwritten principles.

Tragically, with the expansion of European settlement throughout the nineteenth century and a diminishing interest in First Nations partnership, the Canadian government collaborated with churches to institute a residential school system. This system, shamefully designed to eliminate First Nations languages and cultures, not only violated First Nations law but also disregarded the inter-customary protocols that had been established to mutually respect and preserve First Nations and European languages.

CHAPTER 2

LINGUISTIC GENOCIDE

Canada's Educational System

The role that native language repression played in the political oppression of Native Americans and the federal expansion into Indian-held land . . . is a particularly brutal history, but one that all language minorities need to be aware of if they want to know the true nexus between language, politics, and power.

—Sandra Del Valle[1]

I lost my talk
The talk you took away
When I was a little girl
at Shubenacadie school.

You snatched it away:
I speak like you
I think like you
I create like you
The scrambled ballad, about my world.

Two ways I talk
Both ways I say,
Your way is more powerful.

So gently I offer my hand and ask,
Let me find my talk
So I can teach you about me.

—Rita Joe[2]

First Nations languages are a marker of First Nations cultural identities. The language someone speaks identifies the land they come from, and sometimes the dialect pinpoints the specific region. Language not only distinguishes First Nations from one another but also sets them apart from the settler Canadian population. First Nations identity also carries legal, political, and cultural rights. The Canadian government recognized the link between language, culture, and First Nations nationhood, and identified this as a barrier to accessing land and resources. This ultimately led to a national project of displacement and assimilation that targeted children. During the residential school era, First Nations children were removed from their communities and prohibited from speaking their languages. Through education, as well as other assimilation policies, the government aimed to erase all markers of cultural and linguistic differences among First Nations.

Raphael Lemkin, a Polish-Jewish lawyer credited with coining the term genocide, includes actions aimed at destroying a group culturally and linguistically in the definition of genocide. Lemkin's characterization indicates a coordinated plan or process meant to destroy the fundamental aspects of national group life. This includes the destruction of political and social institutions, culture, language, national sentiments, religion, and the economic independence of national groups, alongside personal security, liberty, health, dignity, and lives of individuals belonging to such groups. The second part of this coordinated plan involves imposing the cultural norms of the oppressor onto the oppressed.[3]

The Truth and Reconciliation Commission of Canada (TRC) documented Canada's coordinated plan to destroy First Nations structures and practices essential for their survival as distinct groups during the residential school era. The Final Report of the TRC revealed policies that aimed to destroy political and social institutions through land seizures, forced population transfers, movement restrictions, language bans, persecution of spiritual leaders, and confiscation of spiritual objects.[4] This process resulted in the abuse and death of many First

Nations children as well as the destruction of family and communal bonds, preventing language and cultural transmission. The current educational system's imposition of cultural norms that are not First Nations represents a continuation of the genocidal process and will be examined in subsequent chapters.

Regarding Canada's assimilation policy carried out in residential schools, former chief justice of the Supreme Court of Canada Beverley McLachlin commented that "the objective was—I quote from Sir John A. Macdonald, our revered forefather—'take the Indian out of the child,' and thus solve what was referred to as 'the Indian problem.' 'Indianness' was not to be tolerated. Rather, it must be eliminated. In the buzz-word of the day, assimilation. In the language of the 21st century, cultural genocide."[5] The National Inquiry into Missing and Murdered Indigenous Women and Girls also concluded that colonial structures such as the residential school system resulted in genocide.[6] The late Pope Francis expressed his condemnation of the abuse inflicted by Roman Catholic run residential schools in Canada, acknowledging the profound harm caused to generations of Indigenous peoples. He described the actions of European colonizers carried out with the support of the Catholic Church as a genocide, stating, "I described the genocide and asked for forgiveness, forgiveness for this operation." During his address, he expressed deep remorse, saying, "Today, too, in this place, I want to tell you how very sorry I am and to ask for forgiveness for the evil perpetrated by not a few Catholics." He emphasized the lasting impact of these actions, adding, "How evil it is to break the bonds uniting parents and children."[7]

This chapter provides an overview of Canada's national assimilation framework, which targeted First Nations languages and cultures for destruction. This assimilation project has been detrimental to the ability of First Nations people to communicate and maintain relationships among children, families, and communities. Personal testimonies from former residential school students are included below as vivid depictions of the destructive experiences endured by First Nations children.

Establishing a Genocidal Framework Through Ideology

In the 1867 British North America Act, the federal government was given the power to legislate on matters concerning "Indian lands" and "Indian peoples," as outlined in section 91(24). This was done without seeking consent or involving First Nations. Simultaneously, this constitutional provision placed a legal and moral obligation on the federal government to act in the "best interests" of First Nations peoples.[8] Tragically, Canadian policies were heavily influenced by the theories of British scholar Herman Merivale, who suggested various approaches for interacting with Aboriginal peoples that included assimilation, slavery, and extermination.[9] This ideological influence led to two divergent viewpoints regarding the languages of the First Nations. On the one hand, there was an acknowledgement that the languages held an intrinsic value as a vital component of cultural identity. On the other hand, there was a perception that these languages were hindrances to the colonial objective of assimilation. This dichotomy in perspectives played a significant role in shaping policy: while the legislation itself did not directly address language and culture, the Canadian government's public statements and assimilationist educational policy directives contributed first-hand to the erosion of First Nations languages and cultural practices, leaving a lasting impact on the communities.

In 1857 and in 1869, the Gradual Civilization Act and Gradual Enfranchisement Act were implemented with the objective of eradicating the cultural, political, and legal identities of First Nations peoples.[10] Prior to this, between 1842 and 1844, the Bagot Commission had proposed a residential school system, intending to separate First Nations children from the cultural and linguistic influences of their family and community. This educational system ultimately sought to eliminate First Nations languages and cultures.

In 1883, Sir John A. Macdonald publicly informed the House of Commons of the government's position regarding education:

> When the school is on the reserve the child lives with its parents, who are savages; he is surrounded by savages, and though he may learn to read and write his habits and training and mode of thought are Indian. He is simply a savage who can read and write. It has been strongly pressed on myself, as the head of the Department, that Indian children should be withdrawn as much as possible from the parental influence, and the only way to do that would be to put them in central training industrial schools where they will acquire the habits and modes of thought of white men.[11]

This statement starkly reveals two important aspects of the government's attitude at the time: first, that the government knew how significant close family and social relationships were to maintaining the cultural identities of First Nations; and second, that the government fully intended to remove First Nations children from the cultural connections they had through family and community. Although mothering was not directly mentioned in any legislation, the assimilative policies that followed had a direct impact on mother-child relationships. In First Nations, much like in many other cultures, mothering plays a central role in transmitting both culture and language. The mother-child bond is crucial, as children learn to speak their language by observing and listening to their mother.[12] Learning to communicate in their language is intertwined with learning their culture; the two are deeply connected.[13]

The federal government's annual report of 1885 included a declaration that First Nations children in residential schools should no longer be allowed to speak their mother tongue. John Milloy explains that policy makers had a "multifaceted strategy of re-socialization . . . to stamp out Aboriginal languages within the schools and in children."[14] Federal leaders agreed that teaching children to speak French or English was a critical step in acculturating First Nations children. Language was the vehicle for replacing First Nations culture with core European concepts and values. As Milloy indicates, "that the Department [of Indian Affairs] and the churches understood consciously that culture or, more particularly, that the task of overturning one ontology in favour of another was the challenge they faced is seen in their identification of language as the critical issue in the circle. It was through language that the child gained its ontological inheritance from its parents and community. . . . The civilizers knew it must be cut if any progress were to be made."[15] Senior staff in the Department of Indian Affairs strongly suggested that it would "be found best to rigorously exclude the use of Indian dialects."[16] In 1896, the federal government recommended that in the education of First Nations children, "every effort must be made to induce pupils to speak English and to teach them to understand it, unless they do, the whole work of the teacher is likely to be wasted."[17] An edict of the Department of Indian Affairs declared, "The use of English in preference to the Indian dialect must be insisted upon."[18] The objective was to instruct children in English, except in Quebec where the focus was to instruct in French.

At first, the schools were ineffective in stamping out First Nations languages. The lack of initial success caused some senior government staff in the 1890s to question the likelihood of achieving this policy objective. The federal government appeared to soften its position on language, prompting Hayter Reed, Superintendent General of Indian Affairs, to advise the federal government that "at most the native language is only to be used as a vehicle for teaching and should be discontinued as soon as possible."[19] The government reaffirmed its objective to eradicate First Nations languages and between 1894 and 1908 issued two orders-in-council compelling children to attend residential school.[20]

The policies implemented during this period starkly contradicted the numbered treaties negotiated between 1871 and 1921. First Nations leaders engaged in these treaty negotiations to safeguard the cultural identity of their nations. The sharing of lands and resources was envisioned as a means to ensure economic subsistence and to support the continuity of First Nations cultural identity.

Treaties One to Seven, negotiated during this time frame, explicitly addressed education while establishing the Crown's fiduciary obligation for First Nations education. Sir Adams George Archibald, the lieutenant governor of Manitoba and the Northwest Territories, played a role in the negotiations of Treaty One. He regarded education as a crucial avenue to enable First Nations to live prosperously, emphasizing its importance in the treaties as a means of cultural preservation and economic well-being.[21]

The role of the interpreter played a crucial part in the negotiation of treaties with First Nations. Interpreting went beyond a mere understanding of languages; it required the skills to navigate complex forms of communication, including protocols like offering tobacco, feasting, and pipe ceremonies, as documented in the journals of Kelsey and Isham. Historian Nancy L. Hagedorn aptly characterizes the interpreter as a "cultural broker" or "a person of ability and integrity in whom both sides could place . . . confidence";[22] they required the knowledge of First Nations communications protocols that were inherent in the political processes of negotiating treaties.

Translating a treaty text into First Nations languages demanded great skill, showcasing the intricate role of the interpreter during treaty negotiations. Dialectal variations within a single First Nations language like Cree presented challenges, requiring multiple translators. For instance, aspects of the Swampy Cree dialect in Northern Manitoba may differ significantly from the Cree dialect in Island Lake, also in Northern Manitoba. This diversity necessitated the collaboration of two or more translators. Another potential challenge was the inability of the majority of First Nations people to read Roman orthography during the treaty era, while the syllabic writing system was accessible. As the previous chapter has shown, some First Nations individuals and missionaries possessed the linguistic expertise to translate English into Ojibway and Cree syllabics. Recognizing the role and abilities of interpreters is critical to the work of understanding and preserving treaty rights. Ongoing research with Treaty Elders emphasizes the importance of delving deeper into aspects of treaty breaches, particularly arising from issues related to interpretation and translation.[23]

Breaches of the government's treaty obligations and constitutional responsibilities under the British North America Act to care for and protect First Nations people became apparent in the early 1900s. Dr. Peter Bryce, a medical inspector to the Department of the Interior and Indian Affairs, published a "Report on the Indian Schools of Manitoba and the Northwest Territories" in 1907, revealing that children were dying due to a lack of adequate medical care and unsanitary living conditions.[24] In response, Bryce recommended that the government "undertake the complete maintenance and control of these schools, since it had been promised by treaty." He further urged that the health interests of pupils be safeguarded through proper medical inspection and that local physicians be encouraged to employ fresh air methods in the care and treatment of tuberculosis.[25] Bryce emphasized that the failure to act represented a "criminal disregard for the treaty pledges to guard the welfare of the Indian wards of the nation."[26] He highlighted the constitutional responsibility the government had in caring for First Nations children, stating, "It is indeed pitiable that during the thirteen years since then this trail of disease and death has gone almost unchecked by any serious efforts on the part of the Department of Indian Affairs, placed by the British North America Act especially in charge of our Indian population."[27]

One of Bryce's reports indicated that 24 percent of the children attending the schools died and that over a sixteen-year period, 74 percent of the children from the File Hill reservation had passed away in residential schools.[28] He enquired why the government had not acted on the previous chief medical examiner's 1906 report indicating that "statistics collected from 99 local medical officers having the care of a population of 70,000 have a total of 3,169 cases of tuberculosis . . . and the death rates in several large bands were" over 80 percent.[29] The 1906 report described the detrimental effects of tuberculosis in "diseases of the brain, joints, bones, and to a less degree of the lungs and also if not fatal till adolescence it then usually progresses rapidly to a fatal termination in consumption of the lungs."[30]

By the 1920s, Canada's system of residential and day schools was well established in its task of replacing First Nations languages and cultures with French and English languages and their associated cultures. The regulations for compulsory school attendance were ultimately incorporated into amendments to the Indian Act in 1919–20, stating: "Every Indian child between the ages of seven and fifteen years who is physically able shall attend such day, industrial or boarding school as may be designated by the Superintendent General for the full periods during which such school is open each year."[31] Subsection 10(3) of the Indian Act authorized the government to fine or imprison parents or guardians who failed to send their children to these schools, and to apprehend the children for the purpose of ensuring their attendance:

> Any parent, guardian, or person with whom an Indian child is residing who fails to cause such child, being between the ages of the aforesaid, to attend school as required by this section after having received three days notice so to do by a truant officer shall, on complaint of the truant officer, be liable on summary conviction before a justice of the peace or an Indian agent to a fine of not more than two dollars and costs, or imprisonment for a period not exceeding ten days or both, and such child may be arrested without a warrant and conveyed to school by the truant officer.[32]

During this time, the government was committed "to support, maintain and educate" First Nations children "in a manner satisfactory to the Superintendent General."[33] Although the government's educational goals did not address language specifically, Deputy Superintendent of the Department of Indian Affairs Duncan Campbell Scott revealed the aggressiveness of the federal government's assimilative residential schools policy during a 1920 parliamentary committee meeting. Scott contended that the policy should continue to be implemented "until there is not a single Indian in Canada that had not been absorbed into the body politic, and there is no Indian question, and no Indian Department."[34] The federal government set the general policy for residential schools, but senior government staff did not provide consistent supervision or management. Thus, "the normative policy on language was set in the field by individual school administrators themselves."[35] School principals were left in charge of language training and the development of pedagogy that prevented First Nations children from speaking their mother tongue. Many school administrators held a negative view of First Nations languages and cultures.

According to Elizabeth Graham, author of *The Mush Hole: Life at Two Indian Residential Schools*, the government believed that speaking a First Nations language was not only an impediment to learning but an integral part of the cultural identity of the peoples that had to be eradicated.[36] Most schools made English or French "the only allowed means of communication."[37] Schools varied in their approaches to achieving this goal, but everywhere the effect was the same: First Nations children lost not only their ancestral language, they lost their cultural identity, dignity, and connection to family and community.

Impact: Former Students Recount Their Experiences

Children who resisted speaking French or English encountered a patchwork of punishments deployed by school staff. Some schools enforced their language policies through excessive physical punishment, while other schools used gentler means to induce children to speak English or French, particularly where staff were of First Nations ancestry.[38] Sometimes the punishment was indirect, experienced when the children returned home to discover they were estranged from their families and community. The most compelling accounts of punishment come from former students themselves, who recall extreme physical abuse, ridicule, and simply a profound sense of loss. During this period, the federal government actively sought to eradicate First Nations and Inuit languages within the residential school system.

Physical Punishment

In the 1890s, Mary Tappage attended St. Joseph's Mission School in British Columbia. She recalled, "If we were heard speaking Shuswup, we were punished. We were made to write on the board one hundred times, 'I will not speak Indian any more.'"[39] Tappage questioned why children were not allowed to speak their language.

Eleanor Brass from Peepeekisis reserve in Saskatchewan recalls being strapped when she spoke her language at residential school in 1905.[40] According to Brass, "the Indian language was strictly forbidden and allowed only when relatives came to visit. This was intended only to allow a quicker grasp of the English language; however it also served as a disadvantage to the Indian pupils by forcing them to discard their own native tongue which probably contributed to a feeling of inferiority."[41]

Joseph Francis Dion, a Cree from the Kehewin reserve in Alberta, attended the Onion Lake Mission school and went on to open the first school on the reserve in 1916, where he taught for the next twenty-four years. In Dion's words, he had the children recite "the Lord's Prayer, first in Cree, then I had the children repeat the same in English."[42] One of Dion's greatest challenges was that the children continued to speak Cree when they were together despite the rule that they speak English outside of the classroom.[43] Eventually Dion gave up trying to enforce a strict English-only policy, an exceptional decision that contrasted with the behaviour of non–First Nations staff in residential and day schools across Canada, who in most cases reprimanded First Nations children harshly for speaking their mother tongue.

According to Nelly Stonefish, a former student of Mount Elgin Indian Residential School in Ontario from 1924 to 1927, children were strapped for speaking their language on school grounds.[44] Another former student from Mount Elgin, Dorothy Day, recalled that despite getting strapped for speaking their language, some children resisted. For example, children often spoke among themselves in the absence of school staff, and Day reported speaking with her mother in their language during student-parent visits at school. Nevertheless, children caught speaking their language inside school would get the strap. Day remembered being told, "Don't you know this is an English school you're going to—you're not supposed to talk Indian," and recalled many children being punished for speaking their language.[45]

Peter Smith attended the Mohawk Institute in Brantford, Ontario, from 1926 to 1935. In his recollection, when the small boys came into the school,

> we weren't allowed to talk Indian at all, we couldn't say a word in Indian, just speak English, and these [young] children would come in and maybe have no English at all and they would get in groups like cattle, trying to understand English, because they would give them a licking—or they'd give you a scolding or something like that for not being able to say it in English, and they just wiped out the entire Indian language. It's just the one thing I felt sorry—because you'd see a group of ten or twelve small boys standing in a group trying to learn a little English. Some of them never heard English. I didn't speak any Indian—but it was all the way around us. If we could have utilized our language, probably we would still have our language today—but we don't have a language.[46]

Raymond Hill, a student at the Mohawk Institute from 1929 to 1937, revealed that he lost his language within a year of attending residential school. Hill attributed this quick loss to repeated threats of being strapped if he was caught speaking his Mohawk language.[47] Emmert General, a student at the Mohawk Institute from about 1932 to 1938, had these memories: "I spoke my Native language when I went there but if you tried to speak to someone in your own language, you'd always get the strap or something."[48]

Basil Johnston's autobiography tells of his time at the Spanish Boys School, officially called St. Peter Claver Indian Residential School and renamed after 1945 as St. Charles Garnier. Johnston mentions a young boy who ran away from the school because he was whipped for speaking his language.[49] He also recalls an incident when Father Hawkins came out of his office and enquired if a student had spoken in an "Indian" language. The student responded, "No, Father. Not me. You tol' us not to talk Indian. It is against the rules, you said."[50]

Kenneth George attended the Mohawk Institute from 1953 to 1960. He could only speak Oneida upon first entering the school. Yet upon leaving, he could only understand a few sentences in his language. He attributed this loss to the repeated beatings he received for speaking his language in school. He was hit for helping Cree-speaking children communicate in English, and spoke of seeing a school officer physically punishing kids for speaking their language. The older George got, the worse the beatings became; and things were no better for the

Cree-speaking children who were starting at the school: "It was really bad, because that's all they knew. They were terrified—they were really scared, because all they knew was Cree. Us older guys would kind of pull them aside and try to help them speak English. I always wondered why I ended up getting a ruler across the hand. I didn't know why I was being hit. Now I know why—these guys told me about it. I can't make a sentence in Oneida, but I can pick up words here and there, and that's really sad."[51]

Bob White Eye attended the Mohawk Institute from 1955 to 1964. He spoke mostly Delaware when he arrived at school. He was beaten badly for this, and eventually the only language he knew was English. He remembered having to learn English the very first day of school and the long-term impact this policy had on some children: "The reason we spoke Indian was that Grandmother—that was all that she spoke, she spoke no English at all. Dad spoke English so we had English and Indian, but not fluently. When I was there in the sixties, the Cree children started coming in and they spoke no English, and they literally beat this one child into submission, [as a result] . . . he is in fact mentally [disabled] today."[52]

Lee Snake attended the Mohawk Institute from 1963 to 1965. He recalled being beaten for speaking his Delaware language. However, he was able to pick up some Cree words from a number of Cree children who attended the school. Snake indicated that his language was beaten out of his mom's generation; not everyone from his community had their ancestral language.[53] According to Snake, when language is taken away, a sense of First Nations identity, which includes knowledge of ceremonies and dances, is lost.[54]

Marius Tungilik recalls being punished for speaking Inuktitut at Sir Joseph Bernier residential school he attended in Chesterfield Inlet: "Don't even think Inuktitut was taught in the school. Some students recalled being taught syllabics in the school. I can't recall that myself. I guess that was in the early days. Ten months English two months Inuktitut at home. So difficult. We missed out on how to interact. Suddenly home was an alien environment. We were punished if we were speaking Inuktitut in class. A scolding or beating. We were told not to speak the devil's tongue. Religious instruction was conducted in Inuktitut."[55]

Psychological Punishment

In addition to receiving physical punishment for speaking their ancestral languages, some First Nations students were ridiculed and psychologically abused.

Marjorie Groat, who attended the Mohawk Institute in the 1930s, revealed how children were encouraged to make fun of each other's First Nations languages and cultures in school. Groat recounted an incident with a smaller boy who couldn't speak any English at all. He was teased constantly for this by the older boys, who were bolstered by the other students and teachers, and picked on because he was small. Groat felt sorry for this boy and would have preferred that the older boys protect him.[56]

A woman who attended the Mohawk Institute from 1940 to 1945 recalls being thrown in the clothes closet with another young girl for speaking her language:

> There were rats in there and I remember crying, and I remember wondering: Why was I in there? Why did they put me in there? [W]e were both sitting there crying and afraid that these mice were going to get us, or these rats. I guess we were in there for speaking Indian. I don't remember speaking Indian but my aunt says we used to speak Indian fluently before we went . . . there were a bunch of girls from Walpole Island that used to speak Indian all the time, and they were always getting thrown in there, but they used to go and hide after a while and speak Indian.[57]

Isabelle Knockwood from Wolfville, Nova Scotia, attended residential school in Shubenacadie from 1936 to 1947. She recalled children being punished for speaking Mi'kmaq: "Not only were we forbidden to tell whatever the nuns defined as 'lies'—from our first day at the school speaking our own languages resulted in violent physical punishment. Since we knew no English we had to hide to talk to each other in Mi'kmaq. Even after a few years had passed and we learned enough English to communicate with each other, it still was often dangerous to talk. We were forbidden to talk at night in the dormitory. Brothers and sisters were strictly forbidden to speak to each other."[58]

Georgina Gregory went to File Hills Indian Residential School in Balcarres, Saskatchewan, when she was seven years old. She attended the school for eight years and told of children being "ridiculed and discouraged from speaking their language and [having] no choice but to speak English. . . . I know there is absolutely nothing wrong about learning English, but they saw it that those students forgot their language through humiliation and shame."[59]

Author Maria Campbell, a former student of a residential school in Beauval, Saskatchewan, remembered being allowed to speak only French or English and being put into a small dark closet for hours as punishment for speaking her language: "[I] was paralyzed with fright when they came to let me out. I remember the last day of school and the sense of freedom I felt when Dad came for me. He promised that I would never have to go back."[60]

Theodore Fontaine attended the Fort Alexander Indian Residential School in Manitoba from ages seven to twelve. Like many students, he was punished for speaking Ojibway:

> I inadvertently said something in Ojibway. She'd [the teacher] assumed I was referring to her when a couple of boys laughed at my comment. She yelled that she'd wash out my mouth with soap. . . . I was shoved into a closet behind her chair. It was under the stairs leading to the second floor and was used to store brooms and other cleaning material. I don't remember how long I was in there, but it seemed like an eternity. . . . Eventually she let me out. Her first word was "*Tiens!* (Take that!)" followed by a warning not to speak my "savage" language.[61]

Janie Margaret Matthews, or Geniesh (Little Janie), attended the St. Philip's Indian and Eskimo Anglican Residential School in Fort George, Quebec, in the mid 1940s. She recalled being told: "You are here to learn English in or around the school. You will not speak Cree, and anyone caught speaking it will be severely punished. . . . You are here to be educated. You have been taken out of your homes because it is very difficult to learn under such unfortunate circumstances. It is not your fault . . . and your families don't know any better, so they must be forgiven for their old ways. However, you must forget your old ways."[62]

Andrew Amos lived at Queens Cove reserve on the west coast of Vancouver Island. Amos attended Christie Indian Residential School from 1948 to 1956. When he first went to school, he could not speak English, yet he was no longer allowed to speak his language.[63]

Estrangement and Loss

As a result of the abuse First Nations and Inuit children experienced in residential schools, many lost their ability to communicate with family and community in their birth language. Many former students have commented on their loss of cultural identity and connection to family, making them feel like strangers among their own people.

John Tootoosis from the Poundmaker reserve in Saskatchewan attended St. Michael's and Delmas residential schools in the early 1900s. He recalls that when children returned home, "having lost their Cree language, they could rarely understand what was being said, and could not make themselves understood, and it was months before it began to come back to them. They were strangers in their former homes. Their parents and grandparents, once the centre of their existence, were now diminished, mere remnants of a bygone era and a worthless culture. They no longer could respect their Elders after having been so indoctrinated into the white man's religion. Cree songs and stories, ceremonies or prayers were now, to these young converts, terrifying evidence of souls damned and lost."[64]

A student of Mount Elgin in 1906 recalled that any letter sent by children to their family members had to be written in English. Moreover, "all conversations between the visitors and the children ha(d) to be in English."[65] In consequence, parents who were lucky enough to receive letters from their children were often not able to read them.

Edward Ahenakew, a Cree Anglican minister from Saskatchewan, had these observations about the harmful effects of residential schools: "Again and again I have seen children come from boarding school only to die, having lost during their time at school all the natural joys of association with their own families, victims of an educational policy."[66]

Earl Maquinna George from Clayquot Sound, British Columbia, attended a residential school at Ahousaht in the 1930s. He remarked that the children were not only prevented from speaking their language, they were also denied any opportunity to discuss topics related to the Nuu-Chah-Nulth culture.[67]

Interviews of sixty former students who attended the Mohawk Institute and Mount Elgin revealed that until 1972, most children were restricted to speaking English. Punishment for speaking their language ranged from being strapped to being thrown into the clothes press.[68] Of all the students interviewed from Mount Elgin, only eight claimed they could still speak their mother tongue. All of the students interviewed reported feeling "a deep sense of loss, saying that losing the language, whether individually or collectively, and the associated loss of their culture, was the worst thing about the schools."[69]

One woman who had attended Mount Elgin recalled returning to her community and not being able to communicate with her dad. She recounted one experience when her dad came to visit her and her sister. During the visit, he spoke to them in their traditional language, but they could no longer understand him. As she recounted, she and her sister "couldn't figure out what he was talking about, and he got really angry with us—really angry. Or maybe not so much angry as disappointed. He said, 'Even my dog could understand. . . .' That's what the [school] did to me—it took away my language, and to this day I don't speak Indian."[70]

Bette Spence attended residential school in Brandon, Manitoba, for about six or seven years and recalled not being allowed to speak Cree. In addition, "there was not one single native tradition in the school. They just took you away from home, where you left everything all the Indian-ness back there."[71]

Inez Deiter, from Peepeekisis reserve in Saskatchewan, attended both the Onion Lake and Prince Albert Indian Residential Schools from 1938 to 1946. Prior to attending residential school, Deiter lived in a Métis community until she was eight. At that point, she was taken to an orphanage in Edmonton, where a nun made arrangements to take her to the Onion Lake school. When Deiter was reunited with her brother years later, he noticed that she could no longer speak Cree. He recognized that this was going to be a problem because all their relatives spoke Cree. Deiter recalled hearing the other girls speaking Cree and attempted to copy them. Speaking Cree was forbidden at the school, so the girls would teach her at night.[72]

Albert Canadien attended the Sacred Heart Indian Residential School in Fort Providence, Northwest Territories, when he was seven years old. He recalled the nuns speaking mainly French: "For the first few days of school, communication was very difficult for me as I didn't speak or understand English or French. It took me some time before I learned enough to be able to speak and understand some English.

Soon after that we were forbidden to speak Slavey. . . . It seems ironic when I think about it now, because the Sisters who supervised us at that time spoke only French; they didn't speak English that well. As a consequence, we learned broken English from them."[73]

Canadien also explained the impact that the language restriction has had on his relationship with his family:

> Not being able to speak my own language really created a communication problem for me. It was especially hard when my parents came to visit us. I wasn't quite sure if the restriction applied when speaking to my own parents. I did speak to them in our language only after I was sure the Sisters weren't around or close by. Like most people in Fort Providence at that time, my dad spoke to us in South Slavey when he came to visit us. I don't think he was aware of the language restriction, and I never did tell him about it.[74]

Jennie Blackbird, from Walpole Island, attended the Mohawk Institute from 1942 to 1946. The impact of losing her language rippled throughout her life:

> The thing that shocked me the most was when I was told I could not speak my native language. I was birthed into this language, yet, I was told I was being rude. This really pierced me. Because my native language was all that was spoken at home, the English language was the first foreign language I learned. And we weren't allowed to speak our Indian language?!!! My inner emotions could not accept this, but I could not express myself enough to say what was in my heart in the English language. . . . I knew in my heart that this was wrong and so unfair to us Native children. The emotional shock tremors that I suffered then I still feel to this day. . . . I had to learn all over again to love and to speak my language when I got home to stay. Although I eventually got my language back . . . the tremors from the emotional shock I endured are still with me to this day.[75]

Sylvia Soney was the second generation in her family to attend the Mohawk Institute, and her first language was English. Soney assumed that because both her parents had attended a residential school they wanted to shelter their children from physical punishment for speaking their language, so they never taught them their language.[76]

Harold LeRat attended a residential school in Crooked Lake in the 1930s for ten years. His father, Solomon LeRat, had also attended a residential school. Harold recounted his father's negative experiences speaking the Cree and Saulteaux languages: "When my dad went to school he was not allowed to speak Saulteaux or Cree. The kids would be beaten if they did, so when his older kids went to school, dad said not to speak Cree or you will get beat up. The older ones all spoke the Indian languages at home, but because Elsie and I were in school after our parents died, we lost our language."[77]

Calvin Sault recalled the impact of the Mohawk Institute, which he attended until 1953. He could not speak his language until he was forty-eight years old, and as a result he was prevented from knowing his cultural identity.[78]

Alice Ningeongan, a student at the Churchill residential school from 1964 to about 1970, recalled being encouraged to use syllabics: "I guess it [our own language] wasn't permitted because that was not what we were there to speak, we were there to speak English. But they did encourage us to write syllabics.... I learned to write home to mom using syllabics from the prayer book. It used to take me a long time but at least I learned to write in the writing system that I knew."[79]

At the age of seven, Alice French was taken to the Anglican school in Aklavik, Northwest Territories. People from her community remarked on the fact that she could no longer speak her language when she returned home.[80] French recalled that when she asked her father to speak in Inuvialuktun to her, she "could understand most of the words, but when I tried to answer I found I had first to translate the words from English into Inuvialuktun."[81]

Alice Blondin-Perrin, a Dene from Cameron Bay, attended St. Joseph's Mission School in Fort Resolution from 1952 to 1959. She reported hearing many Aboriginal languages as well as English, French, and Latin. She grew up speaking Slavey at home. Only about fifty people at residential school spoke her language; the other students spoke Dogrib (Tlicho) and Chipewyan.[82] Blondin-Perrin could not understand the other young girls and was physically punished from the age of four for speaking in her mother tongue. After two years, she eventually learned to speak English, a considerable accomplishment considering the older girls spoke Dogrib and Chipewyan, the nuns spoke French to each other, and Latin was read in church.[83] While overcoming these challenges, Blondin-Perrin lost the ability to communicate in her mother tongue. To this day, she does not understand why the children were never told why they were forbidden to speak their language, and believes the language policy had grave consequences. "Their decision," she stated, "created long-term language barriers, problems and grief for me. I would never be able to sit and talk with the Elders. I lost my language."[84] At home, Blondin-Perrin's parents spoke six dialects of the Dene language. She recalled her family teaching her in Dene about the traditional knowledge of the land, including the names of significant places and rivers. By contrast, in residential school,

> our native languages were not to be heard or spoken. Our customs and traditions were denied to all of us. Our Native spirituality denied. Our heritage was denied and not mentioned, because their goal was to take the Indian out of us. We were not taught anything about the land, water or Dene spirituality. We were only taught the white man's way, and a very narrow version of even that. The government and missionaries wanted to civilize us and assimilate us, turn us into white people, make us learn their languages and customs. I am very sad that I lost my native tongue in residential school. All my life I felt like I was looking into the windows of Native peoples' homes because I was not able to participate in any discussions, or laugh at their jokes. It was like a slap in the face. The reality of only speaking English set in when I could not communicate among my people.[85]

Blondin-Perrin's experience when returning home was not an isolated incident. Many former residential school students returned home only to feel like strangers in their own communities. Some of them could no longer communicate with their parents, grandparents, and extended family members in their ancestral language. They also felt a great deal of shame about their Aboriginal identity because of their school experiences. As Milloy explains, "Though children were removed from their parents and communities divorced from direct involvement in their own culture for many years, English and French, and thus western culture, remained quite 'unnatural' to them. They had not been civilized—Canadianized—when they left school. They had not been prepared to live a new life. Indeed, in many cases, as studies in the 1960s revealed, because of their extended isolation from their families, the persistent denial of their culture and abuse, many returned unable to lead any sort of productive life, old or new."[86]

Although the government played a central role in creating a system that facilitated cultural abuse, it did nothing to assist First Nations children after they left the residential school system. A former student from Saskatchewan eloquently described the void many former students felt after leaving school:

> When an Indian comes out of these places it is like being put between two walls in a room and left hanging in the middle. On one side are all the things he learned from his people and their way of life that was being wiped out, and on the other side are the whiteman's ways. . . . There he is, hanging in the middle of the two cultures and he is not a white man and he is not an Indian. They washed away practically everything from our minds, all the things an Indian needed to help himself, to think the way a human person should in order to survive. . . . We were defenseless . . . those who went to school could not even talk when a non-Indian would speak to them, they would hang their heads. I sometimes think that it was planned that way so that the Indian could no longer speak for himself . . . did not believe in himself . . . had to be told what to do.[87]

Some residential school staff also thought that the schools were denying Aboriginal children their culture and language. Miss Eden Corbett, a former teacher in the Aklavik Anglican School, resigned in 1944 on the grounds that the staff were participating in ineffective and immoral teachings practices. On departing from her teaching position, Corbett stated,

> [I am] grieved to think that I must leave these children in the same condition I found them. . . . I consider that the system as it is now in force, definitely does not meet the requirements of the native. Where, in a ten month academic period, does a child get any contact with its practical life? How is a child, after a four to ten year period in a school, supposed to adapt itself to the environment of its parents, when the language,

> habits and arts have been severed, for such a length of time? The child is an alien and the situation is pitiful. Is that practical Christianity?[88]

Harold Cardinal, who attended a residential school in Alberta, described his experiences: "The curriculum stank, and the teachers were misfits and second raters. Even in my own elementary school days, in grade eight I found myself taking over the class because my teacher, a misfit, has-been or never-was sent out by his superiors from Quebec to teach savages in a wilderness school because he utterly failed in civilization, couldn't speak English well enough to make himself understood. Naturally, he knew no Cree. When we protested such inequities we were silenced as 'ungrateful little savages who don't appreciate what is being done for you.'"[89]

Language Resistance

Although many former students of residential schools expressed a deep sense of loss regarding their language and culture, some described powerful instances of resistance. An example of group resistance occurred in 1962 when a riot broke out at the Edmonton Residential School after students were *iced* for speaking their language, which means that other children were not allowed to talk to them for a length of time.[90] In western Canada, children created a sign language that was used in residential schools in Hobbema, Edmonton, Blue Quills, Onion Lake, Prince Albert, Brandon, and Birtle. The signs consisted of a two-handed letter system and body gestures, and allowed children to overcome difficulties learning to speak English at the school. This language also assisted children in situations where students spoke different First Nations languages.[91] Students often used their sign language behind the teacher's back in the classroom. For instance, Inez Deiter reported that students used the language to convey birthday greetings to their siblings, who were generally kept apart from each other and prohibited from speaking together while at school. In Deiter's words, "this language should be a testament to the intelligence, spirit and resourcefulness of First Nations children."[92]

Consequences of the Residential Schools Today

Although the last residential school closed its doors in 1996, it had already become apparent in the early 1960s that First Nations and Inuit communities across Canada were experiencing severe socio-economic problems.

In its final report on residential schools, the TRC concluded that the residential school system was "a systematic, government-sponsored attempt to destroy First Nations cultures and languages and to assimilate First Nations so that they no longer existed as distinct peoples."[93] Residential school survivor Frederick Lee Barney reveals the loss of language and culture resulting from his residential school experience:

> I was deprived of the love and guidance of my parents and siblings for five years. I lost my Native language and Aboriginal culture and was removed from my family roots. The enormity of the loss of both my culture and my connection with my family feels overwhelming and the effects irreversible. I lost my identity as a Native person. I live with a sense of not knowing who I am and how I should be in the world. I lost the friendship and support of my friends and community. I suffered a loss of self-esteem.... I'm angry about my loss of culture.... It's sickening. It was obvious the tremendous effect it has had on me as a person and yes, I get angry as hell.[94]

The TRC has also documented the intergenerational effects of language loss in statements from children of residential school survivors. In one statement, Sabrina Williams from British Columbia described the profound impact loss of language had and continues to have on her connection to her cultural identity: "I didn't realize until taking this language class how much we have lost—all the things that are attached to language: its family connections, its oral history, its traditions, its ways of being, its ways of knowing, its medicine, its song, its dance, its memory. Its everything, including the land.... And unless we inspire our kids to love our culture, to love our language ... our languages are continually going to be eroded over time. So, that is daunting."[95] These statements resonate deeply within me as someone who has been impacted intergenerationally by the residential school system. Their story is my story; my own experience allows me to attest that the impacts of language loss can be all-encompassing, surfacing in unexpected ways.

Like most Canadians, I grew up learning nothing about the history or legacy of residential schools. I never thought about the fact that I often heard my mother speaking Cree and my father speaking Ojibway. I did not identify these languages as my family languages, and I certainly did not consider them as having unique constitutional status. I started to become aware of the source of the cultural shame I had felt as a child during a keynote address my mother gave at a conference in Winnipeg, Manitoba, in the 1990s. She spoke about the physical abuse and denigration she received as a child for speaking Cree while attending a residential school. She told the audience that she was physically punished every time she spoke Cree, a devastating experience because Cree was the only language she knew as a child. Eventually, English would be the only language she used at school.

After I had a few weeks to reflect on what my mother revealed during her talk, I realized that my family's relationship to our languages was far from healthy. We did not cherish the Cree language as my maternal grandparents did, and, in fact, my mother and her siblings appeared to hide the fact that they could speak Cree. They only spoke their ancestral language when they said something private to each other or when my grandparents were present.

Although my generation was not physically abused for speaking a First Nations language, we inherited feelings of cultural shame. Even worse, we never knew where the sense of shame came from, and we never acknowledged it to one another. Some of us went to extremes, denying our First Nations identity, lying entirely and claiming another identity. Part of the problem was that most of us grew up knowing very little about First Nations cultures or histories. For me, my Cree and Ojibway identity meant very little. They became words that I often heard people talk about in places where my mother and father visited friends and family. My parents' generation was somewhat different from the one before them, as many continued to communicate in Cree or Ojibway. In doing so, they maintained a sense of First Nations identity through the language.

The wall that separates my generation from our cultural and linguistic identity became denser when the violence my parents experienced in the schools trickled into our family life. Home was often not safe. We witnessed violence. People changed drastically when alcohol was around. Nothing was predictable. I never knew from one minute to the next whether home life would be calm or chaotic. I did not trust members of my family and never confided in anyone. Most of the time, I kept to myself and tried to be invisible. Some of us eventually became victims of the violence. Although not everyone from my generation has experienced family violence, we have all been denied access to our culture and language in the educational system, and to varying degrees have inherited shame.

I carried this shame into adulthood. A major shift occurred when my mother started to attend our traditional ceremonies. In the process, she learned our teachings and the medicines that come from the land. She also went to see medicine people who were able to assist her in healing from some of the trauma she experienced in the schools. A few of her sisters followed her down this path. My brother, sister, and I became intrigued. My sister became a sun dancer, as did my mother and a few other members of our family. Eventually my brother and I decided to attend ceremonies. Since then, my brother and I have been learning our teachings and the Ojibway language. During this time, the Elders explained many of the customary protocols involving language transmission that Henry Kelsey and James Isham wrote about in their journals three hundred years ago, such as feasting, offering tobacco, and pipe ceremonies. As a result of this educational experience, I eventually became proud of my cultural identity.

In addition to learning about my language and culture, my healing journey included learning about the history of the residential schools and its impact on my life. Before 1990, I had no idea about this history or the policy that targeted the destruction of First Nations languages and cultures. When I first learned about what had happened to my mother and the rest of my family, I was very angry. Soon after, I was able to make the connection between the abuse that happened in the schools and the abuse that was occurring in my home. That knowledge provided me with some freedom. Before gaining this understanding, I walked around in a cloud of silent shame.

Concluding Remarks

We now understand that the Canadian government actively and systematically sought to eradicate First Nations and Inuit cultures, primarily by targeting their languages. In recent years, the number of both personal accounts and scholarly investigations into the legacy of residential schools has significantly increased, shedding light on the profound harm caused by past federal policies and laws, many of which persist today.[96] Actions arising from these policies and laws are no longer viewed as benevolent interventions but rather as intentional tactics to erase First Nations languages, cultures, and identities.[97]

Scholars like Andrea Bear Nicholas, Tove Skutnabb-Kangas, and Robert Dunbar argue that the current educational framework continues to contribute to the decline of First Nations languages. They assert that prioritizing colonial languages over Indigenous ones in the education of First Nations children perpetuates the erosion of their languages and cultures, amounting to linguistic genocide.[98] Linguistic genocide refers to the deliberate destruction of a language by state actors, either through active policies or neglect that leads to language extinction due to resource disparities.[99] This is a significant concern, as it reflects the Canadian government's historical policy in education, which aimed to eradicate and continues to impact First Nations languages and cultures today. The residential school system's core objective was to eliminate First Nations languages by forbidding their use or teaching among children. By seeking to erase First Nations cultures and languages, this system served the purpose of asserting European dominance, aiding in settlement, and securing land rights.

This systematic violence extends globally, affecting Indigenous languages and cultures in various regions worldwide, including in the United States, Central and South America, Australia, New Zealand, Scandinavia, the Russian Federation, Asia, Africa, and the Middle East. Recent research has uncovered histories of abuse, racism, and numerous deaths of Indigenous children in residential schools, further highlighting the extensive and damaging consequences of these institutions.[100] In May 2021, the discovery of 215 unmarked graves at a former residential school site in British Columbia brought renewed global attention to the issue.[101]

In Canada, residential schools, deeply rooted in genocidal policies, processes, and legislation, severely hindered the intellectual and cultural growth of First Nations peoples. There are many communities with no ancestral language speakers, and all First Nations languages are endangered. The loss of language has created a disconnect between generations, including Elders and youth, resulting in a severe decline in transmission of oral history, ceremony, prayer, family knowledge, and the recognition of First Nations presence in Canada's development. Growing up in a community or family impacted by trauma—trauma inflicted simply for being First Nations—becomes even more challenging when that trauma is devoid of historical context. When the education system fails to teach the origins and lasting impact of this trauma, and there is little acknowledgment of one's culture, identity, or language in school, it creates a profound sense of irrelevance.

Former Chair of the Truth and Reconciliation Commission, Murray Sinclair, offers personal insight into the harm from this genocidal legacy based on his experience,

> My education lacked relevance for me, and this was so despite my success at it. That success came at a price. It taught me and others that my people were irrelevant, and, by implication, it caused me to feel that I was too. It taught us to believe in the inferiority of Aboriginal people and in the inherent superiority of white Euopean civilization, and in order to get the grades that I did, I was compelled to repeat that unconscious mantra. This system of my day did not teach us to respect Indigenous people because it never told us anything about the Aboriginal presence in this country that showed the humanity of the people. In public schools, we were all educated to be the same, and if we rebelled, resisted, or rejected that process, we were weeded out or we weeded ourselves out. Of the Indigenous students I started grade school with, few ever graduted from high school. Even my brother and sister did not. But while I and others succeeded in that system, it was not without the cost to our humanity and our sense of self-respect. These are the legacies all of us find ourselves in today.[102]

The harm from this legacy—the loss of purpose and diminished sense of belonging both within the community and the country—is evident today in the over-incarceration rates among First Nations people, the high population of children in the child welfare system, and high suicide rates.[103] Despite the concerted efforts to eradicate First Nations languages and cultures, some communities have persisted in preserving and speaking their native tongues, resisting assimilation.

The upcoming chapter will focus on examples of this resilience. It highlights ongoing initiatives to promote First Nations language transmission within the discourse of constitutional rights and shows how the right to language transmission is inherently linked to First Nations education.

CHAPTER 3

CANADA'S CONSTITUTION

First Nations Language Rights in Education

In 2021, as part of Canada's commitment to address the historical injustices that led to the cultural genocide documented by the TRC, the government implemented the Indigenous Languages Act. This legislation recognizes the language rights of First Nations, Inuit, and Métis peoples under section 35(1) of Canada's Constitution Act, 1982, as an Aboriginal and treaty right. Beyond this constitutional provision, the basis for language transmission is further recognized by the historical inter-customary practices of language exchange established between First Nations and European settlers, as explored in Chapter 1. Moreover, constitutional rights pertaining to language transmission in education have been reinforced by continuous advocacy by First Nations communities and leaders.

This chapter highlights the history of First Nations advocacy for language rights in education through various approaches, including reports, demonstrations, and public statements. The government's response has been to recognize the importance of First Nations languages and the importance of education, particularly in addressing their endangered status through initiatives such as immersion programs. This acknowledgment is reflected in royal commissions, reports, and other federal efforts. The government has also responded through legislation recognizing the significance of First Nations languages.

By focusing on these three areas—advocacy efforts, governmental acknowledgments, and legislative responses—the chapter emphasizes the constitutional framework for First Nations language rights in education. It also provides insights into the ongoing efforts and challenges faced in ensuring the continuity of language transmission by First Nations communities.

An important example of advocacy highlighted at the end of the chapter is Nunavut's leadership in promoting language rights in both education and federal services. Inuit leaders, driven by the vision of Elders committed to protecting Inuktitut, emphasize its central role in preserving land knowledge and cultural identity. The chapter concludes by examining Nunavut's advocacy for language rights, particularly in education, and emphasizes the critical importance of explicit constitutional recognition of First Nations language rights in education under section 35 of the Constitution Act, 1982.

Advocacy, Commissions, and Reports

Royal Commission on Bilingualism and Biculturalism, 1963–67

The push for constitutional discussions regarding language education rights was driven in part by the increasing advocacy for language and cultural protection within the French-speaking community in Quebec during the 1960s. Concerns centred on the socio-economic disparity between the French population in Quebec and the dominant anglophone minority. Consequently, the Royal Commission on Bilingualism and Biculturalism (the B&B Commission) was instituted in 1963 to scrutinize the status of English and French language and culture in Canada.[1] The final report and recommendations of the B&B Commission ultimately led to Canada's Official Languages Act, which recognizes French and English as the official languages of Canada.[2] Although the mandate of the B&B Commission did not include First Nations languages, some First Nations representatives appeared before the B&B commissioners to raise issues related to First Nations languages.

In Sudbury, the B&B Commission heard from a First Nations woman who was appalled that First Nations were excluded from Canada's Constitution. She asked, "Why is the Indian always forgotten? This was the first culture and this was the first language in Canada. We are told the BNA Act [British North America Act] was between the French and the English—where was the Indian during this time?"[3]

In Victoria, a First Nations leader responded to the question of whether French communities' needs should be met linguistically and culturally, stating, "Certainly. If another group can succeed in doing something when we have been condemned to death, we will be glad for them."[4] Then he added, "My grandchildren no longer know the language of my people, but can speak French."[5]

After hearing from the First Nations community, the B&B Commission concluded that Canada's assimilation policy "raises very complex problems. The process of integration calls into question the very nature of the traditions and customs of native society."[6] The commissioners strongly recommended that "everything possible must be done to help the native populations preserve their cultural heritage, which is an essential part of the patrimony of all Canadians. The Commission also feels that the Canadian government, in close co-operation with the provinces concerned, should take the necessary steps to assist the survival of the Eskimo language and the most common Indian dialects."[7]

The B&B commissioners noted that special measures had to be taken to safeguard the cultural contribution of First Nations.[8] They also recognized that a special commission was required to examine the status of Aboriginal cultures and languages: "Though they are the oldest inhabitants—the early Eskimo and the even earlier Indian cultures have existed in Canada for thousands of years—they are less integrated in the life of the Canadian community than any other ethnic group. Their position and future prospects would have to be the object of special study."[9]

Shortly after the release of the B&B Report, the federal government introduced the Official Languages Act in 1969, recognizing English and French as the official languages of Canada. At the same time, the federal government recommended the abolition of the Indian Act and the complete elimination of Indian status, as well as the distinct rights of First Nations.[10] In British Columbia, the Union of British Columbia Indian Chiefs responded with a Declaration of Indian Rights, known as the "Brown Paper." Simultaneously, the Indian Association of Alberta, under the leadership of Harold Cardinal, advocated for securing resources specifically for First Nations education in order to protect

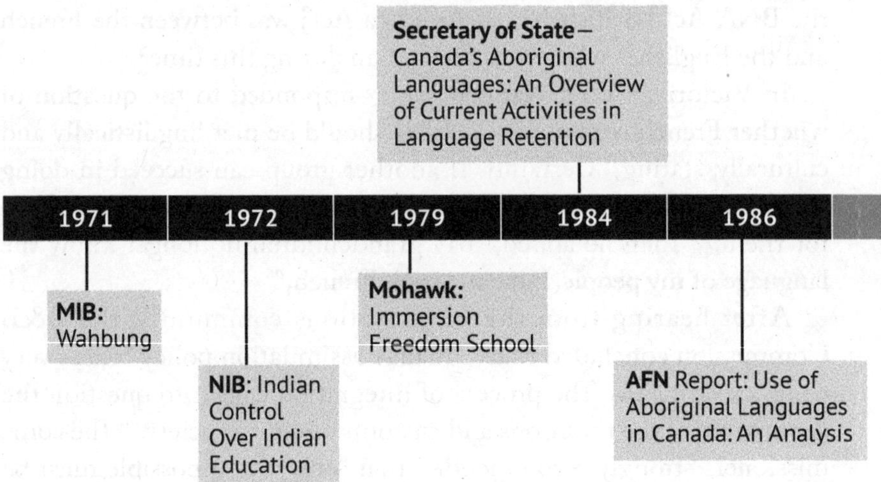

Figure 10. Advocacy by First Nations: Language preservation and promotion. Compiled by author.

and sustain their languages and cultures. They released a report called "Citizens Plus," commonly referred to as the "Red Paper."[11] Both policy papers were in defence of First Nations rights.

Wahbung, 1971

At the same time, First Nations communities in Manitoba were claiming local control over education on reserves, focusing on the importance of teaching First Nations languages in schools. The leaders in Manitoba acknowledged the profound impact of residential schools on First Nations languages and cultures which resulted in asserting jurisdiction over education. In 1971, the Manitoba Indian Brotherhood brought attention to the failings of education in residential schools through the publication of *Wahbung: Our Tomorrows*: "Many non-Indians believe that we have failed education but the truth of the matter is that education has failed us. It has failed us because it was imposed upon us, not relevant to us, nor were we given the opportunity of being involved in designing it. Education has failed to recognize our cultural values and customs, our language, and our contributions to [humankind]. It has led to failure and the lowering of self-esteem."[12]

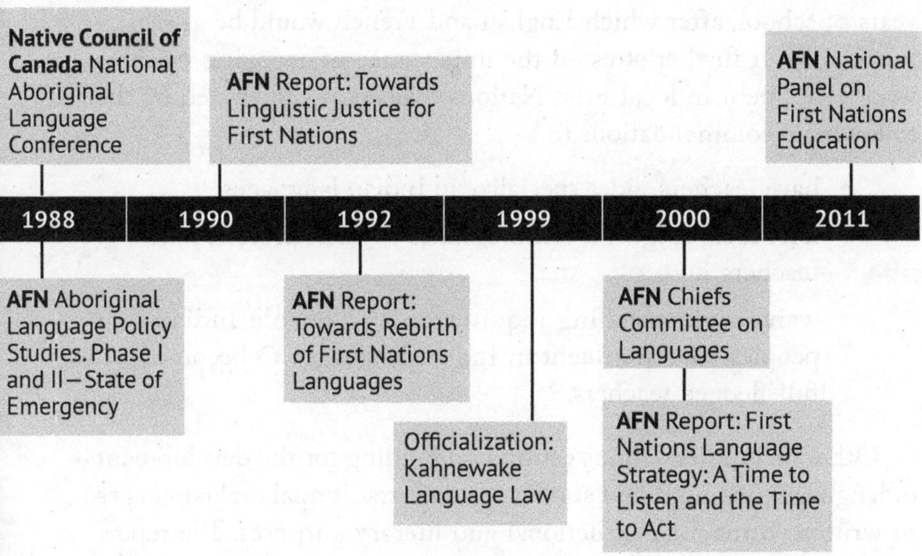

Indian Control of Indian Education, 1972

In 1972, the National Indian Brotherhood (NIB) issued a comprehensive policy document, *Indian Control of Indian Education*. The statement on education, which was presented to the Minister of Indian and Northern Affairs, outlined the philosophies, goals, principles, and directions that would serve as the foundation of future school programs for "Indian" children.[13] The NIB emphasized the importance of language in this context: "Language is the outward expression of an accumulation of learning experience shared by a group of people over centuries of development. It is not simply a vocal symbol; it is a dynamic force which shapes the way [people look] at the world, [their] thinking about the world and [their] philosophy of life."[14]

The NIB also stressed that preserving First Nations cultural identity would require deliberate action to reverse the declining number of language speakers. The report focused primarily on the development of formal language instruction in two key aspects: teaching the language, and teaching *in* the language. The NIB advocated for First Nations children to be taught in their ancestral language for the first four to five years of school, after which English and French would be gradually introduced. It further stressed the importance of engaging teachers who were fluent in local First Nations dialects, as illustrated by the following recommendations to

- have teachers-aides specialize in Indian languages,
- have local language-resource aides to assist professional teachers, and
- waive rigid teaching requirements to enable Indian peoples who are fluent in Indian languages to become full-fledged teachers.[15]

Other recommendations centred on funding for the development of language programs, and studies to adapt traditional oral languages to written forms for instructional and literary purposes. The report also criticized the federal government's reluctance to invest in First Nations languages as shortsighted, arguing that teaching First Nations languages to children would ultimately result in long-term economic benefits.[16]

In response, the federal government prioritized the pedagogical benefits of education for First Nations as defined by government policies, rather than emphasizing the importance of First Nations children learning their language and culture in schools. In 1972, the Department of Indian Affairs acknowledged that for Aboriginal children entering provincial schools, having to function in English (in Quebec, French) was a fundamental challenge. Consequently, it placed significant emphasis on developing a "language arts" program for both day and residential schools. Regional language supervisors were employed to assist children in overcoming language difficulties, with the belief that improved language instruction methods would contribute significantly to progress in "Indian" education.[17]

During this time, a director from the Department of Indian Affairs asserted that the basis of First Nations education was acculturation, "in which the Indian has voluntarily or involuntarily been caught up."[18] Indian Affairs believed that First Nations people would benefit from the influences of European culture and considered the provision of a solid education in the English language as the best course of action.[19]

Mohawk Freedom School, 1979

In 1977, a pivotal moment in language and cultural education occurred when Mohawk students at Howard S. Billings Regional High School organized a walkout. The protest, motivated by the lack of Mohawk language and cultural education in the curriculum, saw students marching from Chateauguay to Kahnawake. This act of advocacy led to the creation of a Mohawk language immersion school: in 1979, the Kanien'kehá:ka Raotitióhkwa Language and Cultural Center was established, dedicated to preserving and transmitting Mohawk language and cultural traditions to upcoming generations. That same year marked the inauguration of Kahnawà:ke Survival School, a forerunner in First Nations language immersion programs in Canada. In a significant legislative step, the Kahnawake community passed the Kahnawake Language Law in 1999, underlining their commitment to language preservation and educational initiatives.[20]

Assembly of First Nations, 1984–2011

In the 1980s, following the 1984 First Ministers Conference on Aboriginal Constitutional Matters, there was a heightened focus on the status of Aboriginal languages. This period saw the release of two pivotal reports: *Canada's Aboriginal Languages: An Overview of Current Activities in Language Retention*,[21] and *The Use of Aboriginal Languages in Canada: An Analysis*.[22] Both reports shed light on a worrying trend of language shift and pointed out significant gaps in federal, provincial, and territorial support for First Nations languages. In response to these revelations, the federal government allocated funding to First Nations organizations to devise language policy proposals. Among these efforts, the Assembly of First Nations (AFN) played a prominent role, producing the influential *Aboriginal Language Policy Studies, Phase I* and *Phase II*. The primary objectives of these studies were to explore and recommend strategies for the preservation and revitalization of First Nations languages, specifically

(1) To study the feasibility of a First Nations Languages Institute within the context of a Comprehensive First Nations Language Policy.

(2) To pursue and investigate the feasibility of on-going mechanism(s) required by First Nations to encourage the

survival and revitalization at the community level of all First Nations languages.

(3) To share and investigate knowledge and skills as it relates to the survival and development of Aboriginal languages at the community level.[23]

After finalizing Phase I of the study in early 1988, which involved a comprehensive review of the First Nation language situation in Canada, the AFN disseminated the findings to one hundred Members of Parliament and various First Nations organizations, with the goal of rallying support for policy recommendations dedicated to preserving First Nations languages. Phase II, conducted from 25 July to 30 September 1988, concentrated on formulating a detailed plan for the revitalization of First Nations languages. This phase also included the development of an educational strategy aimed at fostering understanding and support among the First Nations community and the Canadian public for the AFN's language policy initiatives.[24]

The study uncovered that between 1983 and 1988, federal, provincial, and territorial governments had collectively invested approximately $6.286 billion in programs and initiatives supporting First Nations languages. This included funding for summer camps, workshops, conferences, language classes, publications, and reference materials.[25] However, none of these initiatives were part of a comprehensive language revitalization strategy. One key area that was identified as necessary was the establishment of a language centre that could assist with language planning. The AFN estimated that running a single organization capable of managing all necessary language initiatives—encompassing community education, research, adult instruction, resource development, school materials, and policy and implementation work—would require about $802,500. Additionally, to establish and operate similar organizations nationwide, several million dollars per year would be needed.[26] The study also recommended that language policies be formulated within the context of self-government negotiations. It stressed the importance of promoting First Nations language use in domestic settings and emphasized the need for support and development of First Nations language teachers.

In 1998, Cree scholar Verna Kirkness put forward a proposal for a $100 million endowment fund. This fund was designed to safeguard and rejuvenate First Nations languages and to bolster First Nations language education initiatives at the community level.[27] First Nations Chiefs across Canada also proclaimed a national State of Emergency on Languages. This declaration led to the formation of the Chiefs Committee on Languages and the Technical Committee on Languages by the AFN, with the objective of protecting and promoting First Nations language rights in Canada. In addition, the Native Council of Canada organized a national Aboriginal language policy conference in 1988, highlighting the issue's significance.

During this crucial time, Secretary of State David Crombie, representing the federal government, pledged support for Aboriginal languages in collaboration with the AFN. However, legislative efforts encountered obstacles. A bill proposed to establish a Heritage Languages Institute, which included provisions for Aboriginal languages, was withdrawn. This was a result of strong opposition from the First Nations community, which criticized the bill for inadequate consultation and for its approach of grouping Aboriginal languages with immigrant languages. A subsequent private member's bill, introduced by David Crombie aimed at creating an Aboriginal Languages Institute, also failed to pass, reflecting the importance of effective consultation and collaboration.

Following the federal goverment's unsuccessful attempts to pass legislation to safeguard Aboriginal language, the AFN published three significant policy documents between 1990 and 2000: *Towards Linguistic Justice for First Nations*; *Towards Rebirth of First Nations Languages*; and *National First Nations Language Strategy: A Time to Listen and the Time to Act*.[28] These policy documents drew attention to the alarming decrease in First Nations language speakers and the critical state of all Aboriginal languages. The reports also emphasized the necessity of raising awareness of the significance of these languages at the community level.

At the AFN's Annual General Assembly in July 2000, the Chiefs Committee on Languages and the Technical Committee on Languages recommended the implementation of their language strategy. However, because of funding reductions by the Department of Indian Affairs, the AFN Languages Secretariat was disbanded in early 2000 and consequently, their language strategy was not put into action.

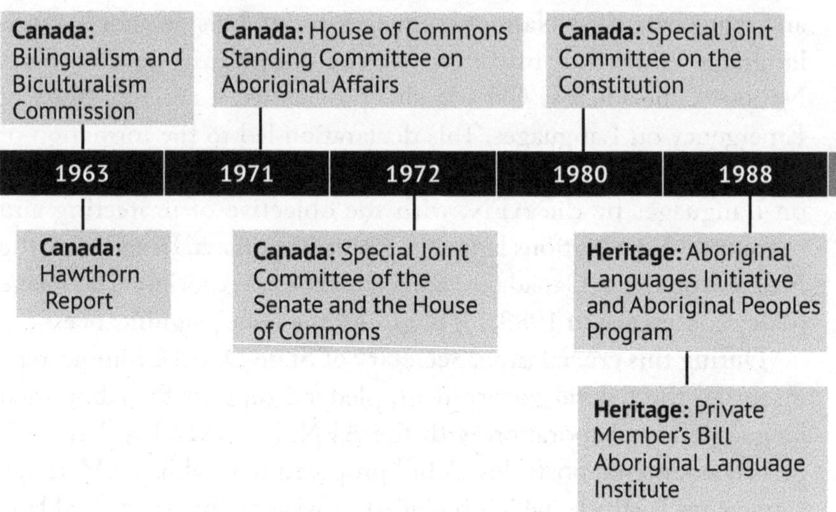

Figure 11. Government recognition and constitutional principles. Compiled by author.

Since 2011, the AFN has been proactive in addressing these challenges. It established a National Panel on First Nation Elementary and Secondary Education for Students on Reserve to provide recommendations on improving education for First Nations students. The panel's findings were critical of the existing education system, pointing out its failure to meet the needs of First Nations people. It highlighted the system's continued governance by legislative provisions that are over a century old, reaching back to the residential school era—an era now widely recognized as deeply harmful and destructive.[29] To address these issues, the panel recommended the inclusion of Aboriginal languages and history in school curricula.[30] This inclusion is seen as a response to the desires of many young people for an education that fosters a sense of belonging and cultural identity.[31]

The persistent advocacy efforts of First Nations have led to the establishment of royal commissions, numerous studies, legislative proposals, and a dedicated federal government program, all aimed at revitalizing and preserving First Nations languages through educational initiatives. Recognizing the essential role of language education in the revival of these languages, the federal government has recognized

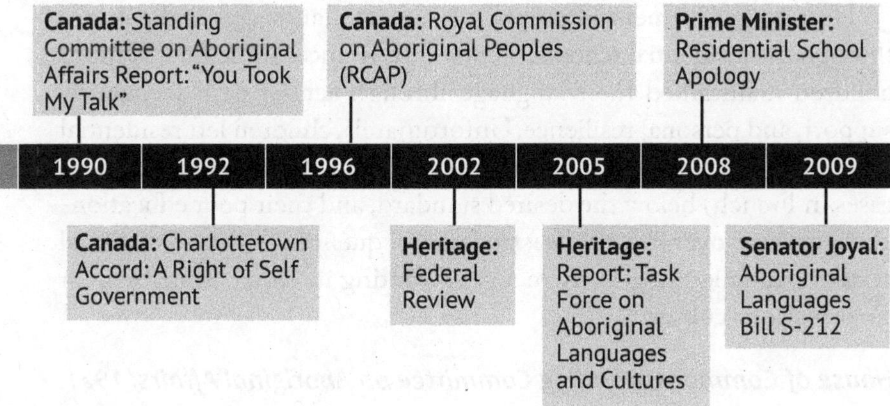

its critical importance in nurturing a sense of belonging among First Nations children within educational environments. Furthermore, these governmental initiatives and studies have brought to light a significant concern: without funding commitments to support immersion programs, there is a real risk of these languages fading into extinction.

Hawthorn Report, 1963

During the 1960s, when the B&B Commission initiated its work, the federal government appointed anthropologist Harry B. Hawthorn from the University of British Columbia to undertake a study of First Nations. Hawthorn's investigation concluded that many of the challenges faced by First Nations were a direct result of the residential school system. His report identified a crucial link between the revival of First Nations languages and culture and the overall well-being of First Nations communities. It suggested that the structure of a language can shape thought processes and influence cognitive development. Furthermore, Hawthorn's report highlighted government policies around First Nations languages, pointing out that the absence of First Nations languages in educational curricula indicated a willingness to let these languages disappear and be replaced by English or French. The report also recognized that the eradication of First Nations languages led to a significant loss of cultural identity and traditions.[32]

Despite government attempts to eradicate languages and cultures through the residential schools, there was resistance. Some First Nations children maintained their language through acts of defiance, family support, and personal resilience. Unfortunately, children left residential schools with a level of language proficiency in English (and in some cases in French) below the desired standard, and their poor educational experience overall had disastrous consequences.[33] The educational system had failed to give them a good footing in either "Canadian" or First Nations culture.[34]

House of Commons Standing Committee on Aboriginal Affairs, 1971

After Hawthorn released his study, the House of Commons Standing Committee on Indian Affairs and Northern Development issued a report on 30 June 1971 that focused on educational rights. In its report, the Standing Committee advised the government to recognize and support the right of First Nations parents to educate their children in their own mother tongue:

> The language of instruction at the pre-school level and up to the first or second year of primary schools should be in the language of the local Indian or Eskimo community with secondary and tertiary languages English and/or French being introduced gradually through the pre-school and primary period and that courses linked to the local Indian and Eskimo culture continue to be taught in the local language throughout the primary level of school. . . . That decision regarding the initial languages of instruction and the timing of introduction of secondary and tertiary languages should only be made after consultation with, and clear approval from a majority of parents in the communities concerned.[35]

Shortly after the the standing committee released its report, constitutional discussion on Aboriginal languages commenced.

Special Joint Committee of Senate and the House of Commons, 1972

In 1972, a Special Joint Committee of the Senate and the House of Commons, commonly referred to as the Special Joint Committee 1972, conducted hearings concerning the constitutional status of Aboriginal languages. The committee ultimately recommended that provincial and territorial governments recognize the rights associated with Aboriginal languages and acknowledge the diversity of Aboriginal cultures throughout Canada. However, the delegation of language rights to provincial and territorial jurisdictions appears incongruous, considering that section 91(24) of the British North America Act, 1867, assigns matters pertaining to Aboriginal peoples to the federal domain.

A potential explanation for this could be that section 93 of the British North America Act placed education primarily under provincial control, barring confessional schools. Additionally, it could be argued that language and culture do not fall within the ambit of "civil rights" as per section 92(13), or constitute matters of a "local or private nature" under section 92(16) of the British North America Act. Nevertheless, the most significant point is the federal government's apparent reluctance to assume responsibility for First Nations languages, demonstrated by its limited efforts to promote them despite the clear recommendations from both First Nations and the Special Joint Committee.

It wasn't until the 1980s, amid the process of patriating Canada's Constitution, that a focused deliberation on the status of First Nations languages took place. During this pivotal period, First Nations leaders emphasized that the rights associated with their languages are deeply rooted in First Nations law and their longstanding history as the original inhabitants of the land. The discussion between First Nations and government representatives highlighted four key constitutional principles that are still pertinent to First Nations language rights in education. The first principle states that these rights have their roots in the First Nations law from pre-European settlement era, serving as a protective measure for First Nations cultures and languages. The second principle points out that the right to preserve language and culture is not static; rather, it is a dynamic right that adapts and evolves to meet current education contexts and needs. The third and fourth principles jointly affirm that essential support for First Nations languages and cultures should be derived from both Aboriginal and treaty rights. Together, these principles provide context to the federal government's duty in section 91(24) of the British North America Act, 1867 to provide financial support for the maintenance and revitalization of First Nations languages and cultures. This financial responsibility plays a pivotal role in sustaining ongoing initiatives aimed at preserving and advancing these languages and cultures.

Special Joint Committee on the Constitution, 1980

Several recommendations related to Aboriginal languages were later made to the Special Joint Committee on the Constitution of Canada in 1980 (Special Joint Committee 1980),[36] with one focused on granting official language status to Aboriginal languages.[37] Maxwell F. Yalden (Commissioner of Official Languages) commented that he "would be tempted to put native languages on the same footing with official languages," stating that "while it is not up to me, as Commissioner of Official Languages, to formally recommend it, I feel it is valid."[38]

George Braden (MLA and Elected Member of the Executive Committee, Government of the Northwest Territories) focused on Aboriginal language issues in his home province, but ultimately recommended that all Aboriginal languages be recognized within Canada's Constitution:

> A matter closely related to Native rights is that of Native languages. The Charter of Rights and Freedoms preserves English and French as the official languages of Canada with equality of status. The Legislative Assembly and the Government of the Northwest Territories both support the preservation of English and French as the official languages. However, the reality in the Northwest Territories is that the people speak several Native languages, the preservation of which is far more crucial to them than the preservation of English and French. I submit that the recognition of the right of Native people to use Native languages is in keeping with their special status. The preservation and indeed the propagation and advancement of Native languages should be an aim to be recognized clearly in the constitution of Canada.[39]

Senator Willie Adams (Northwest Territories) raised the question of language education in the Northwest Territories. He noted that "there are only two official languages, English and French. You are more concerned about language education in the Territories. Right now we are teaching people who go up to Grade III in the local community and who are taught their mother tongue."[40] Braden's response was that the preservation, protection, and the development of Aboriginal languages in a number of areas is an item of great importance to the cultural well-being of Aboriginal peoples:

> We, as a government, are very cognizant of the need to start work right now in developing further, and in some cases, preserving native languages. We generally believe that once a group of people loses their language, they lose a very, very significant and important part of their culture. Believe me, I see the problems that have been created, because kids I went to school with many years ago in the Northwest Territories are no longer able to communicate in the language of their parents or grandparents. So what we have done as an immediate item of action within our government is to establish a small working group with a capability to deliver programs and services in Dene languages such as Dogrib, Slavey, et cetera. We see an immediate need and are going to be establishing a language commission which is hopefully going to provide us with direction of more substance and with the long-term in mind, so that we can start looking at more comprehensive delivery programs and services in all languages in the Northwest Territories. We would like to look at ways and means by which large industries can use Native languages.[41]

In apparent agreement with the language rights proponents, Frank Oberle (MP, Prince George, Peace River) went further to recognize the significance of Aboriginal cultures to the historical context of Canada's Constitution. During discussions, Oberle, and Chief James Gosnell (President, Nisga'a Tribal Council) examined the connection between language rights and Aboriginal title, with Oberle arguing that the source of Aboriginal language rights is based on customary law and the peoples' cultural relationship to the land:

> The constitution, in my opinion, is not the source of rights, it is a result of history and tradition; but if there is any need to entrench anything, surely it must be the need to entrench the rights of native people, the Aboriginal people of this land, because every other ethnic group, every other cultural group in this country does not draw the source of its culture from the North American continent and you do, you have nowhere else to go to replenish your culture. The land is your soul, is your culture, is all of your existence and if there is any need to entrench anything, it should be your rights and the traditions that you have established here. . . . I would like to get

> back, though, and ask you why it is that you have not . . . tied land to culture and to language, why you have not made the connection between your culture, which is part of nature, and which is the land, why you have not made this connection.[42]

Chief Gosnell agreed with Oberle's statement, adding that Aboriginal peoples needed to secure land rights before the federal government would seriously acknowledge and address any derivative rights:

> It is absolutely impossible for us to talk about our language unless we negotiate on a just and equitable basis and there is no way we can do it without Aboriginal title. We intend to do what you have said . . . that is why we are already one step ahead of it in establishing our schools, that is exactly what we are doing, but here again this is what we want to negotiate about. When negotiation comes, then our language is part of that negotiation. It hinges on that entrenchment of our Aboriginal title in the constitution, that is the key. Without that there is nothing we could [do], it is meaningless. We have gone through seven years and we have not gotten anywhere.[43]

In his statement to the committee, Chief Gosnell also observed that communities were not sitting idle but were instead working actively on First Nations language education in schools as flowing from Aboriginal rights to land. He insisted that there is integral connection between First Nations languages and land, and that Aboriginal title is important for the necessary resources that are required to support the continuity of languages and distinct linguistic identities of Aboriginal peoples. The emphasis on resources, Aboriginal rights, and language rights was also present in the National Indian Brotherhood's submission to the Special Joint Committee, noted below. Another important point was that First Nations had never relinquished their language rights, and although these rights were not expressly recognized in Canada's Constitution, Aboriginal language rights nevertheless existed on the basis of Aboriginal title and in part through the establishment of culturally appropriate schools in a number of communities. Chief Gosnell's statement demonstrates the continuity of First Nations efforts to preserve First Nations languages, and the centrality of languages to the creation of schools.

Despite the support for the right to language preservation and transmission expressed by many of the presenters to the Special Joint Committee 1980, Jim Fulton (MP, Skeena) noted in an exchange with Charlie Watt (Co-Chairman, Inuit Committee on National Issues) that submissions to the committee made little reference to language rights:

> One of the things that has profoundly interested me in sitting on this Committee, and I am sure it is something that the other members have thought about, is that the overwhelming majority of native people who have appeared before this Committee have not asked specifically for the entrenchment of their language rights, and I think as all members of this Committee have noted, well within the document, is that one of the potent principles included in it is this specific reference to the inclusion of minority rights specifically for certainly the second largest group in Canada which is the French speaking people of Canada.... Some of the more highly refined [constitutional rights] and perhaps distinct from what you are requesting in terms of language rights has not come forward as one of the most stressed principles before this Committee, and I wonder if you could comment on how far you have gone in terms of what you are requesting before this Committee?[44]

Watt replied that Aboriginal people were busy trying to meet fundamental needs in their communities:

> I guess the reason that it has not come out and I guess has come out from a lot of other groups is because the things that we talk about as far as our survival, really our language is part of that. If we do not survive as a people and if our communities don't survive then our language dies anyway, and you can have all the acts of Parliament and programs and everything else to try and keep our language. It is not going to live if we do not live as a people. What will happen is you will have professors in universities speaking our language and that is about as much as it will be living because if we are not alive as a people, how can our languages live?[45]

Watt's submission suggests that the strategy of leadership during this period was to secure Aboriginal rights as a means for meeting the fundamental needs of the people, which included language rights.

Another submission, by Gilles Tardif (Director, Canadian Federation of Civil Liberties and Human Rights Associations), suggested that Canadians must rise to the occasion and assist Aboriginal peoples in advancing their language rights. "An effort must be made," he argued, "to guarantee native language rights, because some native groups have lost the incentive for making sure that their linguistic rights are guaranteed. So, as someone stated earlier, this means more than just protecting the future, this means a challenge for Canadians."[46]

Finally, a brief statement by René Simon (Chairman, Atikamekw-Montagnais Council) identified the shame around speaking Aboriginal languages that resulted from residential schools: "Presently, we try and speak our languages as much as possible, contrary to what we did before, when Indians were perhaps ashamed, at least embarrassed, to speak their own languages."[47]

In addition to the individual, in-person presentations made to the Special Joint Committee 1980, the NIB submitted proposed amendments regarding Aboriginal rights. The amendments included the right to adequate resources to support the preservation of languages and cultures:

> Within the Canadian federation, the Aboriginal people of Canada shall have the right to their self determination, and in this regard Parliament and the legislative assemblies together with the government of Canada and the provincial governments, to the extent of their respective jurisdictions are committed to negotiate with the Aboriginal people of Canada mutually satisfactory constitutional rights and protections in the following areas: the right to adequate land and resource base and adequate revenues, including royalties, revenue sharing, equalization payments, taxation, unconditional grants and program financing. So as to ensure the distinct culture and economic and linguistic identities of the Aboriginal people of Canada.[48]

Shortly after these constitutional discussions took place, Aboriginal and treaty rights were recognized under section 35 of the Constitution

Act, 1982, but without any specific reference to languages. In 1985, federal and provincial ministers met to examine Aboriginal constitutional rights. During this time, many Aboriginal leaders across the country asserted that Aboriginal rights include language rights. The Inuit Committee on National Issues emphasized the need to define and entrench Aboriginal rights, including the cultural rights, based on Aboriginal peoples' prior occupation of the land:

> It has taken you 52 years to hash out a suitable foundation for this country albeit one in which Quebec and I think it is fair to say the Aboriginal people have been excluded. We know exactly what we want, and we are here to tell you about it. We appeal to all of you around this table not to allow mutual impatience to destroy what we all know ought to be an act of construction. The task at hand is nothing less than identifying, defining and entrenching Aboriginal rights in the Constitution of Canada. . . . We are participating in this conference with the hopes of achieving with dignity, a place in Canadian confederation which recognizes our distinct political, economic and cultural rights as is befitting of our long time occupancy in what is now known as Canada.[49]

A letter written by Charlie Watt and Tagak Curley, co-chairs of the Inuit Committee on National Issues, requested a constitutional amendment guaranteeing resources to meet the cultural and linguistic needs of the peoples based on prior occupation and distinct constitutional status:

> We were . . . never involved or consulted when Canada as we now know it was formed. Even if our existence had been fully known to the Fathers of Confederation at that time, we were not familiar with European ways and would not have been able to understand the proceedings which resulted in the establishment of the Dominion of Canada. Our people, our ways, and our land have slowly become more familiar with European ways. . . . Political and historical tradition in Canada has recognized two founding peoples—the French and the English. You can well imagine that we find this somewhat offensive, considering the fact that we have inhabited this land for many thousands of years. Inuit, together with other Aboriginal people, form a distinct part of the

> Canadian "mosaic." We feel then that this opportunity we now have before us ... should result in the recognition of the rights of our people.... We are seeking amendments which will guarantee Constitutional protection for the following principles:
>
> (1) the collective recognition of the Aboriginal people as distinct peoples in Canada due to our occupation of our lands since time immemorial, including the protection of our cultures . . . to provide Aboriginal people with resources to adequately meet our economic social and cultural needs.[50]

At the conclusion of the federal-provincial discussions, a draft statement of constitutional principles was presented. Four overarching points were made regarding the distinct status of Aboriginal peoples that comes from their prior occupancy of land, and affirming self-governing rights over their cultural life, which includes language. The first point stated: "The special status of Aboriginal people in Canadian Society stems from the fact of their occupation, use and collective ownership of lands in what is now Canada prior to European settlement and the application of European law. The Aboriginal people existed as distinct nations and exercised self-governing powers over their territory and over their religious, cultural, social, economic and political life."[51]

The second point was that Aboriginal rights include "the right to preserve and develop their own distinct aboriginal cultures, languages and religions free from arbitrary interference."[52]

The third point asserted that section 91(24) of the British North America Act, 1867, confers on the federal government a fiscal responsibility to Aboriginal people: "the fiscal and trust responsibility of the Federal Government stems from the devolution of Crown responsibility (which responsibility is defined in part in the Royal Proclamation of 1763); and such responsibility cannot be unilaterally abandoned."[53]

The fourth point emphasized that adequate resources must be provided for services comparable to those provided to all Canadians, while considering the special needs of Aboriginal people. In the case of advancing Aboriginal languages, additional resources may be required to assist with revitalization efforts: "It is further recognized that, when defining and developing aboriginal institutions of self-government, it will be essential that adequate fiscal resources be made available to the Aboriginal people. Such resources are required to provide services reasonably comparable to those available to Canadians generally, taking into account the special social, cultural and economic needs of Aboriginal people."[54] Despite the fact that the suggested amendments did not lead to the explicit recognition of Aboriginal language rights in education under section 35 of the Constitution Act, Aboriginal leaders nationwide have unequivocally stated that these rights are encompassed within Aboriginal rights and title.

Federal Government: Aboriginal Languages Initiative, 1988

The federal government has established two distinct frameworks for resourcing language education in Canada, both primarily overseen by the Department of Canadian Heritage. The first framework is enshrined in section 23 of the Charter of Rights and Freedoms, which mandates federal funding for minority language education. The objective of section 23 is to uphold and advance Canada's two official languages, English and French, along with the cultural identities associated with these languages.

The second framework focuses on Aboriginal languages, using a programmatic approach to safeguard cultural identities. This led to the inception of the Aboriginal Languages Initiative (ALI) in 1988 (now known as the Indigenous Language Component). Consequently, any initiatives pertaining to First Nations language education fall under the purview of Canadian Heritage. The ALI's primary focus is on funding *language projects* that promote, revitalize, and preserve Aboriginal cultures through community-based initiatives. However, the implementation of these programs has been subject to criticism. A significant concern is that the ALI was developed without direct collaboration with Aboriginal leaders, neglecting the essential principle of nation-to-nation relationships between Canada and Aboriginal peoples. Additionally, the ALI was not mandated to provide long-term stable funding and fails to offer adequate opportunities for First Nations to influence decisions regarding funding allocation and program management. Moreover, the ALI's restrictive criteria have placed limitations on vital supports for First Nations language education, such as curriculum development, language teacher training, and immersion program development. There is also no overarching First Nations language revitalization strategy or policy in education. The discrimination—both constitutional and programmatic—inherent within these frameworks will be examined in Chapter 5.

In 2002, the Departments of Canadian Heritage and Indian and Northern Affairs initiated a comprehensive study, known as the Federal Review, focused on reviewing the ALI.[55] A steering committee comprising senior executives from the Departments of Canadian Heritage, Indian and Northern Affairs, and the Treasury Board of Canada was responsible for overseeing the review. The objectives were to assess the support provided by the federal government to Aboriginal languages and cultures, identify areas for improvement in the efficiency of these activities, and contribute to the development of a comprehensive Aboriginal languages and cultures strategy.

The Federal Review identified a significant decrease in the number of Aboriginal language speakers from 1981 to 2001, underlining critical areas for language revitalization. It pinpointed factors such as the aging population of language speakers, limited intergenerational language transmission, and the lack of Aboriginal language programs in urban settings as key contributors to the languages' endangerment. The Federal Review also stressed how vital it was to transmit languages to children as the most effective means of preserving Aboriginal languages.[56]

Although the ALI was acknowledged as an important federal program for language revitalization, the Federal Review pointed out that its funding levels were inadequate to achieve its goals. Moreover, there was still no national Aboriginal language revitalization strategy or framework to promote Aboriginal languages and cultures in Canada. The Federal Review uncovered several challenges and shortcomings in existing efforts, underlining the urgency for a comprehensive strategy to counter the decline of Aboriginal languages and foster their revitalization. In summary, the Federal Review's assessment was that "the slow growth of language programming is not responding quickly enough to the rapidly declining status of the endangered Aboriginal languages. Analysis of the current Aboriginal language activities and relevant program evaluations consistently show that the community-based approach can be effective in addressing specific community needs. However, the community-based approach suffers from the lack of a national language strategy and strategic funding allocations."[57]

The Federal Review also emphasized the vital role of language as the key medium for cultural transmission, stressing that the erosion of languages would significantly impair the ability of Aboriginal people to maintain their cultural identity, history, and traditional knowledge.[58] It further highlighted the essential connection between language retention and cultural reclamation by pointing out the positive influence these have had on the health and social outcomes for Aboriginal communities.[59] Specifically, the Federal Review observed that "strong cultural continuity acts as a protective factor against conditions that could lead to suicide and other adverse social behaviors."[60]

To complement these crucial insights, Canadian Heritage implemented a national consultation strategy, reinforcing its findings and presenting various key recommendations. By recognizing the profound interconnectedness of language, culture, and holistic well-being, the strategy highlighted the urgent need to address the decline of Aboriginal languages and implement impactful measures for their revitalization. Aside from changes to the ALI's name, Canada's programmatic response to Aboriginal language funding has seen minimal change.

Standing Committee on Aboriginal Affairs, 1990

In 1990, the focus on Aboriginal languages pivoted to literacy, as highlighted in the *You Took My Talk: Aboriginal Literacy and Empowerment*, a report by the Standing Committee on Aboriginal Affairs. The committee linked the endangered status of First Nations languages to the literacy challenges faced by First Nations, attributing these difficulties to the government's efforts to extinguish First Nations languages and cultures through residential schools.[61] The report identified several issues connected to these government actions: "Children sent to residential schools returned home unable to communicate with their parents and grandparents—because of the loss of Aboriginal language skills and the almost total disorientation of their cultural value system. Where the system failed to achieve its goal of total assimilation, many children ended up semi-lingual and without a firm cultural identity of any kind. The socio-cultural fall-out from this devastating policy is still very much in evidence and was referred to by most witnesses."[62]

The report emphasized the importance of literacy skills as a vital means to "preserve and promote these endangered languages and boost self-esteem."[63] While recognizing that cultural assimilation should not be an official component of education policy, the committee observed that First Nations languages and cultures were still inadequately integrated within the education system. The Standing Committee's findings were unequivocal: the use of formal education as a tool of assimilation persisted, with little meaningful changes.[64]

Significantly, the Standing Committee also examined the literacy landscape prior to the establishment of the residential school system. A study by social scientists Jo Anne Bennett and John Berry from Queen's University, highlighted in the report, indicated that in the late nineteenth century, Cree-speaking individuals may have had one of the highest literacy rates in the world. They were adept at reading and writing in syllabics, a writing system distinct from the pedagogical tools used in the Euro-Canadian tradition. This study's revelations pointed to the profoundly negative impact of the residential school system on the preservation and transmission of this effective writing system discussed in Chapter 1.[65]

The Charlottetown Accord and Right of Self-Government, 1992

During the constitutional discussions in 1992, Aboriginal language rights were once again raised, particularly during the Charlottetown Accord consultations. Constitutional expert Peter Hogg insists that had the Charlottetown Accord been adopted in the Constitution Act, 1982, it would have included, with the inherent right of self-government in section 35.1(3), the right to safeguard and develop Aboriginal languages, cultures, economies, identities, institutions, and traditions.[66] Although the Charlottetown Accord was defeated in the 1992 constitutional referendum, Hogg suggests that the treatment of Aboriginal people during the negotiations has had some lasting impacts on the status of Aboriginal rights.[67] First, Aboriginal organizations were treated as a virtual "third order" of government in the discussions that led up to the Charlottetown Accord, alongside eleven provincial and two territorial governments. Second, the provincial and the territorial governments agreed that an inherent right to self-government existed. Third, Hogg proposes that even though the Charlottetown Accord was not adopted, its unanimous approval by federal and provincial governments can be regarded as an informal recognition that an Aboriginal language right exists.[68] Hogg's argument is important for advancing Aboriginal language rights in education as part of the right to self-government by Aboriginal nations under self-government agreements.[69] To date there have been very few self-government agreements that have included First Nations language rights to education.[70]

Royal Commission on Aboriginal Peoples Report, 1996

Established in 1991, the Royal Commission on Aboriginal Peoples (RCAP) issued its five-volume report in 1996, in which approximately fifty of the 440 recommendations related to Aboriginal languages and cultures. The RCAP report emphasized the endangered status of Aboriginal languages, noting that once these languages are lost, there is no other place in the world from which they can be retrieved.[71] An endowment of $100 million for an Aboriginal Languages Foundation was recommended.[72] The report highlighted the urgency of language preservation, especially considering the advanced age and fragility of many fluent speakers: "A great many of the elders who constitute the fluent speakers are also fragile with age. This is an area where restorative justice cannot wait while negotiations for a new relationship progress at a deliberate pace. Aboriginal languages have been undermined by government action. They should be conserved, restored or documented for posterity with government support. Because churches have played a critical part in the destruction of languages, we consider that practical support for the restoration of the languages would be a highly appropriate reconciliatory gesture."[73] Other RCAP recommendations included:

- the development of language classes in Aboriginal languages, as determined by the Aboriginal community;[74] and
- that federal, provincial, and territorial governments recognize promptly that determining Aboriginal language status and use is a core power in Aboriginal self-government, and that these governments affirm and support Aboriginal nations and their communities in using and promoting their languages, and in declaring them official languages within their nations, territories, and communities where they choose to do so.[75]

Regrettably, the federal government has largely overlooked these language recommendations over time, perpetuating a pattern of commissioning studies on First Nations issues but failing to act decisively on their findings. This neglect has resulted in the further loss of First Nations languages, with the impacts just as damaging as deliberate policies of language eradication.

Task Force on Aboriginal Languages and Cultures, 2005

In 2003, Canadian Heritage initiated a consultation strategy that included the formation of the Task Force on Aboriginal Languages and Cultures. Comprising ten members representing First Nations, Inuit, and Métis peoples, the task force's mandate was to advise the Minister of Canadian Heritage on the creation of a language centre. In 2005, a comprehensive report, *Towards a New Beginning: A Foundational Report for a Strategy to Revitalize First Nations, Inuit, and Métis Languages and Cultures*, was presented to the federal government. There were twenty-five recommendations regarding national legislation, advocating for equitable funding for language education both on and off reserves and for the establishment of a national organization. More specifically, the Task Force's recommendations were that

- Canada enact legislation to recognize, protect and promote Indigenous languages. This legislation would be developed in partnership with Indigenous peoples; establish a First Nation, Inuit, and Métis Language Commissioner; and provide financial resources for the preservation, revitalization, protection and promotion of Indigenous languages, among other matters;
- a National Language Strategy be developed by Indigenous language communities and representative organizations; and Canada provide funding for Indigenous languages "which is, at a minimum, at the same level as that provided for the French and languages."[76]

Shortly after the final Task Force report was released, the federal government proposed allocating a budget of $160 million over a ten-year period to support the preservation, revitalization, and promotion of Aboriginal languages. However, Prime Minister Harper subsequently withdrew the proposed $160 million, opting instead to maintain the existing $5 million for the 2006/07 fiscal year to the ALI.

It is important to point out that the federal government's 2003 review of Aboriginal languages coincided with a period when there were over 10,000 residential school claims against the federal government, reflecting the profound abuses Aboriginal people suffered in these institutions. The Task Force's report linked the loss of language and culture directly to Canada's policy of assimilation.[77]

A significant step was taken in 2006 when the Minister of Canadian Heritage and Status of Women, the Minister of Indian Affairs and Northern Development, the Federal Interlocutor for Métis and Non-Status Indians, and the Honourable Dennis Fentie, Premier of the Yukon Territory, signed the Canada–Yukon Cooperation Agreement for Aboriginal Languages. This agreement earmarked $1.1 million from the ALI's Community Initiative Program for funding language projects within Aboriginal communities. Since this time, there have been a number of additional regional initiatives implemented to support Aboriginal languages, which will be explored in further detail later in the chapter.

Prime Minister's Statement of Apology, 2008

In 2008, Canada finally publicly admitted to its role in the destruction of Aboriginal languages and cultures through a formal statement of apology to residential school survivors, delivered by the Prime Minister of Canada Stephen Harper. The apology referred to the impact on Aboriginal languages and cultures:

> Two primary objectives of the Residential Schools system were to remove and isolate children from the influence of their homes, families, traditions and cultures, and to assimilate them into the dominant culture. These objectives were based on the assumption Aboriginal cultures and spiritual beliefs were inferior and unequal. Indeed, some sought, as it was infamously said, "to kill the Indian in the child." Today, we recognize that this policy of assimilation was wrong, has caused great harm, and has no place in our country.
>
> . . . First Nations, Inuit and Métis languages and cultural practices were prohibited in these schools. . . .
>
> The government now recognizes that the consequences of the Indian Residential Schools policy were profoundly negative and that this policy has had a lasting and damaging impact of Aboriginal culture, heritage and language.[78]

Both the courts and the federal government have stated that Canada's assimilation policies and attitudes of cultural superiority are no longer acceptable threads in the country's constitutional fabric. Today, language advocates continue to insist that immersion programs are a critical step

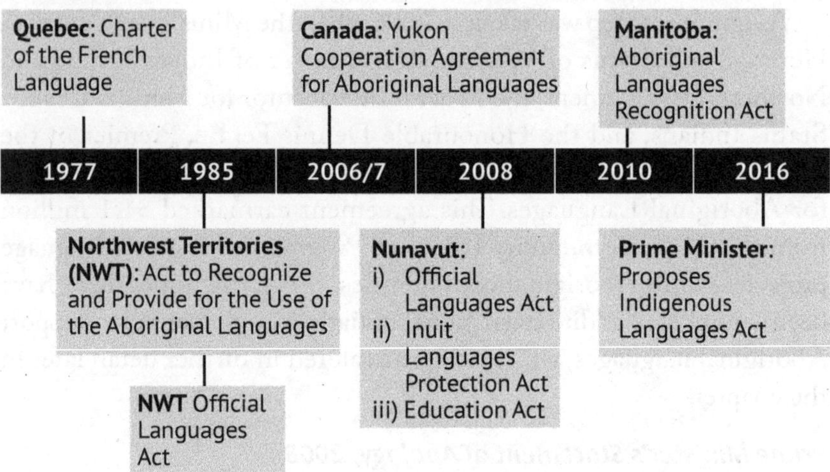

Figure 12. Aboriginal languages: Regional legislation. Compiled by author.

for the revitalization of First Nations languages, and yet provincial and territorial legislation that has been passed has not resulted in adequate support for the revitalization of First Nations languages. Since the statement of apology, there has been minimal support for Aboriginal language education and no federal policy to support immersion programs that are integral if language revitalization is to occur.

Since the mid-1980s, regional Aboriginal language legislation has been implemented in the Yukon, Quebec, Manitoba, the Northwest Territories, and Nunavut. Within these areas, the rights of Aboriginal languages are recognized, ranging from language usage to the right to access specific services in those languages. Notably, in Quebec, First Nations language rights are distinct from minority language rights. However, none of the provincial or territorial legislations address First Nations language rights in education.

Regional Legislation

The next section will offer an overview of language legislation across these provinces and territories, with a particular emphasis on Nunavut. This case study examines the effectiveness of language legislation in preserving Inuktut (Inuktitut is an inclusive term that covers all Inuit languages and dialects) in Nunavut by examining three significant pieces of legislation: the Official Languages Act, the Inuit Language Protection Act, and the Education Act. This analysis is intended to highlight the importance of explicitly defining language rights within Canada's Constitution to ensure that support for language revitalization is based on constitutional rights and not program dollars.

Quebec, 1977

In Quebec, the preamble to the Charter of the French Language recognizes Aboriginal and Inuit peoples as the descendants of the first inhabitants of the country. Aboriginal and Inuit languages are granted certain exemptions from provisions of the Charter of the French Language that make French the language of instruction in elementary and secondary schools.[79] For example, section 88 provides an exception for both Cree and Inuktitut. Section 97 excludes the application of the Charter of the French Language on Indian reserve communities. Section 95 exempts the Cree and Inuktitut speakers who qualify under the agreement concerning the James Bay and North Quebec from using French in the legislature and the courts (with a few exceptions).[80]

Under the Cree-Naskapi (of Quebec) Act, language rights are recognized for the purpose of administering justice. All written judgements and verbal statements made by a judge must be translated into Cree and Naskapi. Section 18 of the Cree-Naskapi (of Quebec) Act recognizes that the language for the administration of justice is Cree and Inuit. All translations in Cree, Naskapi, or an Inuit language are to be provided without cost to Aboriginal people. However, translation is provided for information purposes only. Michel Bastarache notes: "It would seem that . . . the objective underlying these provisions is trial fairness as opposed to the preservation of cultural identity of these Aboriginal people. To preserve aboriginal languages and culture, stronger language use rights in the judicial system would be necessary."[81]

Yukon, 1983

In Yukon, the question of Aboriginal language rights was highlighted shortly after two unilingual traffic tickets were challenged in 1983 by a French-speaking Whitehorse resident on the basis that they violated his language rights under the Charter of Rights and Freedoms.[82] The federal government responded by attempting to amend Yukon's constitution unilaterally by introducing Bill C-26, An Act to Amend the Northwest

Territories Act and the Yukon Act, into the House of Commons. The purpose of Bill C-26 was to apply the official languages provisions of the Charter of Rights and Freedoms and the Official Languages Act to Yukon. Some members of the Yukon Assembly responded that addressing Aboriginal language rights should be a priority, since they were becoming endangered and the Aboriginal population was greater than the francophone population.[83]

In 1984, a Progressive Conservative government formed in the Yukon, followed by the formation of a New Democratic government after a territorial election in 1985. The composition of this newly formed Yukon government was notably diverse, with 50 percent of its members being Aboriginal. During this period, negotiations were ongoing for a land claim agreement that included provisions for Aboriginal language rights. Unfortunately, Bill C-26, which could have furthered these rights, died with the change of government in the 1984 federal election. However, Aboriginal leadership in the Yukon continued to advocate for the inclusion of Aboriginal language rights in their land claim agreements. Several Aboriginal individuals who held positions in the Yukon government were able to continue pushing for these rights. As a result, Aboriginal people were granted special status regarding language services in the Yukon, though the agreement did not clearly define the extent or implementation of these rights. In 1988, the Yukon passed its languages act, section 1(3) of which states: "The Yukon recognizes the significance of Indigenous languages in the Yukon and wishes to take appropriate measures to preserve, develop and enhance those languages in the Yukon."[84] Then, section 11 recognizes that Aboriginal people may receive certain services in an Aboriginal language: "The Commissioner in Executive Council may make regulations in relation to the provision of services of the Government of the Yukon in one or more of the Aboriginal languages of the Yukon."[85]

Northwest Territories, 1984

The French language rights case that occurred in the Yukon also prompted the discussion of Aboriginal language rights in the Northwest Territories. As result, in 1984 the Northwest Territories passed the Official Languages Ordinance, which recognized the special status of Aboriginal languages in addition to English and French as the official languages. Resources were allocated for the creation of a

French school board and the development of Aboriginal languages.[86] In 1985, the Official Languages Ordinance was replaced by the Official Languages Act. Shortly thereafter certain Aboriginal members of the assembly protested because they were not permitted to speak their own language. To assess the status of Aboriginal languages in the Northwest Territories, a Special Committee on Aboriginal Languages was established. Culture Minister Titus Allooloo, in explaining the need to acknowledge Aboriginal languages, stated: "I think it's about time that the aboriginal (people) who have lived in this area for such a long time be given services in their own languages. . . ."[87] The government of the Northwest Territories eventually decided that certain Aboriginal languages and French would be granted official language status in the Territories.[88] In 1990, the Official Languages Act was amended to include Cree, Chipewyan, Dogrib, Inuktitut, Inuvialuktun, Inuinnaqtun, Gwich'in, North Slavey and South Slavey as official languages in addition to French and English. At this time, the Office of the Language Commissioner was also established.

The preamble of the Northwest Territories' Official Languages Act declares that Aboriginal languages constitute a distinct part of Canadian identity and asserts that "the legal protection of languages will assist in preserving the culture of the people as expressed through their language." Under the act, Aboriginal people from the Northwest Territories have a right to use any of the recognized languages in a territorial court or in debates and proceedings of the legislature where it is warranted. Section 9(2) states that "Chipewyan, Cree, Gwich'in, Inuinnaqtun, Inuktitut, Inuvialuktun, North Slavey, South Slavey and Tåîchômay [can] be used by any person in any court established by the Legislature." As for the right to receive public services in an Aboriginal language, section 11(2) of the Official Languages Act states:

> Any member of the public in the Northwest Territories has the right to communicate with, and to receive available services from, any regional, area or community office of a government institution in an Official Language other than English or French spoken in that region or community, where
>
> (a) there is a significant demand for communications with and services from the office in that language; or

(b) it is reasonable, given the nature of the office, that communications with and services from it be available in that language.[89]

Section 11(3) of the Official Languages Act also indicates that "consideration shall be given to collective rights of Aboriginal people pertaining to Aboriginal languages and exercised within the traditional homelands of those peoples, consistent with any applicable lands, resources and self-government agreements, including land claim and treaty land entitlement agreements, and any other sources or expressions of those collective rights."[90]

The significance of the statutory provision lies not only in its support for the continuity of preserving Aboriginal language but also in its recognition of the collective rights that exist on the traditional homeland of Aboriginal peoples. Although there are provisions for Aboriginal languages in certain cases, laws in the Northwest Territories are only legally binding in the French and English versions. Furthermore, the Northwest Territories government is only required to publish laws in the other official languages upon special request of the legislature. Official languages are also only provided when there is a significant demand; English is the only language guaranteed for all services.

Since 2003, the Northwest Territories has advocated for adequate resources to support Aboriginal languages. The Standing Committee on the Review of the Official Languages Act, the report *One Land, Many Voices,* and the report of the Northwest Territories Legislative Assembly's Standing Committee on Government Operations, *Reality Check: Securing a Future for the Official Languages of the Northwest Territories* (2009),[91] resulted in an action plan for preserving Aboriginal languages.

Manitoba

In June 2010, Manitoba implemented the Aboriginal Languages Recognition Act, which recognizes and protects seven Aboriginal languages: Cree, Dakota, Dene, Inuktitut, Michif, Ojibway, and Oji-Cree.[92] The preamble to the Act notes the endangered status of these languages and the government's role in recognizing these languages and promoting their preservation and use. The legislation also recognizes how vital Aboriginal languages are to Aboriginal peoples' culture, self-esteem, and well-being.

Nunavut: A Case Study

With the exception of Nunavut's acts, no provincial or territorial legislation addresses Aboriginal language rights in education. Nunavut's experience with regional and federal constitutional frameworks offers a useful case study of the implementation of the language rights in education. Several Inuit people initiated the Inuit land claims movement in the 1970s.[93] The protection and recognition of language rights are of central importance because language is deeply intertwined with Inuit knowledge of the land and their ability to care for and interpret it.[94]

In 1983, under Nunavut's constitutional discussions, research was conducted to assess the cost of implementing Inuktut in the education system. Inuit leaders strongly advocated for the Inuit language to be used as the language of instruction at all educational levels. They emphasized the necessity of federal funding for Inuit teacher training and curriculum development in Inuktut, and proposed a thirteen-year implementation plan.[95] The goal was to prepare 260 Inuit language teachers by the year 2000, with an estimated budget of fifteen million dollars. Additionally, they recommended the establishment of an Inuit teacher training facility and further resources for curriculum development.[96] However, neither the funding nor the support for Inuktut education were provided or implemented by the federal government.[97] In fact in 1990, Prime Minister Brian Mulroney and his cabinet instructed the federal lawyer negotiating the Nunavut Land claims Agreement not to include any specific language guarantees in the agreement.[98] The document that Nunavut Tunngavik Incorporated (NTI) received under the Access to Freedom of Information Act includes instructions to the federal government's negotiating lawyer that state, "The Final Agreement shall not contain any guarantees for the creation of a Nunavut Territory or provide any linguistic guarantees for use of Inuktitut in government and the legal and educational system in the claims area."[99] As a result, there is nothing included in Nunavut's Land Claims Agreement regarding Inuit language rights in education.

In his 2006 *Conciliator's Report* on the Nunavut Land Claims Agreement, Thomas Berger included a letter addressed to Jim Prentice, Minister of Indian Affairs and Northern Development. In the letter, he emphasized the harmful impact on Inuit youth when schools fail to support their language and cultural identity. Berger drew attention to the alarming statistic that only 25 percent of Inuit children graduate from high school, framing this as a reflection of the broader systemic failure of the education system in Nunavut. He argued that this failure not only contributes to low graduation rates but also undermines Inuit students' self-confidence and belief in their potential. The letter further highlights that exclusion or rejection of Inuit language and culture in educational settings fosters a profound sense of personal inadequacy amongst students. Berger concludes by asserting that,

> In Nunavut this reinforces the colonial message of inferiority. The Inuit student mentally withdraws, then leaves altogether. In such a system Inuktitut is being eroded. Of course, language is only one element of identity, but it is a huge one. The dropout rate is linked to Nunavut's unhappy incidence of crime, drugs and family violence. Ejetsiak Peter, chairman of the Cape Dorset District Education Authority, summed it up for me through an interpreter: "The children who drop out have not developed the skills to live off of the land, neither do they have employment skills." So they are caught between two worlds.[100]

In 2008, the Nunavut Legislative Assembly engaged in several discussions concerning Bill 7, the proposed Inuit Language Protection Act, and Bill 6, the proposed Official Languages Act. Louis Tapardjuk, serving as the Minister of Culture, Language, Elders, and Youth, Minister of Finance, and Chairman of the Financial Management Board (Amittuq), emphasized the crucial significance of the proposed Inuit Language Protection Act. He stressed that for Inuit to maintain their identity as a distinct people, a transformative shift in education must take place that would empower young people to strengthen their language skills and cultural identity:

> Our language is endangered. We cannot take this lightly for language is at the heart of Inuit culture. It reflects the generations who came before and their relationship to our Arctic world. It speaks of who we are, how we view our surroundings, and how we wish our children to know their world. To lose one's language is to lose an essential part of one's identity. In fact, the survival of our language is crucial

> to the survival of Inuit as a distinctive people and to our dream for what Nunavut is and will become. We urgently need to reverse the language shift among our young people and strengthen their use of the Inuit language.[101]

Tapardjuk further elaborated on the objectives of the legislation, emphasizing its focus on language instruction. Bill 7's key objectives are to make the Inuit language a primary language of instruction in schools, ensuring children achieve full proficiency. It also emphasizes using the Inuit language in early childhood and adult education.[102]

Nunavut's Official Languages Act, Inuit Protection Act, and Education Act

As a result of Inuit advocacy, the Legislative Assembly of Nunavut enacted three significant pieces of legislation to protect and promote the Inuit language in education. The Official Languages Act recognizes Inuktitut as one of Nunavut's official languages.[103] The Nunavut Education Act[104] and the Inuit Language Protection Act[105] were implemented to ensure Inuit students receive education in their language and culture, aiming for bilingual education for all students by the 2019/20 academic year.[106] Section 8 of the Education Act outlines the creation of educational programs focusing on Nunavut culture, traditional knowledge, and its unique environmental and land characteristics.

Unfortunately, the 2013 Federal Auditor General's Report revealed shortcomings in Nunavut's legislation, particularly in implementing a fully bilingual school system with Inuit language instruction from kindergarten through grade 12.[107] Some of the challenges identified included a shortage of qualified teachers, inadequate teacher training, limited teaching resources, and a curriculum that inadequately reflected the values and principles of *Qaujimajatuqangit* (that which has long been known) or "Inuit traditional knowledge." The auditor's report also pointed to broader societal issues contributing to the educational challenges, such as housing shortages, food insecurity, health issues, and social problems like teenage pregnancy and substance abuse.[108] In response to these findings, a committee was formed in 2014 to review the Education Act's provisions and effectiveness.[109] One of the committee's key findings was that the Nunavut government did not have the capacity to deliver on its promise of bilingual education.[110]

In 2016, Sandra Inutiq, appointed as Nunavut Language Commissioner, presented a paper at the United Nations International Expert Group Meeting on Indigenous Languages.[111] Inutiq highlighted the significant disparity in government funding for language education in Nunavut compared to funding for other languages. She pointed out that while funding for French language education amounted to approximately $4,000 per person, Inuit language education received only about $40 per person.[112] Inutiq further drew attention to the 2014–15 Canada–Nunavut General Agreement on the Promotion of French and Inuit Languages. This agreement allocated $1.625 million for French language initiatives, despite French speakers in Nunavut constituting a small demographic of about 435 individuals. In contrast, a mere $1.1 million was allocated for Inuit language promotion, emphasizing the stark inequality and apparent discrimination in funding allocation between linguistic communities.[113]

As a potential solution, the Nunavut government proposed Bill 37, which would extend the target date for achieving complete bilingual education from 2019 to 2029. Additionally, the bill suggested modifying the objective of bilingual education to encompass education up to grade 9 instead of grade 12.[114] Kathy Okpik, Deputy Minister of Education, acknowledged the government's significant miscalculation of its capacity to enact certain provisions of the Education Act. She also highlighted the scarcity of Inuktut-speaking educators as one of their most formidable challenges.[115]

Aluki Kotierk, former President of Nunavut Tunngavik Incorporated, the organization that oversees the Nunavut Land Claims agreement, criticized a series of territorial governments for their failure to produce a sufficient number of teachers to fulfill the commitments of the original Education Act. She accused the Government of Nunavut, particularly the Department of Education, of consistently shifting blame onto Inuit.[116] Kotierk argued that the government could not plead resource scarcity as an excuse, pointing out that Nunavut Tunngavik had offered $50 million from the settlement of a lawsuit to support and initiate teacher training programs.[117]

In April 2018, Kotierk presented a report to the United Nations Permanent Forum on Indigenous Issues, revealing a striking imbalance in Nunavut's education system: there were more English-speaking teachers than English-speaking students. She noted that approximately

9,300 students in kindergarten through grade 12 were Inuktut speakers. At the same time, there were only 430 English- and/or French-speaking students and 452 English-speaking teachers—twenty-two more English-speaking teachers than there were English-speaking students. Additionally, thirty-seven out of forty-one school principals in Nunavut were non-Inuit and English speaking.[118] As a result, Inuit children seldom saw their identities, languages, or cultural experiences reflected in their educational environment. The predominance of non-Inuit educators and the limited use of Inuktut in classroom instruction contributed to this disconnect.[119] This situation is particularly concerning given the declining use of Inuktut, which is decreasing at a rate of approximately 1 percent per year, despite its status as one of the most robust Indigenous languages in Canada.

These statistics show that English has been the predominant language in all forty-two schools across Nunavut, overshadowing the needs of the Inuit majority. This situation is particularly startling given that as of 2018, English was serving about 350 anglophone students, who represent a minority in the region. Meanwhile, Inuit students who make up the large majority have been struggling to find their identity and express themselves in their ancestral language within a school system that has been English dominant from the start. These numbers underline the urgent need for a more effective implementation of language policies that truly support and foster Aboriginal languages and cultures in education.[120]

In a presentation to the Senate Standing Committee on Aboriginal Peoples in April 2019 regarding Bill C-91 (now the Indigenous Languages Act), Kotierk mentioned a coalition of Inuit organizations that had dedicated over two years to crafting recommendations for the Indigenous Languages Act, which was supposed to be co-developed with First Nations, Inuit, and Métis leaders. Kotierk noted that none of the Inuit recommendations had been incorporated into the legislation and expressed her overall disappointment in the process:

> We seek, in our homeland, what every Anglophone and Francophone enjoys in Canada, the secure knowledge that our language is one of the essential and enduring building blocks of our country. Our language is central to our identity, but it is also part of Canada's identity as a nation.

> Our language is a gift, not a burden; its future should be a source of hope and inspiration, not defeat and resignation.... As part of the team of Inuit organizations working on this legislative project for more than two years, we offered ... a wealth of legislative provisions which could be added to the Bill to make it work more effectively for Inuktut and for Inuit. You can imagine our disappointment, and frustration that those amendments did not appear to have even been seriously examined by that Committee.... No one suggested that our proposals were unworkable on practical grounds ... or exceed[ed] the authority of Parliament ... or would intrude on provincial or territorial laws ... or would impose unworkable financial demands ... or would cause injustices to current federal works.... Rather, they were just ignored.[121]

In 2020, NTI submitted a complaint to the Office of the High Commissioner for Human Rights stating that Canada had repeatedly failed to fulfill its international obligations regarding Inuit language rights in education. NTI stated that Canada had not taken adequate action to ensure the recognition and realization of the Inuit right to receive public education in the Inuit language. It reported that despite an Inuit majority and the fact that 90 percent of Nunavut students are Inuit,[122] education was delivered primarily in English in kindergarten through grade 12 as well as in postsecondary schooling. As of 2016, only seven schools were offering education in Inuktut up to grade 4, and only one up to grade 5.[123]

In response to NTI's complaint, a letter from UN Special Rapporteurs Fernand de Varennes (UN Special Rapporteur on Minority Issues), Koumbou Boly Barry (UN Special Rapporteur on the Right to Education), Tlaleng Mofokeng (UN Special Rapporteur on the Right of Everyone to the Enjoyment of the Highest Attainable Standard of Physical and Mental Health), and José Francisco Calí Tzay (UN Special Rapporteur on the Rights of Indigenous Peoples) was sent to Marc Garneau, Minister of Foreign Affairs, on 3 August 2021. The four rapporteurs formally asked Canada to respond to NTI's allegations and to provide clarification on specific issues related to Canada's obligations concerning Inuit language rights in education under five international treaties that Canada is a signatory to, in addition to the Universal Declaration of Human Rights and the UN Declaration on the Rights of

Indigenous Peoples (UNDRIP). Among the requests they made were: "Please provide information on the measures taken by the Government to address allegations of lack of adequate actions to ensure access to public education in Inuktut language in Nunavut, particularly after Grade 3, and how to ensure indigenous students are able to receive education in their own language"; and,"Please provide information on funding allocation to support Inuktut as an official language of the Nunavut territory. In particular, in the field of education, please provide a breakdown on the budget for teaching in Inuktut compared to funding for teaching in English."[124]

On 7 June 2022, the Permanent Mission of Canada to the Office of the United Nations and the World Trade Organization responded. Unfortunately, the response did not directly address access to public education in Inuktut after grade 3. Canada's response was that "Nunavut schools offer English and/or Inuktut streams. The difference in streams varies between larger and smaller communities depending on the Language of Instruction chosen by the District Education Authorities. The number of Inuktitut and Inuinnaqtun speaking teachers is limited."[125]

Regarding funding to support Inuktut and the breakdown of the budget for teaching in Inuktitut compared to teaching English, Canada's response was that "Nunavut and Nunavummiut were introduced to formalized classrooms and schools over 100 years after the rest of Canada. Some communities have only had a school since 1962. Nunavut Inuit have seen exponential changes in culture, such as: international whalers; fur traders; missionaries; military and public servants; formation of settlements; dog slaughter; residential schooling and so much more. The pace of change has been challenging for Inuit, their culture, and language; however, the graduation rate is growing and economic opportunities are improving."[126] The only action taken was that Canada's response was posted on the United Nations Office of the High Commissioner's website, under Special Procedures of the Human Rights Council.

In 2021, NTI also filed a lawsuit in the Nunavut Court of Justice against the Government of Nunavut for failing to provide a public school system offering Nunavut Inuit equal opportunities to complete schooling in their own language and culture, thus violating constitutionally protected equality rights of Nunavut Inuit guaranteed under the Canadian Charter of Rights and Freedoms.[127] NTI asserted that the Government of Nunavut failed to meet its legal obligations under the Inuit Language Protection Act and the Education Act and Regulations to provide full language of instruction in Inuktut through to grade 12 by 2020. It also failed to provide implementation strategies and plans for achieving Inuit language education. The claim also indicates that the Government of Nunavut had given itself a new deadline of 2039 and intended to develop Inuit language courses instead of building a functional bilingual education system. In *Nunavut News*, Kotierk highlighted the issue, stating that, "In today's schools, like residential schools of the past, Nunavut Inuit are prevented from learning Inuktut in favour of English or French. Linguicide by any other name is just as damaging. Rather than proactively empowering Inuit students at every level and investing the resources based on Inuit priorities, our government has diminished the existing language rights of Nunavut Inuit. Nunavut's current education system does not meet the needs of Inuit students or equip them to succeed in postsecondary education or thrive in employment and economic opportunities."[128] NTI's claim against the Government of Nunavut was supported by some of the Inuit parents and students who had experienced systemic discrimination in the education system resulting from the lack of Inuktut language instruction in their schools.

The Government of Nunavut's response to NTI's claim was that Inuit rights to language instruction in the Inuit language does not fall within the Charter of Rights and Freedoms and requested a stay on their claim. On 14 May 2024, a panel of judges from the Nunavut Court of Appeal (Dawn Pentelechuk, Suzanne Duncan, and Alice Woolley) overturned a ruling that would prevent NTI from taking further legal action. They noted that prolonging the case could lead to risks like document loss, destruction, or the unavailability of crucial witnesses, emphasizing that delayed justice means denied justice.[129]

A significant observation from this case study is that despite Inuit having negotiated the largest land claim agreement in Canada, in which language was of central importance, the federal government prevented any reference that identified Inuit language rights in education. Since then, there has been a decline in the number of Inuit language speakers, significantly affecting Inuit children and youth who attend schools that do not teach in their language and culture beyond grade 3.

There is a high dropout rate among Inuit, and the education system leaves them without a grounding both in their own language and culture and in the dominant language and culture. This is not to suggest that language rights in education alone will ensure the survival of the Inuit language, but in a country where English and French have dominated and policies have been deliberately designed to eradicate Inuit culture, the situation is unjust. English and French language rights are enforceable, and there is a duty to fund education in these languages. In contrast, Inuit language rights lack equivalent enforcement mechanisms and funding obligations. This disparity exemplifies discrimination, with two distinct constitutional rights to language education: one with enforceable rights and a duty to fund, and the other lacking both.

Canada is currently in a period of reconciling a genocidal history and claims to deal with Aboriginal peoples on a nation-to-nation basis. However, when Inuit leadership is repeatedly ignored and shut out of issues that are central to their self-determination and cultural identity, it raises questions about Canada's sincerity in working toward a nation-to-nation relationship that respects Aboriginal rights under Aboriginal law, Canadian law, or international law.

In a region where Inuit form the majority and Inuktitut is the majority language, it is astonishing that Inuit language rights in education are not respected. Inuit children are the ones who are suffering from the lack of adequate education in their language. Nunavut has an approximate 65 percent dropout rate for Inuit students,[130] who often leave the education system without proficiency in either English or Inuktitut. According to Ian Martin, a York University professor who has taught in Nunavut, the transition for Inuit students entering an education system that teaches only in English, when their home language is Inuktitut, is extremely challenging academically.[131]

Thomas Berger's powerful statement points to the critical link between language education and the educational success of youth. When Aboriginal students do not have access to their ancestral language in school, it sends a message that their language does not matter, reinforcing the colonial narrative that Aboriginal peoples are inferior and that their languages and cultures are insignificant. Most importantly, Aboriginal students do not see themselves reflected in the curriculum, leading many to withdraw or see no point in continuing their education. Education that does not provide Aboriginal youth with a solid foundation in their cultural identity and language leaves them without a footing in either their own culture or the dominant culture. This destructive, subtractive education model not only erodes Aboriginal cultures and languages but also destroys the spirit of the youth. The federal and Nunavut governments have either specified that Inuit language rights not be included in their own Land Claims Agreement or have ignored reports and regional legislative guarantees for language education.

Inuit leadership should be applauded for their advocacy for Inuit language rights. They have worked with both the federal and Nunavut governments, and when that did not result in any action, they filed complaints both internationally and within their domestic court system.

There are two lessons here. One is that the Canadian government's willingness to protect Aboriginal language rights is questionable. The other is that having defined language rights in education with enforceable government duty to provide funding at the federal level is critical.

Concluding Remarks

First Nations leaders have consistently maintained that the federal government has a responsibility for preserving the languages and cultures of Aboriginal peoples under section 91(24) of the British North America Act. They assert that the right to First Nations languages in education is an inherent right that is recognized under section 35(1) of the Constitution Act, 1982, and First Nations law. According to First Nations law, the preservation of cultural identity and the well-being of succeeding generations through the transmission of language is paramount. These leaders also argue for funding support for First Nations language education to be derived from land resource revenues.

Since the 1970s, the Canadian government has recognized the importance of supporting First Nations languages. The need for teacher training, focusing on First Nations languages, has been a central emphasis by First Nations leaders. The 1980s marked Canada's acknowledgement of the endangerment of First Nations languages, prompting a comprehensive governmental review from 1981 to 2001. The 2002 Federal Review highlighted a drastic reduction in the number of First Nations language speakers, underscoring the importance of immersion programs in language revitalization. It also stressed the need to teach First Nations languages to children and pointed out the inadequacy of current funding. A national strategy for language revitalization was recommended.

In 2008, Canada formally recognized its role in the decline of First Nations languages and cultures. Subsequent court rulings and federal statements acknowledged that historical practices of assimilation and cultural superiority conflicted with current constitutional values. Although the government issued an apology, its efforts in supporting First Nations education, particularly in enhancing language instruction in First Nations, have been limited.

The next chapter will explore legislative progress and human rights laws with respect to Indigenous language rights in education in regions outside Canada. This will set the stage for discussing Canada's Indigenous Languages Act in the final chapter.

CHAPTER 4

INTERNATIONAL LAW

Indigenous Peoples' Language Rights in Education

The challenges First Nations in Canada face in advancing language rights in education are indicative of a broader struggle shared by Indigenous peoples globally. With the support of international non-governmental organizations (NGOs), Indigenous communities worldwide are actively advocating for linguistic rights. These efforts include calling for the integration of Indigenous languages and cultural content in school curricula and emphasizing the imperative for substantial government support. Indigenous language rights in education are acknowledged within the broader framework of human rights, Indigenous self-determination, and sovereignty.

This chapter will explore Indigenous language rights in education within three spheres of international law: ratified international treaties with binding obligations; non-binding treaty obligations; and recognized Indigenous language rights in education and culture in countries outside Canada. Surveying these three areas offers insight into the various approaches and practices that have been adopted globally.

International Treaties

Canada has ratified multiple United Nations treaties that recognize language and cultural rights. Prominent among these treaties are the International Covenant on Civil and Political Rights and the International Covenant on Economic, Social and Cultural Rights.

Additionally, Canada is a signatory to the United Nations International Convention on the Elimination of All Forms of Racial Discrimination, and the Convention on the Rights of the Child. These international agreements reinforce Canada's dedication to upholding essential rights related to language and culture.

International Covenant on Civil and Political Rights

In 1976, Canada ratified the International Covenant on Civil and Political Rights,[1] which has three articles that affirm the rights to languages and cultures. Article 1 recognizes cultural rights as a people's fundamental right to self-determination: "All peoples have the right of self-determination. By virtue of that right they freely determine their political status and freely pursue their economic, social, and cultural development."

Article 2 contains a non-discrimination provision regarding language: "Each State Party to the present Covenant undertakes to respect all individuals within its territory and subject to its jurisdiction and to ensure the rights recognized in the present Covenant, without distinction of any kind, such as race, color, sex, language, religion, political or other opinion, national or social origin, property, birth or other status."

Article 27 recognizes the linguistic rights of minorities: "In those States in which ethnic, religious or linguistic minorities exist, persons belonging to such minorities shall not be denied the right, in community with the other members of their group, to enjoy their own culture, to profess and practice their own religion, or to use their own language."

International Covenant on Economic, Social and Cultural Rights

Also in 1976, Canada ratified the International Covenant on Economic, Social and Cultural Rights.[2] Article 2(2) contains a non-discrimination provision regarding language: "The States Parties to the present Covenant undertake to guarantee that the rights enunciated in the present Covenant will be exercised without discrimination of any kind as to race, colour, sex, language, religion, political or other opinion, national or social origin, property, birth or other status."

Article 13(3) states: "The States Parties to the present Covenant undertake to have respect for the liberty of parents and, when applicable, legal guardians to choose for their children schools, other than those established by the public authorities, which conform to such minimum educational standards as may be laid down or approved by the State and to ensure the religious and moral education of their children in conformity with their own convictions."

International Convention on the Elimination of All Forms of Racial Discrimination

In 1981, Canada ratified the International Convention on the Elimination of All Forms of Racial Discrimination, which contains a provision prohibiting discrimination based on culture. Article 5 states: "In compliance with the fundamental obligations laid down in article 2 of this Convention, States Parties undertake to prohibit and to eliminate racial discrimination in all its forms and to guarantee the right of everyone, without distinction as to race, colour, or national or ethnic origin, to equality before the law, notably in the enjoyment of the following rights: . . . (e) Economic, social and cultural rights."[3]

Convention on the Rights of the Child

In 1991, Canada ratified the Convention on the Rights of the Child, which recognizes the language rights of children to be educated in their ancestral language and culture. Article 2 also contains a non-discrimination provision:"(1) States Parties shall respect and ensure the rights set forth in the present Convention to each child within their jurisdiction without discrimination of any kind, irrespective of the child's or his or her parent's or legal guardian's race, colour, sex, language, religion, political or other opinion, national, ethnic or social origin, property, disability, birth or other status."[4]

Articles 28 and 29 focus on children's rights to education. Article 28 holds that "(1) States Parties recognize the right of the child to education, and with a view to achieving this right progressively and on the basis of equal opportunity." Article 29 similarly acknowledges that "(1) States Parties agree that the education of the child shall be directed to . . . (c) the development of respect for the child's parents, his or her own cultural identity, language and values, for the national values of the country in which the child is living, the country from which he or she may originate, and for civilisations different from his or her own."[5]

Finally, article 30 is specific to Indigenous children's rights to their ancestral language: "In those States in which ethnic, religious, or linguistic minorities or persons of indigenous origins exist, a child belonging to such a minority or who is indigenous shall not be denied the right, in community with other members of his or her group, to enjoy his or her own culture, to profess and practice his or her own religion, or to use his or her own language."[6]

UN Reporting Requirements

As a signatory to these international treaties, Canada has reporting obligations to the respective treaty bodies overseeing their implementation. A critical part of this obligation involves reporting on the domestic application of its treaty commitments. For instance, Canada is responsible for providing updates to the Human Rights Committee, an independent body of experts that monitors the implementation of the International Covenant on Civil and Political Rights. In addition, Canada must report to the United Nations Committee on Economic, Social and Cultural Rights, which oversees the implementation of the international Covenant on Economic, Social, and Cultural Rights. These reporting responsibilities highlight Canada's duty to demonstrate its compliance with international human rights commitments, including those pertaining to the protection and promotion of First Nations language rights in education.

In 2006, both the Human Rights Committee and the Committee on Economic, Social and Cultural Rights noted Canada's failure to comply with international standards because the country had not implemented any of the recommendations contained in *Towards a New Beginning: A Foundational Report for a Strategy to Revitalize Indian, Inuit and Métis Languages and Cultures*, a 2005 report by the federal Task Force on Aboriginal Languages and Cultures.[7] Not only had none of the recommendations been implemented, the Committee on Economic, Social and Cultural Rights noted that "no time frame has been set up for the consideration and implementation of the recommendations" in the report.[8] The Human Rights Committee recommended an "increase in Canada's efforts for the protection and promotion of Aboriginal languages and cultures."[9] In one of its comments, the committee recognized the integral connection between Indigenous peoples' culture and language with their existence and well-being.[10]

Non-Binding Treaty Obligations

Canada's engagement with reporting requirements is recognized as non-binding treaty obligations because they do not create legal rights but they can play a crucial role in advancing First Nations language rights in education. This section explores various non-binding treaty mechanisms and processes that are instrumental in promoting First Nations language rights in education within Canada. While international law is often criticized for lack of binding obligations, it does wield considerable moral and political influence.[11]

James Anaya, former Special Rapporteur on the Rights of Indigenous Peoples, argues that nations engaging in international processes contribute to the establishment of customary norms that are generally binding, regardless of any formal recognition.[12] By engaging in these international platforms, Canada not only affirms its recognition of First Nations language rights in education but also acknowledges its responsibility to uphold these rights within both international and domestic contexts.

The Supreme Court of Canada has also recognized the impact of international law on Canadian constitutional law. In a 2015 Saskatchewan Federation of Labour decision, the court discussed the use of international human rights norms in interpreting the Charter of Rights and Freedoms, asserting that it should provide protection on par with or greater than that found in ratified human rights documents.[13] Additionally, the court has examined non-binding instruments, including national constitutions, to discern an "international consensus" regarding the meaning of an international norm.[14] The Supreme Court also considers non-binding instruments in establishing an international consensus.[15] This suggests that Canadian laws and policies supporting First Nations languages in education should align with international standards.

The United Nations has also established international bodies to monitor and support the advancement of Indigenous rights to language in education, including the United Nations Permanent Forum on Indigenous Issues,[16] the Expert Mechanism on the Rights of Indigenous Peoples, and the Special Rapporteur on the Rights of Indigenous Peoples. These bodies, composed of independent Indigenous experts and advisory panels, strive to advance Indigenous language rights in education by assisting in the domestic implementation of these rights.

Canada's active participation in United Nations forums such as the Expert Mechanism on the Rights of Indigenous Peoples and the Permanent Forum on Indigenous Issues emphasizes its commitment to integrating international norms into domestic policies. The recent endorsement of two international declarations that explicitly recognize Indigenous peoples' language rights in education signifies a major step forward in this area.

American Declaration on the Rights of Indigenous Peoples

In June 2016, the Organization of American States (OAS), a body dedicated to human rights issues in the Western hemisphere, ratified the American Declaration on the Rights of Indigenous Peoples (the Declaration).[17] As a participating member of the OAS, Canada played a significant role in shaping the Declaration, reflecting its commitment to advancing Indigenous rights. The Declaration highlights the linguistic rights of Indigenous communities and provides a crucial framework for promoting Indigenous language. It addresses key areas such as the right to use and transmit Indigenous languages, as well as the right to establish and manage educational institutions that provide education in these languages. The details of these principles are outlined in various articles in the American Declaration on the Rights of Indigenous Peoples:

> **Article VI. Collective rights**
> Indigenous peoples have collective rights that are indispensable for their existence, well-being, and integral development as peoples. In that regard, States recognize and respect the right of indigenous peoples to their collective action; to their juridical, social, political, and economic systems or institutions; to their own cultures; to profess and practice their spiritual beliefs; to use their own tongues and languages; and to their lands, territories and resources. States shall promote, with the full and effective participation of indigenous peoples, the harmonious coexistence of the rights and systems of different population groups and cultures.

Article XIV. Systems of knowledge, language, and communication

1. Indigenous peoples have the right to preserve, use, develop, revitalize, and transmit to future generations their own histories, languages, oral traditions, philosophies, systems of knowledge, writing, and literature, and to designate and retain their own names for their communities, individuals, and places.

2. States shall adopt adequate and effective measures to protect the exercise of this right with the full and effective participation of indigenous peoples.

Article XV. Education

3. Indigenous peoples have the right to establish and control their educational systems and institutions providing education in their own languages, in a manner appropriate to their cultural methods of teaching and learning.

4. States, in conjunction with indigenous peoples, shall take effective measures to enable indigenous individuals living outside their communities, particularly children, to have access to education in their own languages and cultures.

There is also a provision for financial and technical assistance so that Indigenous peoples are able to enjoy the rights contained in the declaration:

Article XXXVII

Indigenous peoples have the right to have access to financial and technical assistance from States and through international cooperation, for the enjoyment of the rights contained in this Declaration.[18]

United Nations Declaration on the Rights of Indigenous Peoples

The United Nations Declaration on the Rights of Indigenous Peoples (UNDRIP) was adopted by the United Nations General Assembly in September 2007. Canada's endorsement of UNDRIP has evolved over time. Initially, in 2010, Canada issued a Statement of Support recognizing the principles of UNDRIP as aspirational and non-binding. This perspective shifted in 2015 when Prime Minister Justin Trudeau agreed to implement UNDRIP.[19] This commitment sparked questions about how the federal government would align Canadian law with the principles of international law. Canada formally adopted UNDRIP in 2016.

Key sections of UNDRIP related to Indigenous language rights, particularly in education and culture, are found in articles 13, 14, 15, and 16. These articles affirm the rights of Indigenous peoples to preserve and pass on their histories, languages, oral traditions, philosophies, writing systems, and literatures (article 13); to manage their own educational systems and institutions providing education in their languages (articles 14 and 15); and to establish their own media in their languages and access all forms of non-Indigenous media without discrimination (article 16). On 21 June 2021, the Canadian parliament implemented the United Nations Declaration on the Rights of Indigenous Peoples Act, formally affirming its application in Canadian law and establishing a framework for its implementation.[20] The challenges lie with the implementation of this legislation, particularly Article 14 of UNDRIP, which pertains to Indigenous language rights in education—this will be further discussed in Chapter 5.

United Nations Permanent Forum

Since 2006, the right to Indigenous language education has increasingly become a focus of various United Nations committees, organizations, and NGOs. In January 2016, the Permanent Forum on Indigenous Issues convened an expert group meeting in New York, centred on the theme "Indigenous Languages: Preservation and Revitalization":[21] "Learning in that mother tongue not only strengthens the ability of indigenous children to communicate in their own language but also benefits their overall academic achievements and lowers dropout rates. Furthermore, a strong foundation in the indigenous language has been shown to benefit the ability of those children to learn the dominant non-indigenous language used where they live."[22] The discussions at the expert meeting emphasized the critical importance of mother tongue education as an essential strategy for preserving and revitalizing Indigenous languages.

In addition to focusing on mother tongue education for children, participants at the meeting voiced serious concerns regarding the scarcity of national data on the status of Indigenous languages in most countries. The absence of reliable data presents a major challenge to accurately assess the vitality and usage of these languages and hinders effective planning for their preservation and revitalization: "Participants noted that many countries did not collect any data on the situation of indigenous languages and that, when they did, the methods were faulty. Census questions often fail to accurately reflect to what degree an indigenous language is spoken and used. For this reason census offices must endeavour to work in cooperation with indigenous peoples when conducting censuses and other data collection enterprises, not only in their implementation but also at all stages, including their development."[23]

Several other key areas were discussed. Participants highlighted the widespread threats facing all Indigenous languages and proposed recommendations for their revitalization, promotion, and protection.[24] A strong emphasis was placed on the connection between language rights and broader human rights, including health, employment, and self-determination.[25] In discussions of Indigenous language education for children, participants stressed the importance of Indigenous peoples playing a central role in the development and implementation of education policies. There was unanimous agreement that "Indigenous peoples themselves must claim ownership of their languages and direct the revitalization efforts of their languages."[26]

The Permanent Forum on Indigenous Issues meeting also acknowledged the funding challenges experienced by Nunavut in implementing the Official Languages Act, the Inuit Protection Act, and the Education Act. These legislative frameworks were intended to support the expansion of bilingual (Inuktut-English) education from kindergarten through grade 12, the appointment of a language commissioner to safeguard language rights, the establishment of funding mechanisms for community revitalization efforts, and the development of a centre of excellence for the Inuit language in partnerships with Nunavut Arctic College. However, very few of these initiatives have been implemented.[27]

Additionally, meeting participants recognized the challenges Indigenous peoples in Canada face in securing adequate funding for language education. They emphasized the responsibility of Indigenous communities to provide quality education in ancestral languages to their children, aiming for fluency. This approach is supported by the rationale that mother tongue education improves educational outcomes, reduces dropout rates, and is recognized as a right under article 30 of the Convention on the Rights of the Child.[28]

The Permanent Forum emphasized that governments have an obligation to support language education. It asserted that states must develop language policies that ensure Indigenous children receive instruction and overall education in their ancestral languages. The support for and training of fluent language teachers were highlighted as essential components of this effort. Additional recommendations included promoting the use of language across diverse sectors, including civil service, healthcare, and both public and private industries to create employment opportunities for language speakers.[29] The Permanent Forum also identified priorities for states, including the establishment of language research institutes, the enhancement of capacity-building efforts for language advocates, and support of language standardization initiatives. The creation of Indigenous universities was also identified as critical measures to promote the vitality and sustainability of Indigenous languages.[30]

Expert Mechanism on the Rights of Indigenous Peoples

In 2012, the Expert Mechanism on the Rights of Indigenous Peoples (EMRIP) presented a study to the UN Human Rights Council on the role of language and culture in promoting and protecting the rights and identity of Indigenous peoples.[31] This study offered regional perspectives on the rights of Indigenous peoples to language and culture, explored the relationship between their cultures, languages, self-determination, and rights to lands, territories, and resources, and analyzed the challenges in promoting and protecting Indigenous language and cultural rights.[32] Additional contributions were made by scholars participating in a seminar that same year organized by Brunel University Law School and the Office of the High Commissioner for Human Rights, which focused on Indigenous peoples' languages and cultures.[33]

The EMRIP study concluded that urgent action was required to counteract the historical and ongoing discrimination against Indigenous peoples based on their cultures and languages. It stressed that Indigenous languages and cultures can thrive only in environments where they are respected for their intrinsic value and contribution to human understanding.[34]

EMRIP made several recommendations, including launching an awareness-raising campaign to educate governments, legislators, policy makers, educators, and the public about Indigenous languages.[35] The pivotal role of Indigenous women as primary language transmitters was highlighted, suggesting that the UN Commission on the Status of Women prioritize empowering Indigenous women in language revitalization.[36] Moreover, EMRIP strongly recommended that member countries develop language policies to promote and protect Indigenous languages. These policies should ensure that Indigenous children receive quality education in their mother tongue, facilitated by fluent teachers and in cooperation with Indigenous communities.[37]

Regarding broader UN initiatives, the UN General Assembly drew attention to the endangerment of languages worldwide by declaring 2008 the International Year of Languages. The Permanent Forum on Indigenous Issues subsequently convened a meeting of Indigenous language experts to discuss topics like linguistic diversity and the interrelation between language rights and other fundamental rights.[38] In the same year, UNESCO called for a conference on linguistic diversity, including Indigenous languages.[39] The agenda covered constitutional and legal protections for Indigenous languages, democratic policies for promoting these languages, actions by Indigenous peoples for language protection and promotion, and media support for Indigenous languages.[40] Following this, the Permanent Forum on Indigenous Issues organized an expert group meeting on Indigenous languages.[41]

In a significant move, in November 2016 the UN General Assembly adopted a resolution on the rights of Indigenous peoples, emphasizing the urgent need to preserve, promote, and revitalize endangered languages. It proclaimed 2019 as the International Year of Indigenous Languages and designated UNESCO as the lead agency.[42] UNESCO's key message was the importance of Indigenous languages for various aspects of societal development, including in social, economic, and political spheres, as well as for peaceful coexistence and reconciliation.[43] Most recently, the UN declared 2022 to 2032 as the International Decade of Indigenous Languages as a global call to action to safeguard Indigenous languages.

Canada continues to face significant challenges in meeting international standards for addressing the long-term repercussions of historical polices that were intended to eradicate the use of First

Nations languages in education. In this context, mechanisms established by the UN and the OAS serve a critical function. These international bodies offer vital platforms through which First Nations can advocate for language rights particularly when domestic recognition falls short of international human rights norms. Engagement with these global institutions is thus imperative for advancing a comprehensive, internationally informed approach to redressing the historical injustices associated with the suppression of First Nations languages within the Canadian education system.

Legislative Spaces Outside Canada

In addition to seeing their language rights recognized in international law, numerous Indigenous peoples have successfully secured language rights in education domestically. The next section explores the outcomes of these efforts, concentrating on examples from the United States, Norway, Finland, Sweden, Greenland, Bolivia, and New Zealand. This survey demonstrates the varying degrees of success achieved through domestic language rights legislation and the unique challenges Indigenous peoples around the world have faced.

The United States

In 1990, the Native American Languages Act was adopted by the U.S. government and in October 1992, additional legislation was passed in the state of Hawaii to set up a grant program to ensure the survival and viability of Native American languages across the country.[44] This legislation acknowledges the responsibility of the United States to collaborate with Native Americans in preserving Indigenous languages. It sets forth a federal policy "to preserve, protect, and promote the rights and freedom of Native Americans to use, practice, and develop Native American languages and to encourage and support the use of Native American languages as a medium of instruction."[45]

Section 104 of the Native American Languages Act outlines the policy of the United States, emphasizing the preservation, protection, and promotion of the rights and freedom of Native Americans regarding their languages. It allows exceptions to teacher certification requirements for federal programs and programs funded by the federal government, specifically for instruction in Native American languages. This exception is designed to address challenges related to the employment of qualified teachers who instruct in Native American languages. The legislation also encourages state and territorial governments to make similar exceptions.

In 2003, the U.S. Congress heard testimony from Indigenous leaders in language education regarding proposed amendments to the Native American Languages Act. These amendments were aimed at supporting Native American Language Survival Schools, created as a response to the impact of the No Child Left Behind Act (NCLB) of 2001. NCLB, a comprehensive reform of the U.S. elementary and secondary education system, placed a significant emphasis on standardized testing and accountability measures. This approach often resulted in schools prioritizing English language proficiency and core subjects like math and reading. Consequently, schools serving Native American communities faced difficulties in dedicating time and resources to language and cultural education, which were not the primary focus of federal testing and accountability standards. Although NCLB provided some funding for Native American education programs, the emphasis on meeting specific academic standards often meant that resources were diverted away from Indigenous language education programs. The 2003 hearing before the Committee on Indian Affairs of the United States Senate, which took place on 15 May in Washington, DC, was convened to discuss section 575 of the Native American Languages Act, with the aim of amending the act to bolster support for Native American Language Survival Schools.

Leanne Hinton, President of the Society for the Study of the Indigenous Languages of the Americas and Professor of Linguistics at the University of California, Berkeley, informed Congress that the vast majority of Indigenous language speakers in the United States were not learning their languages at home. She observed that the most effective way to produce new fluent speakers of endangered languages is through school, "the same institution that was used to destroy those languages."[46] She noted the challenge of fluent speakers being too elderly to teach and emphasized the vital role of universities and educational institutions in teaching adult second-language learners and equipping them with teaching skills. Hinton noted that the Indigenous California Language Survival and the University of California had been collaborating on a Master-Apprentice Language

Learning Program, an intensive apprenticeship pairing adult learners with a native speaker to learn their language.[47]

Christine P. Sims, Chairwoman, representing the Linguistic Institute for Native Americans and a member of Pueblo of Acoma in New Mexico, stressed that the "continuance of cultural values, traditions, and belief in governance systems are dependent on this continued transmission of language."[48] She pointed to the threat to Pueblo societies' spiritual belief systems because of the erosion of these languages, advocating for the vital role of immersion programs in preserving Pueblo languages in New Mexico.[49] Sims also discussed the importance of partnerships with the University of New Mexico's faculty in aiding native language planning, teacher training, and language revitalization efforts, including research on the long-term effects of federal and state policies on Native American governance and language sustainability.[50]

Mary Eunice Romero, from the College of Education at the University of Arizona, pointed out the necessity for language teachers, materials, facilities, training, technical assistance, and research in the complex process of language renewal in communities.[51]

William Demmert Jr., Professor of Education at Western Washington University in Bellingham, Washington, reviewed extensive research on Native Americans and the influence of language and cultural programs on academic performance. His findings supported the hypothesis that Native American language and cultural programs improve academic performance, and that children taught in their ancestral language learn it more effectively than those who had been taught in a dominant second language.[52] Furthermore, he found that children proficient in their ancestral language also tend to be more proficient in the dominant language.

The hearings also feature testimony from students who emphasized that learning their ancestral language provides a strong foundation in their identity. A graduating student from the Comanche Nation College in Oklahoma submitted a statement emphasizing the importance of learning the Comanche language and history. Because he could not attend the hearing in person, he requested that his seventy-one-year-old teacher, Ms. Coosewon, the sole Comanche speaker working in the public school system, present his statement at the hearing before the Committee on Indian Affairs. He wrote:

> This Comanche language class has meant a lot to me and the rest of the class. I have learned to speak a new language and learned to be part of a different culture. It has furthered my understanding of Amerca's complex natives. Without classes like this, we as Americans' will forget where we come from. I am a one-fourth Cherokee. . . . Learning about people like me, learning about my ancestors had made me appreciate my culture more. We have learned to speak many sentences and hold conversation. We have learned the history of these people . . . to stop these classes is to stop a culture living on.[53]

Another representation from students was submitted by Hololapaka'ena'enao Kona Ho'opai, a senior attending Ke Kula 'O Nāwahīokalani'ōpu'u, one of few immersion programs in Hawaii. She began her education in the immersion program at age six and graduated in May 2003. She stated:

> I can honestly say that if it was not for this program, I would not have become fluent in my native tongue, nor would I have gained a great awareness of my culture and understanding of who I am, where I am from, where I fit in my community, and what my roots are. The education I received is truly unique and innovative. The immersion education provides a holistic learning environment that [not] only instills cultural values upon students, but also provide quality academic courses. I have no doubt in my mind that I have the ability to succeed in a non-Hawaiian language setting with my recent acceptance to Standford University.[54]

These two statements not only suggest that immersion programs are effective in fostering Indigenous language speakers, but also show that language education plays an equally vital role in preserving cultural identity. This is achieved through a curriculum that educates students about their heritage and culture.

In her presentation at the 2003 hearing, Joycelyn DesRosier, from Piegan Institute's Nizipuhwahsin School in Browning, Montana, emphasized the importance of their educational program: "Our language school has connected my family to our ancestors, as our language is so important to our people and our sacred ways of life."[55]

Keiki Kawai'ae'a, program director of the Hale Kuamo'o Hawaiian Language Center and the Kahuawaiola Indigenous Teacher Education Program, noted significant progress in language revitalization. Since 1983, their initiatives had resulted in approximately 3,000 new speakers. The programs span twenty-two schools, covering educational levels from preschool to postsecondary. Kawai'ae'a shared that their experience has demonstrated the feasibility of implementing immersion programs that cater to a broad spectrum of academic needs while also promoting cultural wellness, all achieved through integrating their language and culture.[56] However, a prominent challenge they face is in generating a sufficient pool of teachers, compounded by constrained resources. To combat this, she suggests the adoption of exemptions or alternative certification pathways for native speakers learning the language as their second language. This strategy aims to bolster teaching capacity in immersion schools by enabling these individuals to join the educational workforce.[57]

Mary Hermes, Assistant Professor of Education at the University of Minnesota, Duluth, concurred with the previously noted perspectives and emphasized the importance of innovative teacher education programs for immersion. She argued that the certification process for teachers in immersion programs should be distinct from regular teacher certification, tailored to the unique demands of the role. Hermes stressed that such programs are not only beneficial but also crucial for effectively imparting cultural knowledge and values. She informed the Committee on Indian Affairs of some particular challenges faced by schools in Native communities:

> We are forced to have certified teachers in our tribal schools. The certified teachers, 80 percent of them are non-native.... They come in at a higher pay rate and a different curriculum than our culture teachers who are native people from the reservation areas ... when I talk to students, many of them read this as an identity choice. So they would read academic success as assimilation. They read this as becoming white if I get good grades. They read in succeeding in the culture-based curriculum, I am being Indian. So it becomes a choice: be Indian or be smart; be assimilated or be native.... Language is an answer to the problem of bringing the culture

> curriculum together. So much research shows us that second language research has many benefits, metacognitive benefits, academic benefits, and yet you can see the world still through that indigenous lens so that the affective benefits of identity, intergenerational connectedness, self-esteem are also there as well. Language brings the two together.[58]

Lawrence D. Kaplan, Director of the Alaska Native Language Centre at the University of Alaska, Fairbanks, emphasized the importance of empowering Indigenous communities to document their languages. He advocated for training students and native speakers in applied language research techniques to collect and archive language materials, which are essential for language revitalization and maintenance.[59]

These testimonies to the 2003 hearing before the Committee on Indian Affairs highlight the ongoing challenges and the critical need for advocacy and support for Indigenous Language Survival Schools within the U.S. education policy framework.

The Nordic Countries

Historically, all Sámi languages have suffered under assimilation policies and dominant educational systems that marginalized these languages. In Norway, for instance, Sámi children were punished for speaking their native language, while in Sweden, the use of Sámi languages in schools was prohibited until 1956.[60] Currently, all Sámi languages are considered endangered. The number of speakers varies widely, ranging from fewer than 30,000 for Northern Sámi (spanning Finland, Norway, and Sweden), to around 400–500 speakers of Inari Sámi in Finland, and approximately 300 speakers of Skolt Sámi in Finland and Russia.[61] Within these regions, there are approximately ten Sámi languages spoken. The most widely used Sámi language is predominant in Norway and Sweden.

The Sámi nationalist movement has been instrumental in advocating for the recognition and support of language rights in education, which is crucial for the revitalization of Sámi.[62] During the 1980s and 1990s, efforts to protect the right to use Sámi and promote its instruction increasingly gained governmental support.[63] Norway led the way by enacting a Sámi language law in 1990.[64] Today, all three

Nordic countries have established directly elected Sámi parliaments,[65] which, though consultative, wield significant influence in matters related to Sámi language policy and revitalization.

Norway

Norway has also made significant progress with Sámi language rights in education.[66] Since 1959, Sámi students have been entitled to receive instruction in their language at the primary school level within their homeland, a right that extends up to grade 10.[67] This provision was formally established in 1969, particularly focusing on the children of Sámi-speaking parents in Sámi districts. The Primary and Secondary Education and Training Act (the Education Act) comprehensively outlines the rights to education in Sámi languages in section 6-2:

> In Sami districts all children at the primary and lower secondary level have the right to receive their education both in Sami and through the medium of Sami.
> Outside Sami districts, if at least ten pupils in a municipality wish to receive instruction in and through the medium of Sami, they have the right to such education as long as there remain at least six pupils in the group.
>
> The municipality may decide to offer Sami instruction at one or more of the schools in the municipality.
>
> The municipality may issue regulations stipulating that all children at the primary and secondary level in Sami districts shall receive instruction in Sami.
> Outside Sami districts, Sami children at the primary and lower secondary level have the right to receive Sami instruction. The Ministry may issue regulations concerning alternative forms of such instruction when it cannot be provided by suitable teachers at the school attended by the children.[68]

From grade 8 onward, students may choose whether to continue with Sámi language instruction, as stipulated in the earlier sections. Additionally, the act addresses rights at the secondary education level in section 6-3:

> Sami pupils in upper secondary education and training have the right to receive Sami instruction. The Ministry may issue

> regulations concerning alternative forms of such instruction when it cannot be provided by suitable teachers at the school attended by the pupils.
>
> The Ministry may issue regulations stipulating that certain schools shall provide instruction in or through the medium of Sami or in specific Sami subjects in upper secondary education within certain courses or for certain groups. The county authority may also elect to offer such instruction.[69]

For Sámi in Norway living outside their homeland, there is a provision for language lessons, ensuring the preservation and promotion of their linguistic heritage.[70]

Finland

Finland's Basic Education Act 1988/1288 (revised in 2003) recognizes the Sámi people's right to receive education in their language within their homeland.[71] Sámi students may receive education in their mother tongue or as an elective.[72] In 1992, Sámi was recognized as an official language in Finland and in 1996 the Sámi Parliament was established. One of the challenges, however, is that government resources are primarily allocated for initiatives within the Sámi Homeland.[73] For Sámi living outside of their homeland, municipalities can provide two hours of supplementary Sámi language classes per week, supported by the Ministry of Education.[74] Only about 10 percent of Sámi take these classes, since the majority of Sámi in Finland live in urban areas where there is advocacy for online education and pedagogy development for endangered languages.[75] At the postsecondary level, Sámi can be studied at the Universities of Oulu and Helsinki, and at the University of Lapland in Rovaniemi.[76]

Sweden

In Sweden, the Sámi language is recognized as a minority language along with Finnish, Yiddish, Romani, and Meänkieli. The Swedish government is responsible for protecting and promoting these languages. The right to receive instruction in the Sámi language was established in 1976 and it was taught as a subject in 1977.[77] However, the use of Sámi as a medium of instruction is limited; it is available only in five schools and only up to grade 6. A specific curriculum for Sámi language education was established in 2011.

In 1993, Sweden established a Sámi Parliament, which primarily serves as an advisory body on matters including language education.[78] The Swedish Education Act legislates the right to use the Sámi language in schools, further emphasizing the state's commitment to supporting Sámi.[79] Despite these legal frameworks the Sámi population in Sweden faces challenges similar to those in Norway and Finland, including a shortage of qualified language teachers and systemic challenges to securing adequate support for the preservation and revitalization of endangered Sámi language.[80]

Greenland

The Inuit population in Greenland has experienced cultural and political movements similar to those of Sámi peoples, however, comparable developments such as land claims and efforts toward self-governance began earlier in Alaska and parts of the Canadian Arctic.[81] The establishment of a national newspaper in 1861, in Kalaallisut, the Greenlandic Inuit language, sparked a renewed interest in language and culture, while also fostering political debates about Greenland's future. Greenlanders have demonstrated considerable skill in using media platforms, including state-owned radio and television through the Greenlandic Broadcasting Corporation, as well as newspapers and book publishing. The Greenland Home Rule Act of 1979 marked a significant milestone recognizing Greenlandic, rather than Danish, as the principal language of the country. Section 9 states that "(1) Greenlandic shall be the principal language," and that "(2) Either language [Greenlandic or Danish] may be used for official purposes."[82] Since the passage of the Act, substantial progress has been achieved. Greenlandic has been established as the primary language of instruction in schools, and there is broad societal consensus that children of Danish parents residing in Greenland should also acquire proficiency in Greenlandic.[83]

Bolivia

Bolivia, which has largest Indigenous population in Latin America, has made notable advancements in recognizing the rights and cultures of these communities.[84] The 1994 educational reform introduced intercultural bilingual education for Indigenous children, incorporating curricula that reflect Indigenous knowledge, values, and cultures, while integrating Indigenous pedgogies for language instruction.[85] In 2009, the Bolivian Constitution officially declared thirty-six Indigenous languages, alongside Spanish.[86] This constitutional reform mandated that government officials be proficient in at least two official languages, including Spanish.[87] Collectively, these legislative and educational initiatives have significantly enhanced the social and political status of Indigenous languages in Bolivia.[88]

The 2009 Bolivian Constitution also formally established the country as a pluri-national state, acknowledging the pre-colonial existence of Indigenous peoples and affirming their right to self-determination. Education is a conceptualized tool for decolonization, intended to safeguard Indigenous cultures and identities while promoting active community and parental involvement.[89] The overarching goal is to develop an educational system that is rooted in both Bolivian and Indigenous cultural identities.

According to the Education Law, instruction in schools is to be conducted in students' ancestral languages. In regions where Indigenous languages predominate, education is to start in the local Indigenous language, with Spanish introduced as a secondary language. In contrast, in predominantly Spanish-speaking areas, Spanish serves as the primary medium of instruction, complemented by an Indigenous language. This bilingual model reflects Bolivia's commitment to fostering linguistic diversity.[90]

Despite the robust legal framework, the implementation of these educational reforms has faced considerable challenges. Although parents are legally entitled to choose educational models appropriate for their children, available options have frequently failed to fully realize the cultural and linguistic rights of Indigenous peoples.[91] The integration of Indigenous knowledge and locally relevant content in the curriculum has been insufficiently executed.[92] In April 2003, the discontinuation of pedagogical advisors, as an essential element of the educational reform, was a major setback, attributed to a lack of political will, resistance from teachers' unions, and the withdrawal of external funding.[93] In 2009, the UN Committee on the Rights of the Child criticized Bolivia for inadequately adapting its national education system to accommodate Indigenous cultures, exposing a significant gap between policy and practice.[94] Although Indigenous languages were introduced in schools, their public presence and everyday usage outside educational institutions have remained limited.[95]

New Zealand

The 1840 Treaty of Waitangi formally acknowledges Māori language rights. However, subsequent legislation that mandated the use of English contributes to a significant decline in the number of Māori language speakers, particularly in the northern regions.[96] By the 1970s, growing Māori assertiveness brought attention to the Crown's failure to uphold the Treaty, particularly in relation to the protection of the Māori language. A pivotal moment occurred in 1972 when a petition with 30,000 signatures was presented, calling for the inclusion of Māori language education in all schools.[97] The establishment of the Waitangi Tribunal in 1975, a commission mandated to address Māori claims of treaty breaches, marked another milestone. In 1986, the Tribunal acknowledged the Crown's failure to adequately protect the Māori language, leading to the Māori Language Act, 1987.[98] This legislation recognized acknowledged Māori as an official language of New Zealand and established the Māori Language Commission (Te Taura Whiri) to develop and implement a national language revitalization strategy.[99]

Following these legal advancements, a range of initiatives followed, including the creation of Māori-language immersion programs in early childhood, school, and tertiary education providers; the establishment of Māori-language radio and television stations; funding for community-driven Māori language projects, and regular surveys assessing public attitudes towards the language.[100] Thanks to the Māori Language Commission's efforts, many Māori people have been empowered to learn and take pride in their language.

Despite these efforts, including the Māori-language programs in education and the media, the percentage of Māori speakers continues to decline, raising concerns about the effectiveness of the Māori Language Commission's strategies. While the Waitangi Tribunal has declared the te reo Māori a national treasure, language rights, though recognized under the Treaty of Waitangi, lack enforceability in New Zealand.[101] The Waitangi Tribunal can advise the government but does not have the authority to mandate legislative action.

In response to concerns over the effectiveness of the Māori Language Commission, the New Zealand government established *Te Paepae Motuhake* in 2010 to evaluate the alignment of government services with iwi and Māori aspirations for language revitalization.[102] The recommendations put forward by Te Paepae Motuhake informed the development of the Māori Language Act 2016, which reaffirmed te reo Māori as an official of New Zealand and recognized it as a *taonga* (treasure) under the principles of the Treaty of Waitangi.[103] While the Act affirms the right to use te reo Māori in legal proceedings and mandates the provision of support services, it stops short of guaranteeing the right to be addressed in the language in all official contexts. Developed through extensive consultation with Māori communities, the Act also established Te Mātāwai, an independent body mandated to represent Māori interests in the revitalization of language. The Act is distinctive in its dual legal authority where both Māori and English versions hold equal status, with Māori version taking precedence in cases of conflict and in its creation of two parallel language strategies (Crown-led and Kiwi-led). Together, these provisions reflect a uniquely collaborative and comprehensive approach to Māori language revitalization.[104]

The revitalization of the Māori language within the education sector faces several persistent challenges, including a shortage of fluent speakers and qualified teachers, inconsistencies in instructional quality, and varying degrees of community engagement. Additionally concerns involve balancing contemporary education practices with traditional Māori pedagogies as well as addressing significant resource limitations.[105] Overcoming these challenges requires sustained commitment, adequate funding, and coordinated efforts among the government, educational institutions, and Māori communities. Such collaborative action is essential to support the continued advancement of te reo Māori within New Zealand's educational framework.

Concluding Remarks

This chapter highlighted the Indigenous language rights in education in five international treaties that Canada has ratified. These treaties create international obligations for Canada to not only honour but also ensure that First Nations language rights in education are implemented in an effective and non-discriminatory manner. The expectation to honour First Nations language rights in education under international law has increased domestically since Canada committed to align all federal laws with UNDRIP through the introduction of the United Nations Declaration on the Rights of Indigenous Peoples Act. A close look at Canada's Indigenous Languages Act will be required as part of this process. Currently this legislation has no enforceable rights to language education or a duty to fund language programs. This issue will be explored in greater depth in Chapter 5.

In addition to considering binding treaty obligations, this chapter also examined non-binding treaty obligations. Canada has played a role in shaping international declarations such as the OAS's American Declaration on the Rights of Indigenous Peoples. This declaration provides a framework for Canada to consider as it aligns federal laws with the principles of UNDRIP. The OAS declaration mandates that member countries adopt adequate and effective measures to protect Indigenous peoples' rights. Moreover, it recognizes that Indigenous peoples are entitled to financial and technical assistance for implementing their rights, as outlined in the declaration. Accordingly, Canada has a responsibility to provide resources and support to First Nations when implementing international rights into domestic law.

There are also UN treaty bodies and bodies specific to Indigenous issues that monitor how Canada is addressing (or not addressing) First Nations' rights under international law. Independent Indigenous experts and advisory panels strive to advance First Nations' rights by monitoring Canada's actions and assisting to ensure that implementation is carried out according to international law and standards.

Over the past fifty years, the active engagement of countries in developing international legal principles recognizing the rights of Indigenous peoples has contributed to a significant shift in both international and domestic attitudes.[106] Countries such as Canada have moved from viewing Indigenous peoples merely as objects of international law to acknowledging them as holders of distinct international rights. Notably, international customary norms related to Indigenous language rights in education have increasingly been recognized as integral to the broader right of self-determination.[107]

A comparative analysis of how various states have recognized Indigenous language rights in education highlight the central role of government support and legislative action. In the United States, while community-based schools that employ Native American languages as a medium of instruction have achieved notable success. Provisions under federal language legislation have allowed for flexibility in teacher certification, however, ongoing challenges persist, particularly in relation to funding and institutional support. In Norway, Sweden, and Finland, ensuring sufficient resources and the availability of qualified Sámi language teachers remains essential, especially in regions outside the designated Sámi Homeland. Greenland has prioritized the integration of Greenlandic in both media and education and has undertaken initiatives to normalize its everyday use. Bolivia has advanced Indigenous language rights through policies that mandate proficiency in Indigenous languages for government officials and by framing education as a mechanism for decolonization, an approach that has significantly elevated the status of its multiple Indigenous languages.

New Zealand's experience with te reo Māori emphasizes the importance of investing in teacher training and fostering meaningful community engagement in the development of language policy, curricula, and pedagogical approaches. Across all these cases, the successful revitalization and maintenance of Indigenous languages in education depend on long term commitment, sufficient resources, well resourced teaching training programs, and collaborative efforts among governments, Indigenous communities, and educational institutions.

CHAPTER 5

INDIGENOUS LANGUAGES ACT

Section 35 of Canada's Constitution Act, 1982

The preceding chapters outlined the foundation of First Nations language transmission in Canada, starting with inter-customary language transmission practices on the Prairies involving the Hudson's Bay Company and missionaries. Language transmission remained pivotal for First Nations, despite the linguistic genocide carried out through Canada's educational system. Constitutional rights for First Nations language education were further reinforced by advocacy from First Nations leaders, constitutional principles presented by them, as well as findings from royal commissions, reports, and regional Aboriginal language legislation from provincial and territorial governments. Indigenous peoples' right to language education is also recognized under international law. In this final chapter, the Indigenous Languages Act will be critically examined in the context of First Nations law, constitutional law, and international law.

Between 2009 and 2016, two bills addressing Indigenous languages were introduced. The first, known as Bill S-212, the Act for the Advancement of Aboriginal Languages of Canada and to Recognize and Respect Aboriginal Language Rights, was introduced by Honourable Serge Joyal (Senator, Kennebec) in 2009.[1] The second, Bill C-91, An Act Respecting Indigenous Languages, was put forward by the federal government in 2016.[2] The following section surveys the discussions and debates surrounding Bill S-212, followed by an examination of the co-development process that the federal government proposed for Bill C-91 and other factors that led to the Indigenous Languages Act.[3]

Senate Bill S-212

The objective of Bill S-212 was to broaden the acknowledgement of Aboriginal language rights under the umbrella of self-government and right of use. During the bill's second reading in May 2017, Senator Joyal referred to the constitutional status of Aboriginal languages, as well as the significance of Canada's signing on to the United Nations Declaration on the Rights of Indigenous Peoples (UNDRIP):

> In 1982, we entrenched the treaty rights in section 35 of the Constitution Act, so treaty rights include not only recognition of the possession of the lands, of the property of the land and its resources, but also the recognition of the Aboriginal identities.
>
> That is recognized by the Royal Proclamation since 1763. The Royal Proclamation marks the definition of the status of Aboriginal people through the British Crown. We entrenched the Royal Proclamation also in 1982.
>
> When Senator Sinclair mentioned in his report that Aboriginal language rights are reinforced by the treaties, he [spoke] of the nature of our constitutional law in Canada. Honourable senators, this is very important. It is at the heart of the United Nations Declaration on the Rights of Indigenous Peoples, which the Canadian government endorsed finally on May 10 of this month, only a week ago. The Minister of Justice and the Minister of Indigenous and Northern Affairs were in New York to sign formally the recognition by Canada of the United Nations Declaration on the Rights of Indigenous Peoples. Before that, we recognized the UN declaration, but with a proviso of reserve. There were four countries that reserved their approval of the UN declaration. Canada was one of them. Last week we lifted that reserve and are now fully under the principle of the United Nations Declaration on the Rights of Indigenous Peoples.[4]

In 2018, before the Standing Committee on Procedures and House Affairs, Joyal acknowledged the historical significance of First Nations languages:

> When the missionaries came to Canada in those years, they had to hire people to use as interpreters because none of the European settlers spoke aboriginal languages. The first thing they had to do was to learn aboriginal languages, because aboriginal languages were spoken. In those years, during the French regime and up to the Treaty of Paris of 1763, aboriginal leaders were speaking their aboriginal languages and not learning French; it was the French who were learning the aboriginal languages. It's the situation now that they are trying to reintegrate into the Canadian mainstream, with their identity, with pride in speaking their languages. Of course, it is the responsibility of the Government of Canada, which through the residential school system obliterated aboriginal languages, to take the initiative and steps to reinstate for them the right to speak their languages.[5]

Joyal also acknowledged that Canada was facing a new era and a new challenge to re-establish First Nations languages rights. He strongly advocated for the adoption of Bill S-212, believing it would demonstrate Canada's ability to embrace cultural diversity while upholding the principles of freedom and democracy.[6] He also indicated that First Nations languages are "better taught, not only through the oral tradition, but also through the education system of the indigenous peoples themselves."[7]

In expressing his endorsement of Bill S-212, Honourable Dennis Glen Patterson (Senator, Nunavut) offered a historical perspective on the territories' commitment to Aboriginal language rights during a period of contemplating official bilingualism. He shared that at one point, certain members of the territorial government, himself included, vehemently opposed the entrenchment of French language rights unless equal, if not greater, attention was given to Aboriginal languages.[8] Senator Patterson also recalled that during the 1980s,

> there was a push from the government of Pierre Elliott Trudeau to make the NWT officially bilingual. New Brunswick had just become officially bilingual, and the

> government of the day was urging other provinces and territories to follow suit. There was a lot of pressure on us in the NWT to become officially bilingual. At the same time, we had a number of MLAs whom we described as unilingual. They spoke only aboriginal languages, or if they could speak English or French, they were clearly handicapped. At the time, as my colleague said, there were also nine aboriginal languages spoken in the NWT that we were very concerned about supporting and enhancing. The prospect of becoming officially bilingual in English and French without also recognizing and supporting the aboriginal first languages of the majority of our population was unacceptable.[9]

As a result of sustained advocacy for Aboriginal language rights during that period, the Northwest Territories' Official Languages Act of 1985 granted official status to English, French, and several Aboriginal languages.[10] According to Patterson, this legislative recognition contributed to the inclusion and support of Aboriginal languages in key domains such as land claims negotiations and other significant political processes:

> Members of both of those assemblies could then—and can now—fully participate in their first languages in a fulsome debate on the complex issues that mattered most to them and their constituents. There is, at significant cost I will say, simultaneous interpretation available in both of those assemblies in the official aboriginal languages of the NWT and Nunavut. We were able to debate complex land claims and political development of the NWT, including a major proposal to divide the NWT and create the new territory of Nunavut, with the full participation of unilingual MLAs who were also respected elders. I think this background may be helpful to you in your discussion of this issue as it pertains to the House of Commons.[11]

Patterson also emphasized that "aboriginal languages are a fundamental expression of aboriginal rights."[12] Despite Senator Patterson's concern about inadequate funding for Aboriginal languages nationwide, he ultimately supported Bill S-212.

Senator Murray Sinclair (former Chair of the TRC) also endorsed Bill S-212, characterizing it as an act of reconciliation. However, he issued a caution, stating that the bill fell short for a few reasons. First, he pointed out that a Senate bill lacked the authority to mandate the government to allocate funding. Consequently, Bill S-212 could not impose an obligation on the federal government to provide funding for language education, including immersion programs. Another inherent limitation was that Bill S-212 could solely affirm the existing powers of the government to fund language programs it deemed suitable.[13] Sinclair noted the challenges First Nations had faced in securing funding for language revitalization efforts over the past decade:

> At a time when government funding is most needed to protect Aboriginal languages and culture, Canada has not upheld commitments it previously made to fund such programs.
>
> In 2002, the federal government under Prime Minister Chrétien promised that $160 million would be set aside for the creation of a centre for Aboriginal languages and culture and a national language strategy. But in 2006, the government retreated from that commitment, pledging instead to spend only $5 million per year in permanent funding for the Aboriginal Languages Initiative (ALI), which had been started in 1998. The ALI is a program of government-administered heritage subsidies. It is not based on the notion of a respectful nation-to-nation relationship between Canada and Aboriginal people. Nor does it provide Aboriginal people with the opportunity to make decisions for themselves about how to allocate scarce resources and how to administer programs. Other than ALI, the only significant programs for language preservation are the Canada Territorial Language Accords, with a $4.1 million budget, which support territorial government-directed Aboriginal language services, which support as well community projects in Nunavut and the Northwest Territories. In Yukon, language revitalization and preservation projects there are supported through transfer agreements, with 10 of the 11 self-governing Yukon First Nations becoming eligible.[14]

Sinclair concluded that the legislation should go beyond merely acknowledging Aboriginal language rights; it must also incorporate the principles outlined in UNDRIP and in the TRC's Calls to Action. This entails, among other provisions, the allocation of adequate resources to support the revitalization of Aboriginal languages. Additionally, it should recognize the educational rights associated with Aboriginal languages while providing the necessary support for language programs to develop and thrive.

In addition to comments regarding the limitations of Bill S-212, Sinclair included a poignant personal statement. He explained to the Senate how, during one of the TRC gatherings, he came to realize his grandmother's motivation for not passing on his ancestral language to him as a child:

> My grandmother, for example, who raised me and my siblings from the time that I was an infant, could speak Ojibway and Cree, as well as French and English. She taught all of those languages to me as a young boy, but she insisted that we only speak English once I started school. I always wondered why she did that and came to some understanding when one survivor told us during our hearings of the Truth and Reconciliation Commission that he had a similar experience. When he asked his mother why she had never taught him the language, she told him simply, "Because I wanted to save your life." In the Catholic school where she had been raised, she was taught that if she continued to practise her culture and to speak her language, she would end up in purgatory or in hell, places of eternal damnation. She simply wanted her children to have a chance at eternal life in heaven, so she refused to teach them their language.[15]

Sinclair attributed his grandmother's insistence on English only to the federal government's genocidal policy: "Residential schools were a systematic, government-sponsored attempt to destroy Aboriginal cultures and languages and to assimilate Aboriginal people so that they no longer existed as distinct peoples."[16] He emphasized that, given the federal government's central role in the destruction of Aboriginal languages, it bears a duty to provide sufficient funding for their revitalization and maintenance. Despite Sinclair's reservations about the Senate Bill's capacity to fully acknowledge Aboriginal language rights in education, he advocated for its progression.

Although there was ample support for Bill S-212 and it was adopted in the second reading, it was referred to the Standing Committee on Aboriginal Peoples for study, where it remained.

Commitment from the Federal Government

In November 2015, the Departments of Canadian Heritage and Indigenous and Northern Affairs received directives from Prime Minister Justin Trudeau to provide support and funding for the promotion, preservation, and enhancement of Aboriginal languages.[17] On 6 December 2016, Trudeau delivered a speech to the Assembly of First Nations Special Chiefs, expressing his commitment to engage with First Nations on a nation-to-nation basis. In his address, he acknowledged that the laws of Canada "were, and in many ways still are, used to control and constrain" First Nations.[18] The prime minister pledged to implement UNDRIP, recognizing that "residential schools and other decisions by governments were used as a deliberate tool to eliminate Indigenous languages and cultures. If we are to truly advance reconciliation, we must undo the lasting damage that resulted."[19] With these considerations in mind, Trudeau announced that the federal government would collaboratively develop Indigenous languages legislation.[20]

Glendon College, York University

Shortly prior to Prime Minister Trudeau's announcement regarding Indigenous languages legislation, more than eighty Aboriginal and non-Aboriginal scholars and language activists convened at a national colloquium at Glendon College, at York University, Toronto. The purpose of the gathering was to examine the role and the responsibilities of postsecondary educational institutions in the revitalization of Aboriginal languages. The colloquium culminated in a Declaration on Indigenous languages, which outlined specific recommendations to postsecondary instutions for promoting the advancement of Aboriginal languages and cultures:

1. Post-secondary Institutions must develop collaborative funding models to support Indigenous language initiatives open to research, pedagogy, and partnerships.
2. TRC Committees must be established in all post-secondary institutions.

3. Post-secondary institutions must engage in Community building: both inside the university and between the institution and Indigenous communities and Indigenous community-based organizations.
4. Varying qualifications and credentials of Indigenous people must be recognized and honoured.
5. There must be cross-(cultural) training and collaboration across university administrations, programs, and faculty.
6. Post-secondary institutions must develop programs in Indigenous language studies with a view to promoting full oral proficiency and literacy in Indigenous languages, with certification through college and university diplomas and degrees in Indigenous languages.
7. There must be Indigenous Cultural Competency Training for all post-secondary institutions which would include Governors/Regents, Administration, Faculty, and Staff.[21]

The participants also recognized an urgent need for the right to education in Aboriginal languages to be recognized in Canada's Constitution.[22]

First Peoples' Cultural Council, British Columbia

A few months after Glendon College's colloquium, in June 2016, the First Peoples' Cultural Council (FPCC) hosted an Indigenous languages event in Victoria, British Columbia. The gathering brought together twenty Aboriginal language experts and representatives from Canadian Heritage to discuss strategies for the revitalization of Aboriginal languages in Canada. Key recommendations stemming from these discussions included the necessity for consultation with Aboriginal language educators, particularly those who had achieved language fluency, before drafting Aboriginal languages legislation. Another recommendation emphasized that the legislation should be shaped by successful language revitalization models. Additionally, the recognition of adequate financial support for educational Aboriginal language programs as a right within the legislation was highlighted. The final report outlined the following principles:

1. All decisions and actions for Indigenous language development and implementation must be a collaborative process led by Indigenous language experts and Indigenous people of each Indigenous language.
2. All Indigenous people must have accessibility and opportunity to learn their Indigenous homeland language regardless of place of residence, and all who choose for their children (from preschool to Grade 12) to be educated in the medium of their mother-tongue must have that option. To this end, legislation must be enacted immediately according that right to all Indigenous People. The legislation must, thus, include guarantees of adequate funding to prepare curriculum, train fluent speakers to be immersion teachers, train non-fluent teachers to be speakers, and provide for parallel programs (immersion and non-immersion) in communities where not everyone will opt for immersion. Additionally, funding must be made available for immersion proponents to be involved in the development of this legislation as soon as possible.
3. Funding must be permanent, sustainable and encompassing to support Indigenous people in implementing their homeland language goals and objectives. Funding must be based on the cost of what is needed to implement initiatives to recover, restore and maintain the vitality of Indigenous languages wherever Indigenous people reside.
4. Our teachings are "we belong to the language"; the language does not belong to us, but we must ensure that the appropriate principles of ownership, control, access and possession (OCAP) apply to Indigenous languages.
5. Indigenous languages in Canada encompass a diversity of worldviews, histories, identities, cultures and knowledges that are vital to the identity of Indigenous peoples, and are intrinsic and inherent in each of these languages.
6. We envisage legislation that will include a national office of an Indigenous Language Commission with regional offices to support each Indigenous homeland language and

will provide a *statutory guarantee of the funding necessary to support language revitalization initiatives.* We need a coordinated and collaborative approach and investment across all ministries, institutions and organizations.[23] (my emphasis)

The recommendations resulting from the FPCC and Glendon College sessions were submitted to the Department of Canadian Heritage for consideration in the development of the Indigenous Languages Act.

Bill C-91: Indigenous Languages Act

Following these national dialogue sessions, the federal government declared its intention to collaboratively develop language legislation with leaders from the Assembly of First Nations (AFN), the Métis National Council (MNC), and the Inuit Tapiriit Kanatami (ITK). In June 2017, several statements were issued, emphasizing support for the revitalization of Indigenous languages, including a statement from the Minister of Canadian Heritage that declared: "The responsibility to protect and promote Indigenous languages and cultures is a critical one, and a priority for our government. The Truth and Reconciliation Commission laid out a clear path for the Government of Canada through its Calls to Action. By helping preserve and restore Indigenous languages, Canadian Heritage is following through on our government's commitment to implement these Calls to Action in the spirit of reconciliation."[24] Carolyn Bennett, the Minister of Indigenous and Northern Affairs, echoed the support expressed by Canadian Heritage for Aboriginal languages, emphasizing the connection between language revitalization and the improvement of social, economic, and health outcomes in the following statement:

> The preservation and revitalization of Indigenous languages, cultures and traditions plays a pivotal role in the expression of nationhood and identity. The evidence is clear that a secure personal and cultural identity is a critical determinant of improved health, economic, educational outcomes. We are proud to work with First Nations, Inuit and Métis partners to co-develop legislation that addresses the promotion, protection and revitalization of First Nations, Inuit and Métis languages in this country. These partnerships, which include communities and their representative groups, as well

as language experts and grassroots organizations, contribute to the vital work of reconciliation and are essential for Indigenous Peoples' participation in a strong and prosperous Canada.[25]

Aboriginal leaders representing national organizations also expressed their support while emphasizing the importance of a transparent process. Principles were developed to guide the co-development of language legislation, and included the following points:

- The intent is to develop legislation that includes common and overarching legislative content as well as *three distinct First Nations Inuit and Métis sections to meet the distinct legislative and policy needs of each language group* within diverse geographic, political, and cultural contexts. . . .
- *A "pan Aboriginal" approach was not seen as appropriate* given the significant differences in the state of readiness of languages depending on: distinction; geographic area; measures already in place (such as territorial Official Languages Acts); and the existence of Languages Commissioner and Commissions. It is the intent that the legislation would need to support or be consistent with these measure that are already in place in some jurisdictions. . . .
- *Article 14 of the UN Declaration is an important component of the overall framework* to achieve revitalization and maintenance of indigenous languages. . . .
- The *government of Canada's commitment* [will be] *to providing adequate and long-term funding* for the reclamation, revitalization, maintenance and strengthening of Indigenous languages.[26] (my emphases)

Aboriginal leaders urged that the legislation prioritize the distinct status and needs of the Inuit, Métis, and First Nations. Clément Chartier, President of the Métis Nation, backed the legislative process but insisted that reconciliation for the Métis people hinges on addressing their exclusion from all aspects of the Residential School Settlement Agreement.[27] Natan Obed, President of ITK, echoed support for the legislation while emphasizing the necessity for a distinct process for the Inuit in drafting the legislation.[28] Perry Bellegarde, National Chief of the AFN, emphasized jurisdiction over languages, the inherent nature of language rights, and First Nations' right to self-determination. Bellegarde also highlighted the importance of recognizing that Indigenous languages are the original languages of the country.[29]

Canadian Heritage Engagement Sessions

Between 2017 and 2018, the Department of Canadian Heritage organized a number of regional engagement sessions involving First Nations, Métis, and Inuit peoples. These sessions explored ten issues, including the present state of Indigenous languages, the potential role of a language commissioner, Aboriginal language rights, and the use of technology in advancing the teaching of Aboriginal languages. Canadian Heritage's summary of the preliminary findings emphasized the significance of Aboriginal language revitalization as being integral to the cultural identities, philosophies, and world views of Indigenous peoples. The summary stressed that all these aspects must be taken into consideration in the development of legislation.[30] The findings also highlighted participants' desire for the recognition of Aboriginal language rights both on and off reserves and underscored the need for adequate funding for language revitalization efforts in both areas.[31] Additionally, it was noted that the management of any new language institutions should be Aboriginal-led, less bureaucratic than current governmental bodies, and non-political.[32] Inclusivity in Indigenous language programming was deemed crucial, with specific consideration for individuals with special needs and disabilities, a point that must be acknowledged and accommodated in the legislation.[33]

Assembly of First Nations: Engagement Sessions

Between June and October 2017, the AFN conducted a series of independent engagement sessions on the language legislation, involving regional chiefs, chiefs, councillors, Elders, fluent speakers, knowledge keepers, language activists, scholars, and linguists. From these sessions, the AFN identified four overarching principles:

1. **Recognition.** The Indigenous languages of this land have existed since time immemorial and pre-exist Canada; they must be recognized, protected, respected, valued, promoted, acknowledged, supported and used.

2. **Indigenous Rights and Control.** It is the constitutional and inherent right of each Indigenous government to direct, maintain and develop their own language and culture (Indigenous control of Indigenous languages).
3. **Access.** All Indigenous languages need to be accessible to all Indigenous people regardless of where they reside.
4. **Establishment of a Language Structure(s).** Legislation must mandate the establishment of a language body or bodies that orchestrate the following four critical roles: government accountability, funding, support for language learning, and public promotion and awareness.[34]

Additional topics included the need to enhance the use of statistics to support language revitalization endeavours. There were also discussions regarding the recognition of Aboriginal languages as official languages of Canada.

During the consultation period for the development of Indigenous language legislation, both the federal government and Aboriginal organizations conducted parallel sessions. Although some individuals, either as organization representatives or community members, participated in both processes, notable discrepancies emerged between preliminary reports produced by Canadian Heritage and the AFN's reports. Canadian Heritage emphasized the importance of flexibility and diversity in funding and language revitalization approaches. In contrast, the AFN emphasized the necessity of centering Aboriginal language rights under section 35 of the Constitution Act, 1982. Notably, Canadian Heritage's reports offered little focus on language rights in education, despite the fact that Indigenous organizations, scholars specializing in endangered language revitalization, and previous government reports commissioned by Canada Heritage had consistently identified immersion programs as essential for effective Aboriginal language revitalization efforts.[35]

On 5 February 2019, Bill C-91 An Act respecting Indigenous languages (the Indigenous Languages Act) was introduced by the Minister of Canadian Heritage and Multiculturalism. The purpose of the legislation was to facilitate the use of Indigenous languages and bolster language revitalization endeavours. While many First Nations welcomed the legislation, concerns were also raised.[36] While the Bill specified the recognition of Indigenous (Aboriginal) language rights under section 35(1) of the Constitution Act, 1982, it unfortunately did not explicitly recognize Aboriginal language rights in education or provide any funding guarantees. Section 5 declared the federal government's commitment to

> (c) *establish a framework* to facilitate the effective exercise of the rights of Indigenous peoples that relate to Indigenous languages, including by way of agreements or arrangements referred to in sections 8 and 9;
>
> (d) *establish measures* to facilitate the provision of adequate, sustainable and long-term funding for the reclamation, revitalization, maintenance and strengthening of Indigenous languages. . . .
>
> (e.1) *Facilitate meaningful opportunities* for Indigenous governments and other Indigenous governing bodies and Indigenous organizations to collaborate in policy development related to the implementation of this Act.[37] (my emphases)

Section 6 affirms that Indigenous languages are recognized as a right under section 35 of the Constitution Act, 1982, however the legislation itself does not establish any enforceable rights. Nor does it impose any explicit positive obligations on the federal government, such as a requirement to provide sustained funding for Indigenous languages. Section 7 merely requires the Minister of Heritage to "consult" with Indigenous peoples to determine appropriate funding, without mandating a binding commitment. This limited framework stands in contrast to the Supreme Court of Canada's interpretation of language rights require active government involvement to be meaningful. As the Supreme Court has stated, "freedom to choose is meaningless in the absence of a duty of the State to take positive steps to implement language guarantees."[38]

Following its second reading, Bill C-91 was referred to the Standing Committee on Canadian Heritage for examination. Several committee meetings were held to discuss the Bill. On 28 February 2019, the Senate also adopted a motion for the Standing Senate Committee on Aboriginal Peoples to conduct a pre-study on the Bill. The AFN insisted that the legislation recognize language rights in education on and off reserve and stressed the importance of immersion schools, beginning with primary-age children.[39] The Chiefs of Ontario raised concerns that the Bill did not identify a specific right.[40] The Canadian Bar Association agreed, asserting that the Bill required a clause defining a justiciable right, enabling "Indigenous peoples to seek out court remedies for violations of the rights it recognizes. Without this important amendment, the Indigenous Languages Act risks being little more than another hollow promise."[41] Ellen Gabriel, representing Kontinónhstats—the Mohawk Language Custodian Association from Kanehsatà:ke—emphasized the need for rights to core funding for language transmission:

> The religious doctrines of superiority and racism have brought us to the point where we are looking at Canada to say, "Please help us with our languages because you hold the purse strings"—if we had the money to be able to pay, as we do post-secondary students, the youth or even adults to go to school, then let's do it, because that's what is needed. We are not going to be successful in revitalization and maintenance if we don't have adult speakers to teach the children, if we don't have those first-language speakers to teach the second-language speakers exactly the meaning of what they are saying.... We need core, long-term, sustainable funding for experienced Indigenous languages organizations that have led the way in Indigenous languages preservation and revitalization ... can't emphasize enough that this is an urgent situation. Language must be given priority and a special place because, without our languages, we have lost who we are as Indigenous people.[42]

Similarly, Robert Matthew, the principal of T'selcéwtqen Clleq'mel'ten/ Chief Atahm School, emphasized the critical importance of securing adequate resources to support language education. He expressed concern over the disproportionate time spent securing funding rather than focusing on educational initiatives:

> So money is very important.... The problem is you spend so much time raising the money. Where should my energy be going? It should be going into the educational plan of the school and it should be going into the research.... I spend six months finding money and another six months accounting

for it and only a month to spend it. My point is the legislation, to show real commitment to our language, it should be expressed in adequate and sustainable long-term funding.[43]

This emphasis on securing stable funding is critical. One of the key reasons for advocating a right to funding within the Indigenous Languages Act is to move away from short term proposal driven program models. For the most part, Aboriginal communities are forced to compete for limited resources by submitting language proposals. Funding allocations are determined annually at the discretion of the government during the budget process, leading to inconsistent and often inadequate support for language revitalization initiatives. This approach created disparities and undermined long term planning sustainability. Between 2009–2010 and 2013–2014, for instance, 952 applications requested a total of $68.2 million, although there was less than $5 million in funding available per year (which amounts to approximately $450,000 per year). As a result, the evaluation reported that only 28 percent of submitted applications received funding through the program.[44] Canada proposed to invest $89.9 million in 2017 over three years to support Indigenous languages and cultures.[45] In sharp contrast, Canada's *Action Plan for Official Languages 2023–2028* allocated four billion dollars to support official-language minority communities (French outside of Quebec and English in Quebec) and promote bilingualism across the country.[46]

When questioned about the absence of funding rights in the Indigenous Languages Act, Pablo Rodriguez, Minister of Canadian Heritage and Multiculturalism, indicated that funding arrangements can be negotiated with government. Rodriguez stated that, "We will work with these groups to clearly define funding mechanisms that make sense for their circumstances and needs because, in many cases, stability is key. I agree with this committee that year-to-year project funding can put a lot of smaller Indigenous organizations in precarious positions. Yes, it's very difficult for schools to hire teachers when they don't have the funding to plan for the future. It's not good for the kids, either. That is why the multi-year agreement in proposed sections 8 to 10 offer flexible funding mechanisms."[47] Senator Doyle questioned whether Rodriguez thought the funding was adequate, pointing out that, "in looking at the amount of funding in the budget for supporting

Indigenous languages, $333 million over a five-year period, if we take that number and divide it by 260,000 Indigenous language speakers, that amounts to about $256 per year per speaker if you spread it equally between the strong languages and the dying languages. Is that adequate and sustainable funding, in your opinion?"[48] Rodriguez responded that the amount was a good start.

Senator Sinclair highlighted that, beyond the absence of funding guarantees, the legislation also fails to recognize any enforceable language rights.[49] Notably, the Indigenous Languages Act omits explicit provisions concerning language education and linguistic sovereignty that are identified in UNDRIP. These rights are explicitly recognized in articles 13, 14, 15, and 16 of UNDRIP, and they are implicitly rec-ognized in articles 2 (anti-discrimination), 11 (cultural traditions), and 12 (spiritual traditions). The right to language transmission is defined in article 14:

> 1. Indigenous peoples have the right to establish and control their educational systems and institutions providing education in their own languages, in a manner appropriate to their cultural methods of teaching and learning.
> 2. Indigenous individuals, particularly children, have the right to all levels and forms of education of the State without discrimination.
> 3. States shall, in conjunction with indigenous peoples, take effective measures, in order for indigenous individuals, particularly children, including those living outside their communities, to have access, when possible, to an education in their own culture and provided in their own language.[50]

Article 14 of UNDRIP emphasizes that the revitalization of Indigenous languages in Canada depends on intergenerational continuity. It recognizes that, in today's context, this requires state-supported educational systems and institutions that teach Aboriginal children their ancestral languages in the required subjects, both on and off reserve.

Several commitments have been made in Canada to implementation UNDRIP. The TRC Calls to Action identify UNDRIP as the framework for reconciliation.[51] Similarly, the Indigenous Languages Act recognizes the revitalization of Indigenous languages as key component of implementing UNDRIP.[52] Furthermore, Canada's United Nations Declaration on the Rights of Indigenous Peoples Act, 2021, requires that the federal government take "effective measures" to ensure federal laws are consistent with UNDRIP. In accordance with this mandate, the Department of Justice released the *United Nations Declaration on the Rights of Indigenous Peoples Act Action Plan 2023–2028* (UNDRIP Action Plan),[53] which sets out a roadmap for implementing UNDRIP in partnership with Aboriginal peoples and advancing reconciliation through concrete ways.

Despite these commitments, the UNDRIP Action Plan faces significant challenges in advancing Aboriginal language rights in education. Presently, there is no coordinated structure or process that enables Aboriginal leaders to engage meaningfully with all three relevant ministries to ensure that the Indigenous Languages Act aligns with Article 14 of UNDRIP. Jurisdiction over Aboriginal language education and language rights remains fragmented: Canadian Heritage is responsible for Indigenous Languages, the Department of Justice oversees the implementation of the UNDRIP Act and Action Plan, and Indigenous Services Canada manages elementary and postsecondary education.[54] The federal government's current emphasis on regional education agreements is at odds with the priorities of many Aboriginal communities who are advocating for legislative amendments to the Indigenous Languages Act. These communities seek formal recognition of Aboriginal language rights in a manner consistent with the principles of Article 14 of UNDRIP, rather than reliance on piecemeal agreements.

A study conducted by the Standing Committee on Indigenous and Northern Affairs further identifies these concerns. The Standing Committee received several briefs highlighting the Indigenous Languages Act's misalignment with UNDRIP, particularly in relation to language rights in education. For instance, constitutional lawyer David Leitch emphasized in his submission that "the revitalization of Indigenous language rights in Canada depends, as it always has, on intergenerational transmission. In the modern context, this requires state supported educational systems that both teach Indigenous children in their own ancestral languages and that teach other subjects in those languages. Importantly for Canada, Article 14 of UNDRIP recognizes such systems must exist both on and off reserve."[55]

Despite significant apprehension expressed regarding the Bill's lack enforceable language rights and rights to funding for Aboriginal languages, Senator Sinclair acknowledged that the legislation represents an important initial step. He emphasized the urgency of action, stating, "The important thing we have to do is get through the door or knock down the door. This legislation does that."[56] Senator Sinclair proposed a three-year review, arguing that for a young child, five years can mean the difference between fluency and language loss. The proposed shorter review period, he contended, would allow for timely amendments to ensure that enforceability and a duty to fund Indigenous language education. The Indigenous Languages Act received royal assent on 21 June 2019[57] and mandates a parliamentary review to occur after the third anniversary in 2024.[58] Unfortunately, there has not been meaningful progress on this review, particularly with respect to examining potential amendments related enforceability or funding obligations. This delay raises concerns about the government's commitment to the legislation's implementation and highlights the urgent need to address systemic gaps in the protection and revitalization of Aboriginal languages.

In response to ongoing discussions regarding issues related to the Indigenous Languages Act, Minister of Canadian Heritage, Pascale St-Onge, indicated that any proposed amendments to the Indigenous Languages Act would be considered in the independent mandatory five-year review.[59] St-Onge also stated that the federal government, through Indigenous Services Canada, is responsible for language education of Aboriginal students residing on-reserve while provincial or territorial governments are responsible for those living off-reserve.[60] This position raises several concerns, particularly the assertion that language education for off-reserve Aboriginal students falls within provincial or territorial jurisdiction. Under section 91 (24) of the Constitution Act, 1867, the federal government holds jurisdiction over "Indians and Lands reserve for the Indians" a provision that extends beyond geographical boundaries. Given that language is a foundational element of Aboriginal cultural identity, delegating this responsibility to the provinces or territories risks undermining the federal government's constitutional and fiduciary responsibility. Furthermore, Aboriginal language rights are not only recognized and protected in section 35 of the Constitution Act, 1982, they are also grounded in Aboriginal law, inter-customary practices, Aboriginal and treaty rights, as well as international legal frameworks such as UNDRIP. These legal foundations highlight the necessity of substantive federal support in education where meaningful implementation of Aboriginal language rights in education occurs.

Additionally, the intrinsic connection between language rights in education and the resources required to implement culturally and linguistically relevant programming is critical to the health, well-being, and self-determination of Aboriginal peoples. There exists a clear legal and moral obligation for the federal government to provide adequate funding for such initiatives. Empowering communities to design and deliver their own language education programs is essential for fostering resilience, identity, and sense of belonging. Building on this foundation it becomes evident that the benefits of Aboriginal language education extend beyond academic achievement. Canadian research demonstrates that students in Aboriginal language immersion programs tend to excel academically, and report improved health, well-being, and stronger community ties.[61] Research consistently demonstrates a strong correlation between language revitalization and improved well-being in Aboriginal communities,[62] highlighting the role of education in both cultural preservation and the promotion of community health.[63]

These findings highlight that language education is not only about communication—it is fundamental to cultivating individual and communal resilience. Increased cultural identity, heightened pride, and stronger community connections are frequently observed as direct benefits of such programs. In this sense, Aboriginal language knowledge holds broader significance in fostering cultural resilience and well-being.[64] The connection to identity is particularly reinforced through educational initiatives that integrate Aboriginal pedagogical frameworks, Indigenous languages and cultural knowledge.[65]

To fully realize these benefits, it is also essential to focus on the content and design of language programs. The effectiveness of Aboriginal language initiatives depends on how meaningfully they connect language learning with cultural values and lived experiences. Programs that reflect Indigenous worldviews and practices allow students to see their identities and histories reflected in the curriculum. These culturally grounded approaches are critical not only for advancing language revitalization, but also for promoting the health and well-being of Aboriginal learners. As Senator Murray Sinclair emphasized,

> Language and culture are keys to personal identity. Personal identity is key to a sense of self-worth, and spiritual and mental wellness hinge on one's sense of self-worth.
>
> Everyone wants to feel worthy and to belong to something valid. Education is the key by which we make our society and our membership within it seem valid.
>
> Identity also gives one a sense of being valued and worthy if one's language and culture are considered valuable and worthy. If the language you speak and the culture you follow are denigrated or otherwise portrayed as unworthy of respect from your neighbours, disrespect is reciprocated and tension between you is inevitable.[66]

Building on these insights, it is evident that promoting language vitality requires more than symbolic gestures or isolated initiatives, it requires sustained, systemic support and attention to the progress of language transmission.[67] Aboriginal language education must be recognized not only as an optional enrichment but as a foundational component of a health, self-determining community.

The federal government has acknowledged the connection between education and health and well-being of Aboriginal people. A 2010 study conducted by Canadian Heritage emphasized the critical role of using Aboriginal languages as the primary medium of instruction in revitalization efforts.[68] It found that students in immersion programs not only performed better academically than their peers but also experienced higher levels well-being. These findings affirm that language immersion is one of the most effective strategies for revitalizing Aboriginal languages, especially when embedded within community led educational models.[69]

Success, however, depends on more than immersion alone—it requires meaningful collaboration with Aboriginal communities. Effective revitalization strategies must reflect community priorities, values, and linguistic goals.[70] The establishment of clear, culturally relevant indicators is essential for evaluating progress and adapting strategies to meet evolving needs.[71] As sociolinguist Joshua Fishman argued, revitalizing endangered languages is not just about preserving vocabulary it depends on daily use, social function and especially intergenerational transmission.[72]

Comprehensive approaches are therefore essential. These include supporting second language learners, expanding immersion opportunities, and promoting the use of Aboriginal languages in homes and everyday community life. Promotion language use in daily context ensures that language remains spoken, respected and passed on.[73] Ultimately, language vitality is not merely a linguistic issue—it is a reflection of the cultural resilience and self-determination of the communities that speak it.[74]

To support this ongoing vitality, robust and sustained structural support is critical. The success of language transmission in education is significantly influenced by the availability of stable, long-term funding and institutional support. When language education is meaningfully implemented, it can facilitate revitalization that extend beyond short term programmatic responses. Yet, the absence of guaranteed core funding has constrained the ability of First Nations to develop and sustain long term education initiatives such as immersion programs.[75]

Financial limitations continue to present substantial barriers to both implementation and sustainability of educational initiatives across communities. While some economically stable First Nations, such as Onion Lake First Nation in western Canada have managed to developed language programs through self-funding, many others face significant financial insecurity. Immersion programs at places such as the Opaskwayak Cree Nation,[76] the Mohawk Freedom School,[77] and Mi'kmaq Immersion in Nova Scotia[78] frequently operate under uncertain conditions, dependent on discretionary government funding or short-term project-based allocations. In the absence of enforceable rights to sustain funding, these programs remain vulnerable and at risk of interruption or collapse.

This lack of reliable support reflects a broader pattern of governmental neglect that continues to undermine language revitalization efforts. Many Aboriginal languages across Canada are experiencing gradual declines, despite formal recognition of language rights. While the Indigenous Languages Act represents a symbolic step forward, meaningful implementation remains critically insufficient. Effective language revitalization requires more than symbolic recognition, it requires sustained core funding for immersion programs, as well as comprehensive policies that prioritize teacher training, curriculum development, and community-led initiatives.

Alongside these educational reforms, broader societal change is necessary. The normalization of Aboriginal languages must become a central objective of revitalization efforts. Normalization involves transforming public perception and societal practices to recognize the educational, cultural, and intellectual value of Aboriginal languages. This transformation requires support from both private and public sectors to engage in creating environments where Aboriginal languages are not only accepted but visibly present and actively used. Practical measures such as bilingual signage, official documents in Aboriginal languages, and policies that reinforce these languages into educational, cultural, and civic institutions are essential to this goal. Normalization not only to affirms Aboriginal identity but also contributes to building a more inclusive national identity one that respects and upholds the linguistic heritage of Aboriginal peoples as integral to Canadian identity.

Discrimination: Implications of Section 23 Charter of Rights and Freedoms

Despite the growing recognition of the importance of Aboriginal language revitalization, Canada's constitutional framework continues to reflect inequalities in how language rights are recognized and protected. One key example lies in section 23 of the Charter of Rights and Freedoms, which grants Canadian citizens meeting specific criteria the right to have their children educated in either English or French, depending on the linguistic minority in their province.[79] This provision acknowledges minority language rights in education, particularly concerning English and French language instruction in various provinces.[80] Section 23 also imposes a duty on the government to fund educational programs for these languages, ensuring substantial institutional support and reflecting their status as Canada's official languages.[81]

In contrast, while Indigenous language rights are recognized under section 35(1) of Canada's Constitution Act, 1982, and referenced within the Indigenous Languages Act, the legislation lacks specific enforceable obligations or clearly defined rights concerning Aboriginal language education. This absence constitutes discrimination in Canadian law for the protection and promotion of Aboriginal languages, especially in educational contexts. Unlike official minority languages, such as French in anglophone provinces, Aboriginal languages do not benefit from a comparable level of governmental commitment, institutional support, sustained resource allocation—elements that are essential for meaningful revitalization and long-term preservation.

One of the goals of section 23 of the Charter of Rights and Freedoms is to address the historical suppression of French language education in minority communities, thereby serving a remedial purpose.[82] The Supreme Court of Canada has emphasized the connection between language rights to the preservation of cultural identity, which is particularly significant given Canada's historical efforts to assimilate and eradicate Aboriginal languages and cultures. The Supreme Court's purposive interpretation of section 23 of the Charter of Rights and Freedoms is to address past injustices and prevent the assimilation of minority language communities affirms the fundamental importance of access to minority language educational institutions. This interpretation carries significant normative weight in the broader effort to safeguard linguistic diversity and cultural heritage in Canada.[83]

Section 23 of the Charter of Rights and Freedoms mandates that minority language groups are entitled to a degree of management and control over their educational institutions "where the numbers warrant."[84] This clause has been interpreted to mean that where there is a sufficient population of minority language speakers in a given area, the government has a constitutional obligation to provide education in that language.[85] This provision reinforces the intrinsic connection between language preservation and institutional autonomy. Moreover, the Supreme Court of Canada has acknowledged that Aboriginal people often seek constitutional protection for their rights under section 35 of the Constitution Act, 1982, but also through broader constitutional principles. As the Supreme Court has noted, the protection and recognition of Aboriginal rights earned through hard struggles and only recently, whether considered independently or within the broader context of minority rights, reflects a fundamental constitutional value. In this context, the interpretive approach applied to section 23 of the Charter of Rights and Freedoms offers a compelling constitutional framework for addressing the systemic discrimination of Aboriginal languages in Canadian law, affirming the principle that language rights require substantive rights rather than mere symbolic recognition.[86]

Given the absence of enforceable rights or defined government duties in the Indigenous Languages Act, the rational and objectives of section 23 of the Charter of Rights and Freedoms should be considered in any future amendments to the legislation. Incorporating a similar rights-based framework could not only provide redress for past assimilation policies, but also be a step to aligning federal legislation with Aboriginal law surrounding language transmission. Such an approach would address some of the current inequities embedded in Canadian law concerning language rights.

If the federal government continues to ignore repeated calls from Aboriginal leaders to amend the Indigenous Languages Act to include enforceable rights and a legal obligation to provide sufficient resources for language education, the prevailing structure that prioritizes French and English will continue to contribute to the destruction of Indigenous languages. As the Nunavut case study (Chapter 3) demonstrates, the pattern of disregarding substantive recommendations or implementing superficial solutions has contributed to decline of Inuit language use. In response, governments have often relied on producing reports, action plans, and recommendations that ultimately resulted in limited implementation. The negotiations and outcome of the Indigenous Languages Act are revealing in several respects. Aboriginal leaders were invited to co-develop the legislation, clearly emphasizing the importance of language rights in education and the necessity of guaranteed funding. Prime Minister Trudeau's government articulated a commitment to fostering a new, nation-to-nation relationship, acknowledging that Canadian laws have historically constrained Aboriginal rights. This spirit of reconciliation was intended to inform the co-development of the Indigenous languages Act.

A central question remains: does Canada's commitment to a "new relationship" extend to the providing the necessary resources for meaningful language education? Genuine support for Aboriginal languages requires Canada to move from passive deference or indifference to the active implementation of rights. Only through such sustained dedication can Canada begin to address its colonial legacy and honour a nation-to-nation relationship that respects Aboriginal and internation law, recognizing the fundamental importance of language transmission.

The government has acknowledged its historical role in undermining Aboriginal languages, especially through an educational system that punished children for speaking their ancestral languages. There is now a broad recognition of the responsibility to repair this harm, with both the government and Aboriginal leaders agreeing that investment in education is central to the success of language revitalization efforts. Canada has a clear understanding of how to address language endangerment, as evidenced by its own research, which confirms that immersion programs are the most effective approach—an understanding reflected in the country's ongoing support for French language education, an approach that should similarly be extended to Aboriginal languages.

It is also widely recognized by the government, courts, and Aboriginal leaders that language legislation is ineffective without enforceable rights and guaranteed funding. Thus, the legislation must move beyond symbolic recognition of language rights. During consultations, Aboriginal leaders and language experts consistently identified two critical requirements for effective legislation: the right to guaranteed funding for language education and the explicit recognition of language rights within educational settings. Following the completion of the draft legislation, the government solicited feedback from leaders and experts, who once again emphasized the need for including these provisions. Yet when the Indigenous Languages Act was implemented, it lacked both guaranteed funding and explicit recognition of language rights in education. In fact, it failed to provide any concrete language rights guarantees, instead offering only a commitment to pursue further negotiations with Aboriginal leaders—falling significantly short of the protections that had been consistently advocated.

What kind of nation-to-nation relationship exists when one party retains the financial control and power, has caused significant harm, and ignores the other's calls for support? How do we characterize a country that, after acknowledging its role in cultural destruction—even genocide—seeks guidance on how to repair the harm, only to disregards the response it receives? These questions are crucial to an examination of the Indigenous Languages Act. Does Canada's commitment to a "new relationship" extend to the language rights in education of Aboriginal peoples? Will the government provide the core funding necessary to support the type of education that can meaningfully revitalize Aboriginal languages?

As the TRC warns, "if the preservation of Aboriginal languages does not become a priority for both governments and Aboriginal communities, then what the residential schools failed to accomplish will come about through a process of systematic neglect."[87]

The negotiations surrounding the Indigenous Languages Act, and the legislation itself, reveal a relationship between Aboriginal nations and Canada that falls short of a respectful, nation-to-nation partnership. This relationship requires urgent re-evaluation, and a vital first step is recognizing Aboriginal language education as a constitutional right within the Indigenous Languages Act.

AFTERWORD

In the Preface to this book, I described a dream that revealed that our languages, inherently tied to the land, are fundamental to reviving the spirit of First Nations languages. These languages are born from the land and evolved according to the peoples' relationship to the territory. The history of Canada is embedded in these relationships, making the country unique. As the original languages of Canada, not only are they are foundational to First Nations but also to the identity of the country.

Since having the dream, I've also grown to understand the pivotal role women play in transmitting language, particularly in my Cree culture. Cree women, through language, have traditionally been instrumental in nurturing and imparting cultural values to children. This language-based bonding starts with sensory interactions like touch and eye contact, especially during nursing, and evolves into verbal communication. This verbal dimension, encompassing sounds that gradually form into words, imparts a world view rich in values, ways of behaving, and connections with all beings—humans, plants, animals, and even water. This learning process is deeply entwined with rituals, songs, and storytelling.

My own journey into the world of maternal linguistic bonding began with my daughter. In her first year, we developed a unique language, comprehensible only to us. As I navigated the complexities of teaching her about life, I often reflected on how I was mothered. My mother's childhood was deeply rooted in Cree language and culture, a bond forged by my grandmother, where language was an essential part of their connection to the land and their survival as a trapping culture. This language-land relationship was their life force.

Our Creation story tells us that Swampy Cree, our language, emerged from our ancestors' interactions with the land. The evolution of the language was shaped by experiences with the land—with the swamps, rivers, wildlife, trees, plants, and even the spirits of our ancestors. This connection underwent a drastic change when the federal government began placing First Nations children in residential schools, distancing them from their mothers and the land. This policy severely impaired the ability of Cree women to pass on their language and culture. I am a descendant of this resilient yet fragmented history. My grandmother's determination to preserve our language and culture manifested in her efforts to keep some of her children out of residential schools and immerse them in the Cree language and culture on our family trapline. This defiance of the Indian Act, which could have led to fines or imprisonment, ensured that my mother and her siblings remained fluent in Cree. However, the abuse my mother suffered in residential school left deep scars, preventing her from passing the language on to me and my siblings. Thankfully, we were still surrounded by Cree cultural values and occasionally heard the language in our childhood. I carry this legacy of harm and shame but also of determination and resilience. I raised my daughter with an understanding of her Cree and Ojibway heritage, bringing her to our ceremonies and providing her with a naming ceremony. She recognizes the importance of our ancestral languages, not only for worldview and prayer but for understanding our beautiful teachings. Although fluency has eluded us, the cultural values embedded in these languages remain central to our identity. We understand our responsibility to preserve them for future generations.

My hope is that Canada will fully recognize Aboriginal constitutional rights to language education and treat these languages as treasures, providing adequate support within educational systems. Ideally, our ancestral languages will not only thrive within Aboriginal communities but also become a living part of Canadian society.

Mi iw.
Ekosi.

APPENDIX

George Simpson, Character Book of 1832

The following individuals are included in the Character Book of George Simpson, Governor of Hudson's Bay Company (HBC). The book lists individuals who joined the HBC anywhere from 1790–1821, noting details such as their nationality, capacity, the length of service, salary, in addition to Aboriginal language skill. Numbers in parentheses refer to page numbers in the Character Book.[1]

Chief Factors

Stewart Alexander—served NWC from 1796 until 1821 when he became chief factor of the HBC—speaks Cree well with good relations with Aboriginal people (170–71).

Keith George—born in Scotland—joined NWC before 1813 and then joined HBC in 1821—speaks Cree and understands Chipewyan (172–73).

John Dugald Cameron—born in Canada—joined NWC in the 1790s. He became Chief Factor of HBC at the coalition of 1829—speaks Saulteuax and is one of our best Indian Traders—stemmed from the fact that he had an Indian wife, probably Ojibway or Saulteuax (173).

John Charles—speaks Cree and Chipewyan and has a good deal of influence with Indian (174).

Edward Smith—joined NWC before 1806 and became wintering partner in 1814. He was appointed as Chief Factor of HBC in 1821 coalition—speaks Cree and Chipewyan and is an excellent trader (175).

John McLoughlin—joined NWC in 1803 and then HBC in 1821—speaks Saulteaux (176).

James Millan—from Scotland—NWC sometime before 1804 and then with the HBC after the coalition in 1821 Chief Trader and then Chief Factor in 1827. Speaks several Indian Languages (183–84).

Duncan Finlayson—from Scotland—Joined HCB as a clerk in 1815—and became chief trader in 1828 and then Chief Factor in 1831—Speaks Cree (186).

Chief Traders

Thomas McMurray—Orkneyman—served HBC since 1790 and was appointed as chief trader in 1821 Speaks Cree and Saulteaux (187).

Donald McIntosh—NWC since 1806 and appointed Chief Trader for HBC in 1821 during Coalition—speaks Saulteaux (188).

John Peter Pruden—joined HBC in 1791 and was appointed chief trader in 1821—speaks Cree (188).

Angus Cameron born in 1782 in Scotland, joined NWC in 1801 and then HBC in 1821 retired in 1845. Speaks Algonquin and has much influence with Indians (189).

Cuthbert Cumming—from Scotland—entered into service with NWC in 1804 and joined HCB during 1821 coalition and then onto Chief Trader in 1827—best Saulteaux speaker in the Country (194).

Colin Campbell—Born in Canada—Joined NWC in 1804 and HBC in 1821 and Chief Trader in 1828—speaks several Native Languages (196).

Clerks

Nicholas Brown joined HBC in 1828—An Irishman—speaks Algonquin (203).

Williams Cowie joined HBC in 1822—Scotchman—Speaks Chippewyan (203).

George Delormier. Joined HBC in 1830—A Canadian—speaks a little Algonquin having been brought up in an Indian village of Cocknawgan opposite of La Chine where his Father is the Government Interpreter (205).

NOTES

Preface

1 Kathleen E. Absolon, *Kaandosswin: How We Come to Know* (Winnipeg: Fernwood Publishing, 2011); Jo-Ann Archibald, *Indigenous Storywork* (Vancouver: University of British Columbia Press, 2008); John Borrows, *Drawing Out Law: A Spirit's Guide* (Toronto: University of Toronto Press, 2010); Linda Tuhiwai Smith, *Decolonizing Methodologies: Research and Indigenous Peoples*, 3rd ed. (London: Zed Books, 2021).

2 First Nations, as defined under Section 35 of Canada's Constitution Act, 1982, fall within the broader category of "Aboriginal peoples," which also include the Inuit and Métis. However, this terminology often fails to fully acknowledge the vast array of distinct nations that constitute the First Nations people, inadvertently glossing over the rich diversity of cultural and linguistic identities present within these groups. In Canada, there are more than eleven Indigenous language families, each contributing to the country's rich linguistic tapestry. This diversity underscores the importance of recognizing and preserving the unique cultural and linguistic identities of each First Nation in Canada.

3 Under the Settlement Agreement, Aboriginal people had three options. (1) Receive a settlement payment: Former students seeking a payment from the settlement and who did not wish to sue the Government of Canada or the churches had to register and request a claim form, sent by mail after 20 August 2007. The claimant was to complete and return the form. (2) Remove oneself (opt out): Those not wanting a payment, or who were interested in suing the government or the churches on their own, had to remove themselves from the agreement by submitting an Opt Out Form postmarked by 20 August 2007. (3) Do nothing, receive no payment, and give up rights to sue. See the authorized court notice.

4 *Calder et al. v. Attorney-General of British Columbia*, [1973] S.C.R. 313.

5 Virginia Arthurson, *First Nation Languages: Why We Need Them* (Winnipeg: Manitoba First Nations Education Resource Centre, 2012), 3.

6 Ibid.

7 Statistics Canada, "Aboriginal People: Inuit: Fact Sheet for Nunavut," Catalogue 89-656-X2016017. 2016.

8 Statistics Canada, *Census in Brief: Indigenous Languages Across Canada; Census of Population, 2021*, Statistics Canada and Minister of Industry, 2023, accessed 2 January 2024, https://www12.statcan.gc.ca/census-recensement/2021/as-sa/98-200-x/2021012/98-200-x2021012-eng.pdf.

Introduction

1 "Nishnaabe" refers to an Aboriginal person or a person of Ojibway ancestry.

2 Quoted in Brian D. McInnes, *Sounding Thunder: The Stories of Francis Pegahmagabow* (Winnipeg: University of Manitoba Press, 2016), 60. This statement was made by Duncan Pegahmagabow in 1995 at a language conference in Sault Ste. Marie. McInnes interprets the meaning of the language as a spiritual expression that "provided the people with a special connection to their identity and purpose. Only through the language . . . could we be sure that our thinking was reflective of the values and teachings given to the Nishnaabe people in the beginning."

3 Ibid., 77.

4 Task Force on Aboriginal Languages and Cultures, *Towards a New Beginning: A Foundational Report for a Strategy to Revitalize First Nation, Inuit and Métis Languages and Cultures*, Report to the Minister of Canadian Heritage (Ottawa: Task Force on Aboriginal Languages and Cultures, June 2005), 23.

5 Ibid., 23.

6 Sabrina Williams, quoted in Truth and Reconciliation Commission of Canada, *Canada's Residential Schools: The Legacy*, vol. 5 of *The Final Report of the Truth and Reconciliation Commission of Canada* (Montreal and Kingston: McGill-Queen's University Press, 2016), 138–39.

7 Marianne B. Ignace, *Handbook for Aboriginal Language Programming in British Columbia*, report prepared for the First Nations Education Steering Committee, Aboriginal Languages Sub-committee (North Vancouver, BC: First Nations Education Steering Committee, April 1998).

8 Herman M. Batibo, *Language Decline and Death in Africa: Causes, Consequences and Challenges* (Clevedon: Multilingual Matters, 2005), 37.

9 Joshua Fishman, "Maintaining Languages: What Works and What Doesn't," in *Stabilizing Indigenous Languages*, ed. Gina Cantoni, Northern Arizona University Center for Excellence in Education (Flagstaff: Northern Arizona University, 1996), 21.

10 Ibid., 40.

11 Truth and Reconciliation Commission, "Chapter 26, Suppressing Aboriginal languages: 1867–1939," *Canada's Residential Schools: The History, Part 1, Origins to 1939*, Vol. 1 of the *The Final Report of the Truth and Reconciliation Commission of Canada* (Montreal and Kingston: McGill-Queen's University Press, 2015).

12 Truth and Reconciliation Commission, "Suppressing Aboriginal languages: 1867–1939"; Woolford, *This Benevolent Experiment.*

13 An official definition of Indigenous peoples has not been adopted by any United Nations body. The following criteria, however, have been developed to identify Indigenous peoples as characterized by their

- "self-identification as indigenous peoples at the individual level and accepted by the community as their member
- historical continuity with pre-colonial and/or pre-settler societies
- strong link to territories and surrounding natural resources
- distinct social, economic or political systems
- distinct language, culture and beliefs
- forming non-dominant groups of society
- resolve to maintain and reproduce their ancestral environments and systems as distinctive peoples and communities."

See United Nations, *Who Are Indigenous Peoples?*, 15th Session of the United Nations Permanent Forum on Indigenous Issues. Fact Sheet 1, Secretariat of the Permanent Forum on Indigenous Issues, 2015, accessed 3 October 2024, https://www.un.org/esa/socdev/unpfii/documents/5session_factsheet1.pdf. Canada has defined Indigenous ("Aboriginal") peoples under section 35 of Canada's Constitution Act, 1982 as the Inuit, Métis, and First Nations peoples of Canada.

14 Rodolfo Stavenhagen, *Report of the Special Rapporteur on the Situation of Human Rights and Fundamental Freedoms of Indigenous People, Rodolfo Stavenhagen* (6 January 2005), United Nations Commission on Human Rights, Economic and Social Council (E/CN.4/2005/88), para. 42.

15 Luis Enrique López, "Reaching the Unreached: Indigenous Intercultural Bilingual Education in Latin America" (2009), paper commissioned for the Education for All Global Monitoring Report 2010, *Reaching the Marginalized* (UNESCO, 2010/ED/EFA/MRT/PI/29), 38–40; Lars-Anders Baer, with Ole Henrik Magga, Robert Dunbar, and Tove Skutnabb, "Forms of Education of Indigenous Children as Crimes Against Humanity?" expert paper submitted to United Nations Permanent Forum on Indigenous Issues, 8 February 2008 (E/C.19/2008/7), paras 2–7, 25, 34.

16 Robert Phillipson, "Indigenous Children's Education as Linguistic Genocide and a Crime Against Humanity? A Global View," *Journal of Contemporary European Studies* 20, no. 3 (2012): 377–81.

17 United Nations Permanent Forum on Indigenous Issues, "Expert Group Meeting on the Theme Indigenous Languages: Preservation and Revitalization (Articles 13, 14 and 16 of the United Nations Declaration on the Rights of Indigenous Peoples)," Economic and Social Council, February 2016 (E/C.19/2016/10), para. 12.

18 Ibid., 2.

19 UNESCO, International Decade of Indigenous Languages 2022–2032, https://en.unesco.org/idil2022-2032.

20 *R. v. Van der Peet*, [1996] 2 S.C.R. 507 at para. 55.

21 *R. v. Van der Peet*; Brian Slattery, "A Taxonomy of Aboriginal Rights," in *Let Right Be Done: Aboriginal Title, the Calder Case, and the Future of Indigenous Rights*, ed. Hamar Foster, Heather Raven, and Jeremy Webber (Vancouver: University of British Columbia Press, 2007), 118.

22 *R. v. Van der Peet* at para. 160.

23 Constitution Act, 1982: Amended by Constitution Amendment Proclamation, 1983 (S1/84-102), section 35.

24 John Borrows, "Indigenous Love, Law, and Land in Canada's Constitution," in *Fragile Freedoms: The Global Struggle for Human Rights*, ed. Steven Lecce, Neil McArthur, and Arthur Schafer (Oxford: Oxford University Press, 2017), 123–66.

25 Section 35(1) provides the constitutional framework for reconciling pre-existing distinctive Aboriginal societies occupying the land with Crown sovereignty. In his comment on *Delgamuukw v. British Columbia*, Mark Walters suggests that the essence of Aboriginal rights is their bridging of Aboriginal and non-Aboriginal cultures: "The challenge of defining aboriginal rights stems from the fact that they are rights peculiar to the meeting of two vastly dissimilar legal cultures; consequently there will always be a question about which legal culture is to provide the vantage point from which rights are to be defined . . . a morally and politically defensible conception of aboriginal rights will incorporate both legal perspectives." Walters, "British Imperial Constitutional Law and Aboriginal Rights: A Comment on

Delgamuukw v. British Columbia" *Queen's Law Journal* 17 (1992): 412–13. Similarly, Brian Slattery has suggested that the law of Aboriginal rights is "neither English nor aboriginal in origin: it is a form of inter societal law that evolved from long-standing practices linking the various communities." Slattery, "The Legal Basis of Aboriginal Title," in *Aboriginal Title in British Columbia: Delgamuukw v. The Queen*, ed. Frank Cassidy (Montreal: Institute for Research on Public Policy, 1992), 120–21. Slattery further notes that such rights concern "the status of native peoples living under the Crown's protection, and the position of their lands, customary laws, and political institutions." See Brian Slattery, "Understanding Aboriginal Rights," *The Canadian Bar Review* 66 (1987): 737.

26 John Borrows, *Canada's Indigenous Constitution* (Toronto: University of Toronto Press, 2010).

27 Brian Slattery, "The Organic Constitution: Aboriginal Peoples and the Evolution of Canada," *Osgoode Hall Law Journal* 34 (1996): 112.

28 Brian Slattery, "A Taxonomy of Aboriginal Rights," in *Let Right Be Done: Aboriginal Title, the Calder Case, and the Future of Aboriginal Rights*, ed. Hamar Foster, Heather Raven, and Jeremy Webber (Vancouver: University of British Columbia Press, 2007).

29 Brian Slattery, "The Generative Structure of Aboriginal Rights," *Supreme Court Law Review* (2d) 38 (2007): 608.

30 Denise Réaume, "The Demise of the Political Compromise Doctrine: Have Official Language Use Rights Been Revived?" *McGill Law Journal* 47 (2001): 618.

31 Leslie Green, "Are Language Rights Fundamental?" *Osgoode Hall Law Journal* 25, no. 4 (1987): 651.

32 Réaume, "The Demise of the Political Compromise Doctrine," 618–19.

33 Denise Réaume and Leslie Green, "Education and Linguistic Security in the Charter," *McGill Law Journal* 34 (1988): 790.

34 United Nations General Assembly, *Declaration on the Rights of Indigenous Peoples: resolution / adopted by the General Assembly*, A/RES/61/295, 2 October 2007, accessed 3 October 2024, https://www.un.org/development/desa/indigenouspeoples/declaration-on-the-rights-of-indigenous-peoples.html.

Chapter 1. Inter-Customary Law

1 Language exchange refers to a method of learning and adapting to another language.

2 Sean P. Harvey, *Native Tongues: Colonialism and Race from Encounter to the Reservation* (Cambridge, MA: Harvard University Press, 2015), 3.

3 Inter-customary law is a body of law that emerges from the interaction between First Nations and settler legal traditions, particularly through shared practices like language transmission. In the prairie region, this included trade, missionary education, and the development of syllabics, forming a framework for recognizing First Nations language rights.

4 Mary Jane Norris, Report and Reference Manual on Documentation and Classification of Aboriginal Languages in Canada, 3rd ed, Unpublished report originally prepared for Aboriginal Affairs Directorate, Department of Canadian Heritage (Norris Research Inc, 2016).

5 The Algonquian language family includes Blackfoot, Arapaho, Gros Ventre, Cheyenne, Cree, Menominee, Ojibwe, Pottawatomi, Sauk-Fox, Kickapoo, Shawnee, Miami-Illinois, Mi'kmaq, Abenaki, Malecite-Passamaquoddy, Massachusett,

Carolina Algonquian, Powhatan, Etchemin, Loup A, Loup B, and Shinnecock languages.

6 Some of these languages are referred to as Catawba and Woccon.

7 Harold Cardinal, *Treaty Elders of Saskatchewan: Our Dream Is That Our Peoples Will One Day Be Clearly Recognized as Nations* (Calgary: University of Calgary Press, 2000), 10. These terms are in the Plains Cree dialect.

8 Quoted in ibid., 30.

9 Doris Young, personal communication, September 2007.

10 Ruth Norton, "Aboriginal Languages: Multiplicity and Insufficiencies," in *Les droits linguistiques au Canada: ou collusions?* Proceedings of the First Conference, University of Ottawa, 4–6 November 1993, ed. Sylvie Léger (Ottawa: Centre canadien des droits linguistiques, University of Ottawa, 1995), 153.

11 Vine Deloria and James Treat, *For This Land: Writings on Religion in America* (New York: Routledge, 1999), 252.

12 I am grateful to have received these teachings from my late aunt Esther Sanderson and in consultation with Elders of the Opaskwayak Cree Nation.

13 Brian Slattery, "Aboriginal Language Rights," in *Language and the State: The Law and Politics of Identity: Proceedings of the Second National Conference on Constitutional Affairs*, edited by David Schneiderman. Centre for Constitutional Studies (Montreal and Cowansville: Editions Yvon Blais, 1991), 373.

14 Ibid.

15 John Borrows, *Canada's Indigenous Constitution* (Toronto: University of Toronto Press, 2010), 23–24.

16 Aimée Craft, *Breathing Life into the Stone Fort Treaty: An Anishnabe Understanding of Treaty One* (Saskatoon: Purich, 2013).

17 Jean Friesen, "Magnificent Gifts: The Treaties of Canada with the Indians of the Northwest 1869–1876," *Transactions of the Royal Society of Canada* 1 (1986).

18 Craft, *Breathing Life into the Stone Fort Treaty*.

19 Howard Robert Baker II, "Law Transplanted, Justice Invented: Sources of Law for the Hudson's Bay Company in Rupert's Land, 1670–1870" (MA thesis, University of Manitoba, 1996).

20 Arthur Silver Morton and Lewis Gwynne Thomas, *A History of the Canadian West to 1870–71: Being a History of Rupert's Land (the Hudson's Bay Company's Territory) and of the North-West Territory (including the Pacific Slope)*, 2nd ed. (Toronto: University of Toronto Press, 1973; published in cooperation with University of Saskatchewan), 110.

21 James Dempsey, "Effects on Aboriginal Cultures Due to Contact with Henry Kelsey," in *Three Hundred Prairie Years: Henry Kelsey's "Inland Country of Good Report,"* ed. Henry Epp (Regina: Canadian Plains Research Center, University of Regina, 1993), 132.

22 Arthur J. Ray, *Indians in the Fur Trade: Their Role as Trappers, Hunters, and Middlemen in the Lands Southwest of Hudson Bay, 1660–1870; With a New Introduction* (Toronto: University of Toronto Press, 1998).

23 Dale R. Russell, *Eighteenth-Century Western Cree and Their Neighbours* (Hull: Canadian Museum of Civilization, 1991).

24 Ray, *Indians in the Fur Trade.*

25 British House of Commons, Report from the Committee Appointed to Inquire into the State and Condition of the countries adjoining to Hudson's Bay, and of the trade carried on there, in ([London: House of Commons], 1749), 274, accessed 3 October 2024, https://www.canadiana.ca/view/oocihm.9_02954/2.

> We perceive our Servants are unwilling to travel up into Country, by reason of Danger, and want of Encouragement. The Danger we judge is not more now than formerly; and, for their Encouragement we shall plentifully reward them when we find they deserve it by bringing down Indians to our Factories, of which you may allure them. We judge Robert Stanford a fit person to travel, having the Lingua and understanding the Trade of the Country; and upon a Promise of Mr. Young (one of our Adventurers) that he should travel for which Reasons we have advanced his Wages to Thirty Pounds per Annum.

26 Ibid., 274. "I Shall not be neglectful, as soon as I find any Man capable and willing to send up into the Country with the Indians will and may produce, and to use their utmost in bringing down the Indians to our Factory; but your Honours should give good Encouragement to those who undertake such extraordinary Service, or else I fear that there will be but few that will embrace such Employment."

27 Ibid.

28 Ibid. "Mr. Stanford does not accept the Term your Honours provide, but rather chooses to go home; neither he nor any of your Servants will travel up Country, altho' your Honours have earnestly defined it, and I pressed it upon those proposals you have in mind."

29 John Warkentin, Arthur G. Doughty, and Chester Martin, *The Kelsey Papers* (Regina: Canadian Plains Research Center, University of Regina, 1994), xxx.

30 Ibid., 1.

31 Kelsey also identified six different groups: the Nayhaythaway Indians, the Home Indians, the Stone Indians, the Eagles Birch Indians, the Mountain Poets, and the Naywatame Poets. Scholars have identified the first two groups but the identities of the others are not yet known for certain, despite many theories. Kelsey likely anglicized the words he selected when referring to the first two groups as the Nayhaythaway, from the plural Cree word *Nehithawak* (those who speak the same language) or in the singular *Nehithawew*. The HBC commonly referred to these Cree as "the Home" or "Homeguard Indians." See Russell, *Eighteenth-Century Western Cree*, 77, 78.

32 This area has been parcelled into approximately eighteen First Nations reserve communities: Chemawawin Cree Nation, Cumberland House Cree Nation, Fisher River Cree Nation, Fort Severn First Nation, Fox Lake Cree Nation, Marcel Colomb Cree Nations (also Rock Cree), Mathias Colomb First Nation, Misipawistick Cree Nation, Mosakahiken Cree Nation, Opaskwayak Cree Nation, Red Earth Cree Nation, Sapotaweyak Cree Nation, Shamattawa Cree Nation, Shoal Lake Cree Nation, Tataskweyak Cree Nation, War Lake First Nation, Wuskiwi Sipihk First Nation, and York Factory First Nation.

33 This area has been parcelled into approximately six First Nation reserve communities: Albany River Cree or Kashechewan First Nations, Attawapiskat, Flying Post or Mattagami River Cree, Nipigon Cree, Severn River Cree, and Weenusk First Nation.

34 Russell, *Eighteenth-Century Western Cree*, 79.

35 Warkentin, Doughty, and Martin, *The Kelsey Papers*, 8.

36 Russell, *Eighteenth-Century Western Cree*, 80.

37 Samuel Hearne and Joseph Burr Tyrrell, *A Journey from Prince of Wales's Fort in Hudson's Bay to the Northern Ocean* (London: Printed for A. Strahan and T. Cadell, 1795), 12.

38 Lawrence J. Burpee, *The Search for the Western Sea: The Story of the Exploration of North-western America* (Toronto: Musson, 1908), 111.

39 Morton and Thomas, *A History of the Canadian West*, 113.

40 James W. Whillans, *First in the West: The Story of Henry Kelsey, Discoverer of Canadian Prairies* (Edmonton: Applied Art Products, 1955), 145.

41 Russell, *Eighteenth-Century Western Cree*, 79.

42 Henry Kelsey, *A Dictionary of the Hudson's-Bay Indian Language* (London, 1710).

43 Warkentin, Doughty, and Martin, *The Kelsey Papers*, xxxvii.

44 Joseph Robson, *An Account Of Six Years Residence In Hudson's-Bay, From 1733 to 1736, and 1744 to 1747* (London, 1759), 72.

45 "Now being in the Enemies Country I had eight Indians for my conduct one of which Could speak both Languages for to be my interpreter so set forward and having traveled to day near 30 miles in ye Evening came to small poplo Island which standeth out from ye main Ridge." Warkentin, Doughty, and Martin, *The Kelsey Papers*, 9.

46 Arthur G. Doughty, Chester Martin, and Arthur Dobbs, *The Kelsey Papers* (Ottawa: Public Archives of Canada and Northern Ireland Public Record Office; F.A. Acland, printer, 1929), 15.

47 "This morning they provided a feast for me to hear what I had to say so told them my message which was to stay for those which I came from now I understanding their drift was to come altogether for to go to wars so I told them they must not go to wars for it will not be liked by the governor neither would he trade with them if they did not cease from warring." Ibid., 15.

48 Ibid., 16.

49 Ibid., 17.

50 Ibid., 19–20.

51 Ibid., 20.

52 Ibid., 24.

53 Ibid., 21.

54 Ibid.

55 Ibid., 22–23.

56 Ibid., 23.

57 Ibid.

58 Warkentin, Doughty, and Martin, *The Kelsey Papers*, ix.

59 Ibid.

60 James Isham, Edwin Ernest Rich, and A.M. Johnson, *James Isham's Observations on Hudsons Bay, 1743* (Toronto: published by the Champlain Society for the Hudson's Bay Record, 1949), 113.

61 Ibid., 177–78.

62 Ibid.

63 Ibid., 57.

64 Ibid., 59.
65 Ibid., 7.
66 Ibid.
67 Ibid., 8.
68 Ibid., 15.
69 Ibid., 51.
70 Ibid., 83–84.
71 Ibid., 85.
72 Ibid., 87.
73 Ibid, 88.
74 Governor and Committee to George Simpson, 11 March 1823. Hudson's Bay Company Archives, A.6/21, folder 50.
75 Winona L. Stevenson, "The Church Missionary Society Red River Mission and the Emergence of a Native Ministry 1820–1860, with a Case Study of Charles Pratt of Touchwood Hills" (MA thesis, University of British Columbia, 1988), 57.
76 Ibid.
77 Ibid., 53; citing John West, Report to the Hudson's Bay Company and the Church Missionary Society, 3 December 1823, Public Archives of Canada, Church Mission Society Archives, A. 98, 96.
78 Ibid., 53.
79 Ibid., 58.
80 Ibid.
81 Stevenson, "The Church Missionary Society"; Tolly Bradford, *Prophetic Identities: Indigenous Missionaries on British Colonial Frontiers, 1850–75* (Vancouver: University of British Columbia Press, 2012).
82 Stevenson, "The Church Missionary Society."
83 John Webster Grant, *Moon of Wintertime: Missionaries and the Indians of Canada in Encounter since 1534* (Toronto: University of Toronto Press, 1984), 101.
84 T.C.B. Boon, *The Anglican Church from the Bay to the Rockies: History of the Ecclesiastical Province of Rupert's Land and Its Dioceses from 1820 to 1955* (Toronto: Ryerson Press, 1962).
85 Isaac Kholisile Mabindisa, "The Praying Man: The Life and Times of Henry Bird Steinhauer" (PhD diss., University of Alberta, 1984).
86 James Michael Reardon, *George Anthony Belcourt: Pioneer Catholic Missionary of the Northwest, 1803–1874; His Life and Times* (St. Paul: North Central Publishing Company, 1955), vii.
87 Ibid., 12–13.
88 Ibid., 30.
89 Stevenson, "The Church Missionary Society," 100–101.
90 Ibid., 108.
91 Ibid., 111.
92 Stevenson, "The Church Missionary Society"; Bradford, *Prophetic Identities*; and Katherine Pettipas, *The Diary of the Reverend Henry Budd, 1870–1875* (Winnipeg: Manitoba Record Society, 1974).
93 Bradford, *Prophetic Identities*, 122.

94 Ibid.

95 Stevenson, "The Church Missionary Society"; Bradford, *Prophetic Identities*; Pettipas, *The Diary of Henry Budd*; Mabindisa, "The Praying Man"; Donald B. Smith, *Sacred Feathers: The Reverend Peter Jones (Kahkewaquonaby) and the Mississauga Indians* (Lincoln: University of Nebraska Press, 1987).

96 As J. Keith Hyde notes, "When Rev. Henry Budd (c. 1812–1875) was establishing Anglican missions at The Pas, MB, and Nepowewin, SK, he chronicled his activities in a series of journals for the Church Missionary Society. Because only the journals from 1870–1875 have been transcribed, I plan to begin transcribing the earlier years dating back to Dec. 1850. This undertaking will provide further insights into Budd's preliminary years of ministry following his ordination, as well as facilitating further scholarship into Budd and his legacy as one of the first Indigenous Anglican priests in North America." J. Keith Hyde, *St. John's College Assembly Minutes*, May 2019, St. John's College, University of Manitoba, Winnipeg, accessed 3 October 2024, https://umanitoba.ca/st-johns-college/sites/st-johns-college/files/2021-04/Assembly%20Agenda%20September%2017%202019.pdf.

Additionally, according to Pettipas, "Native candidates for the ministry were trained by European missionaries but the objective was not assimilation" (xiv).

"Once a native Christian community had been established, the role of the missionary was reduced to that of a mediator and guide rather than a leader in religious functions" (xiv).

"That members of the native ministry were never regarded as sharing the same relationship with the Society as their European counterparts is revealed in the discrepancy in salaries and contingent privileges. In Venn's communication of native policy to Bishop David Anderson of Rupert's Land in 1849, he specified that the salaries of native ministers should be adjusted in accordance with '. . . Native wants and habits and not to European requirements'" (xiv).

"Within this paternalistic system of education, Henry acquired the values of the middle class Victorian as they were communicated by the individual missionaries. This dissemination of Christian morality was imparted not only to uplift the native, but also to promote the emergence of an efficient Christian native leadership in the Canadian Northwest. That Henry was able to assimilate and retain these values won him recognition as an exceptional student. In comparison, other native pupils had been a source of discouragement for their instructors. Although they tended to view the European missionary as their 'adopted' parent, who supplied them with the basic necessities of life, these students were reported to be 'as fond of the Indian maxims, fashions and customs as ever'" (xviii). "The type of education received by Henry and his peers was modeled after the English parochial boarding school system" (xvi). Pettipas, *The Diary of the Reverend Henry Budd, 1870–1875*.

97 Stevenson, "The Church Missionary Society."

98 Ibid., 164.

99 Jean Usher, "Apostles and Aborigines: The Social Theory of the Church Missionary Society," *Histoire Sociale/Social History* 7 (1971): 41.

100 Miscellaneous Papers from the Diocese of Moosonee, Correspondence overseas with General Secretary, GY C1 6a, 1865.

101 Ryan Eyford, *White Settler Reserve: New Iceland and the Colonization of the Canadian West* (Vancouver: University of British Columbia Press, 2016), 96.

102 Stevenson, "The Church Missionary Society"; Jerry Saddleback, "Cree Syllabics" (paper presented at conference on the Origins of Cree Syllabics, Edmonton,

Alberta, 4–5 June 2013); Neal McLeod, *Cree Narrative Memory: From Treaties to Contemporary Times* (Saskatoon: Purich, 2007).

103 Saddleback, "Cree Syllabics."

104 Participants who registered for and attended a workshop by Elder Jerry Saddleback at the conference on the Origins of Cree Syllabics (Edmonton, 4–5 June 2013) were given permission to write about the general discussion that took place on the history of syllabics. The information provided here is based on notes I took during the workshop in addition to the written material that Saddleback provided prior to the workshop.

105 Saddleback, "Cree Syllabics," 3–5.

106 Ibid., 4.

107 John Murdoch, "Syllabics: A Successful Educational Innovation" (MA thesis, University of Manitoba, 1981); Rev. Nathanael Burwash, "The Gift to a Nation of Written Language," *Royal Society of Canada: Proceedings and Transactions*, 3rd series, 5 (1911).

108 Burwash, "The Gift to a Nation," 5.

109 Murdoch, "Syllabics," 22.

110 Ibid., 21.

111 James Evans, *The Speller and Interpreter, in Indian and English: For the Use of the Mission Schools, and Such as May Desire to Obtain a Knowledge of the Ojibway Tongue* (New York: D. Fanshaw, 1837).

112 Burwash, "Gift to a Nation," 6.

113 Murdoch, "Syllabics," 23.

114 Ibid., 24.

115 Ibid., 26.

116 Burwash, "Gift to a Nation," 9.

117 Ibid., 10.

118 Ibid., 15.

119 Ibid., 11.

120 Murdoch, "Syllabics," 176.

121 Burwash, "Gift to a Nation," 12.

122 William Mason, letter from Hudson's Bay Territories to the Church Missionary Society. Church Missionary Society Archives, C1/042/3a, GY C1 042 3, 1854.

123 Although this section takes us outside the scope of the prairie region, it demonstrates the influence that the prairie region had on other languages in other regions.

124 E.A. Watkins, J.A Mackay, R. Faries, and Church of England in Canada, General Synod, *A Dictionary of the Cree Language: As Spoken by the Indians in the provinces of Quebec, Ontario, Manitoba, Saskatchewan and Alberta* (Toronto: Published under the direction of the General Synod of the Church of England in Canada, 1938).

125 Ibid.

126 Ibid., v.

127 Murdoch, "Syllabics," 34.

128 Letters from Reverend Horden and E.A. Watkins 1865–1866 relating to syllabics used for the Cree and Eskimo languages with printed. Syllabrium and conference minutes, Church Missionary Society Archives, G Y C1 F1 1, 1865.

129 Ibid., 1866.

130 Ray, *Indians in the Fur Trade.*
131 Slattery, "Aboriginal Language Rights," 372.
132 Ibid., 372.

Chapter 2. Linguistic Genocide

1 Sandra Del Valle, *Language Rights and the Law in the United States: Finding Our Voices* (Clevedon: Multilingual Matters, 2003).
2 Rita Joe, "Four Poems," in *Canadian Women Studies/Les cahiers de la femme* 10, nos. 2/3 (Summer/Fall 1989): 28.
3 Raphael Lemkin, *Axis Rule in Occupied Europe: Laws of Occupation, Analysis of Government, Proposal of Redress* (Washington: Carnegie Endowment for International Peace, 1944), 79.
4 Truth and Reconciliation Commission of Canada, *Final Report of the Truth and Reconciliation Commission of Canada. Volume One, Summary: Honouring the Truth, Reconciling for the Future* (Toronto: James Lorimer and Company, 2015), 1.
5 The Right Honourable Beverley McLachlin, "Reconciling Unity and Diversity in the Modern Era: Tolerance and Intolerance." The Global Centre for Pluralism, Aga Khan Museum, Toronto, Ontario, 28 May 2015.
6 National Inquiry into Missing and Murdered Indigenous Women and Girls, *Reclaiming Power and Place,* vol. 1a (Gatineau: National Inquiry into Missing and Murdered Indigenous Women and Girls, 2019), 50, https://www.mmiwg-ffada.ca/final-report/; National Inquiry into Missing and Murdered Indigenous Women and Girls, *Supplementary Report—A Legal Analysis of Genocide* (Ottawa, 2019), 1, 8, 26–27, https://www.mmiwg-ffada.ca/wp-content/uploads/2019/06/Supplementary-Report_Genocide.pdf.
7 Jason Harrowitz, "Francis Calls Abuse of Indigenous People in Canada a 'Genocide,'" *New York Times,* 30 July 2022.
8 *Guerin et al. v. The Queen* (1984), 2 SCR 338 at 340. Many of the Supreme Court of Canada decisions have reviewed cases dealing with lands and resources. This constitutional provision also has implications for the best interests of Aboriginal peoples' well-being in terms of culture and identity.
9 David McNab, "Herman Merivale and the Native Question: 1837–1861," *Albion: A Quarterly Journal Concerned with British Studies* 9, no. 4 (Winter 1977).
10 Genocide occurs from "the violence that comes from an unwillingness to acknowledge different ways of seeing the world." Andrew Woolford, "Unsettling Genocide Studies at the Eleventh Conference of the International Association of Genocide Scholars, July 16–19, 2014, Winnipeg-Canada," *Genocide Studies and Prevention: An International Journal* 9, no. 2 (2015).
11 *Official Report of the Debates of the House of Commons of the Dominion of Canada,* 1st Session, 5th Parliament, 8 February–19 April 1883 (Ottawa: MacLean, Roger, 1883), 1107.
12 Dawn Memee Lavell-Harvard and Jeannette Corbiere Lavell, eds., *"Until Our Hearts Are on the Ground": Aboriginal Mothering, Oppression, Resistance and Rebirth* (Coe Hill: Demeter Press, 2006).
13 Task Force on Aboriginal Languages and Cultures, *Towards a New Beginning: A Foundational Report for a Strategy to Revitalize First Nation, Inuit and Métis*

Languages and Cultures, Report to the Minister of Canadian Heritage (Ottawa: Task Force on Aboriginal Languages and Cultures, June 2005).

14 John Sheridan Milloy, *A National Crime: The Canadian Government and the Residential School System, 1879 to 1986* (Winnipeg: University of Manitoba Press, 1999), 39.

15 Ibid., 38.

16 Ibid., 39.

17 Ibid., 38.

18 Ibid., 39.

19 Ibid., 45.

20 Order in Council, Privy Council, 3327, 10 November 1894; and Order in Council, Privy Council, 1685, 6 October 1908.

21 Alexander Morris, *The Treaties of Canada with the Indians of Manitoba and the North-West Territories, Including the Negotiations on Which They Were Based, and Other Information Relating Thereto* (Toronto: Belfords, Clarke and Co., 1880; repr. Saskatoon: Fifth House Publishers, 1991), 28.

22 Nancy L. Hagedorn, "A Friend to Go Between Them: The Interpreter as Cultural Broker During Anglo-Iroquois Councils," 1740–70. *Enthnohistory* 35, no. 1 (1988): 61.

23 Harold Cardinal, *Treaty Elders of Saskatchewan: Our Dream Is That Our Peoples Will One Day Be Clearly Recognized as Nations* (Calgary: University of Calgary Press, 2000); Treaty 7 Elders and Tribal Council, with Walter Hildebrandt, Sarah Carter, and Dorothy First Rider, *The True Spirit and Original Intent of Treaty 7* (Montreal and Kingston: McGill-Queen's University Press, 1997).

24 Peter Bryce, *The Story of a National Crime: Being a Record of the Health Conditions of the Indians of Canada from 1904 to 1921*, Library and Archives Canada, Ontario, Canada.

25 Ibid., 4.

26 Ibid., 14.

27 Ibid.

28 Ibid., 4.

29 Ibid., 11.

30 P.H. Bryce, *The Story of a National Crime: An Appeal for Justice to the Indians of Canada* (Ottawa: James Hope and Sons, 1922), 11.

31 An Act to Amend the Indian Act, S.C. 1919-20, c.50 (10-11 Geo. V), s. 10 (1).

32 Ibid., s. 10 (3).

33 Milloy, *A National Crime*, 184.

34 Ibid., 46.

35 Ibid., 185.

36 Elizabeth Graham, *The Mush Hole: Life at Two Indian Residential Schools* (Waterloo: Heffle Publishing, 1997), 220.

37 Milloy, *A National Crime*, 39.

38 Ibid., 183–84.

39 Mary Augusta Tappage Evans and Jean E. Speare, *The Days of Augusta* (Vancouver: J.J. Douglas, 1973).

40 Eleanor Brass, *I Walk in Two Worlds* (Calgary: Glenbow Museum, 1987), 25.
41 Ibid., 6.
42 Joseph F. Dion and Hugh Aylmer Dempsey, *My Tribe, the Crees* (Calgary: Glenbow Museum, 1979), 158.
43 Ibid., 161.
44 Graham, *The Mush Hole*, 430.
45 Ibid., 436.
46 Ibid., 360.
47 Ibid., 368.
48 Ibid., 374.
49 Basil Johnston, *Indian School Days* (Toronto: Key Porter Books, 1988), 104.
50 Ibid., 105.
51 Graham, *The Mush Hole*, 409–10.
52 Ibid., 418.
53 Ibid., 422.
54 Ibid., 423.
55 David Paul King, "The History of the Federal Residential Schools for the Inuit Located in Chesterfield Inlet, Yellowknife, Inuvik and Churchill, 1955–1970" (MA thesis, Trent University, 1999), 229.
56 Graham, *The Mush Hole*, 362.
57 Ibid., 380.
58 Isabelle Knockwood and Gillian Thomas, *Out of the Depths: The Experiences of Mi'kmaw Children at the Indian Residential School at Shubenacadie, Nova Scotia* (Lockeport: Roseway, 1992), 10.
59 Constance Deiter, *From Our Mothers' Arms: The Intergenerational Impact of Residential Schools in Saskatchewan* (Toronto: United Church Publishing House, 1999), 63.
60 Maria Campbell, *Halfbreed* (Lincoln: University of Nebraska Press, 1982), 44.
61 Theodore Fontaine, *Broken Circle: The Dark Legacy of Indian Residential Schools: A Memoir* (Surrey: Heritage House, 2010), 106–7.
62 Jane Willis, *Geniesh: An Indian Girlhood* (Toronto: New Press, 1973), 45.
63 Agnes Grant, *Finding My Talk: How Fourteen Native Women Reclaimed Their Lives After Residential School* (Calgary: Fifth House, 2004), 25.
64 Norma Sluman and Jean Goodwill, *John Tootoosis* (Winnipeg: Pemmican Publications, 1984), 105.
65 Graham, *The Mush Hole*, 220.
66 Edward Ahenakew, *Voices of the Plains Cree*, ed. Ruth Matheson Buck (Regina: Canadian Plains Research Center, University of Regina, 1995), 132.
67 Earl Maquinna George, *Living on the Edge: Nuu-chah-nulth History from an Ahousaht Chief's Perspective* (Winlaw: Sono Nis Press, 2003), 38.
68 Graham, *The Mush Hole*, 22.
69 Ibid., 220.
70 Ibid., 383.
71 Deiter, *From Our Mothers' Arms*, 51.
72 Ibid., 51.

73 Albert Canadien, *From Lishamie* (Penticton: Theytus Books, 2010), 56.
74 Ibid.
75 Graham, *The Mush Hole*, 388–89.
76 Ibid., 392.
77 Harold LeRat and Linda Ungar, *Treaty Promises, Indian Reality: Life on a Reserve* (Saskatoon: Purich, 2005), 128.
78 Graham, *The Mush Hole*, 400.
79 LeRat, *Treaty Promises*, 229.
80 Alice French, *My Name Is Masak* (Winnipeg: Peguis, 1997), 4.
81 Ibid., 8.
82 Alice Blondin-Perrin, *My Heart Shook Like a Drum: What I Learned at the Indian Mission Schools, Northwest Territories* (Ottawa: Borealis Press, 2009), 16.
83 Ibid., 22.
84 Ibid.
85 Ibid., 23–24.
86 Milloy, *A National Crime*, 185.
87 Sluman and Goodwill, *John Tootoosis*, 106.
88 Milloy, *A National Crime*, 185.
89 Harold Cardinal, *The Unjust Society* (Madeira Park: Douglas and McIntyre, 1999), 46.
90 Deiter, *From Our Mothers' Arms*, 75.
91 Ibid., 75–76.
92 Ibid., 77.
93 Truth and Reconciliation Commission of Canada, *Canada's Residential Schools: The Legacy*, vol. 5 of *The Final Report of the Truth and Reconciliation Commission of Canada* (Montreal and Kingston: McGill-Queen's University Press, 2016), 6.
94 Ibid., Statement to the TRC from Frederick Lee Barney, 122.
95 Truth and Reconciliation Commission of Canada, *Honouring the Truth, Reconciling for the Future: Summary of the Final Report of the Truth and Reconciliation Commission of Canada* (Toronto: James Lorimer and Company, 2015), 157.
96 Brian E. Titley, *A Narrow Vision: Duncan Campbell Scott and the Administration of Indian Affairs* (Vancouver: University of British Columbia Press, 1986); J.R. Miller, *Shingwauk's Vision: A History of Native Residential Schools* (Toronto: University of Toronto Press, 1996).
97 Andrew John Woolford, *This Benevolent Experiment: Indigenous Boarding Schools, Genocide, and Redress in Canada and the United States* (Lincoln: University of Nebraska Press, 2015); David A. Nock, *A Victorian Missionary and Canadian Indian Policy: Cultural Synthesis vs Cultural Placement* (Waterloo: Wilfrid Laurier University Press, 1988); Roland David Chrisjohn, Sherri Lynn Young, and Michael Maraun, *The Circle Game: Shadows and Substance in the Indian Residential School Experience in Canada* (Penticton: Theytus Books, 1997).
98 Tove Skutnabb-Kangas, *Linguistic Genocide in Education—or Worldwide Diversity and Human Rights?* (Mahwah: Lawrence Erlbaum Associates, 2000); Tove Skutnabb-Kangas and Robert Dunbar, *Indigenous Children's Education as Linguistic Genocide and a Crime Against Humanity? A Global View* (Guovdageaidnu/Kautokeino: Gáldu,

Resource Centre for the Rights of Indigenous Peoples, 2010); Andrea Bear Nicholas, "Linguicide: Submersion Education and the Killing of Languages in Canada," *Briarpatch* 40, no. 2 (2011): 4; Andrea Bear Nicholas, "Linguistic Decline and the Educational Gap: A Single Solution Is Possible in the Education of Indigenous Peoples," March 2009; Andrea Bear Nicholas, "Canada's Colonial Mission: The Great White Bird," in *Aboriginal Education in Canada: A Study in Decolonization*, ed. K.P. Binda and Sharilyn Calliou (Mississauga: Canadian Educators' Press, 2011).

99 Tove Skutnabb-Kangas and Robert Phillipson, "Linguicide," in *Concise Encyclopedia of Sociolinguistics*, ed. Rajend Mesthrie and R.E. Asher (Elsevier Science and Technology, 2001).

100 Office of the Independent Special Interlocutor for Missing Children and Unmarked Graves and Burial Sites associated with Indian Residential Schools, "Sites of Truth, Sites of Conscience: Unmarked Burials and Mass Graves of Missing and Disappeared Indigenous Children in Canada," 2024. Miller, *Shingwauk's Vision*; Titley, *A Narrow Vision*; James Sakej Youngblood Henderson, "Treaties and Indian Education," in *First Nations Education in Canada: The Circle Unfolds*, eds. Marie Ann Battiste and Jean Barman (Vancouver: University of British Columbia Press, 1995); J. Rick Ponting, *Arduous Journey: Canadian Indians and Decolonization* (Toronto: McClelland and Stewart, 1988); Chrisjohn, Young, and Maraun, *The Circle Game*; Nock, *A Victorian Missionary and Canadian Indian Policy*; Mick Dodson, "Bringing Them Home: Report of the National Inquiry into the Separation of Aboriginal and Torres Strait Islander Children from Their Families" (Canberra: Australian Human Rights Commission, 1997).

101 Antonio Voce, Leyland Cecco and Chris Michael, "'Cultural Genocide': The Shameful History of Canada's Residential Schools—Mapped," *The Guardian*, 6 September 2021.

102 Murray Sinclair, Mazina Giizhik, *Who We Are, Four Questions for a Life and a Nation* (Penguin Random House McClelland and Stewart, 2024), 8.

103 Darcy Hallett, Michael J. Chandler, and Chistopher E. Lalonde, "Aboriginal Language Knowledge and Youth Suicide," *Cognitive Development* 22, no. 3 (2007).

Chapter 3. Canada's Constitution

1 Royal Commission on Bilingualism and Biculturalism, *Report of the Royal Commission on Bilingualism and Biculturalism*, vol. 1 (Ottawa: Queen's Printer, 1967).

2 The Official Languages Act was proclaimed in 1969, giving French and English equal status. As a result, both languages have preferred legal status over all other languages. It is also considered the keystone of bilingualism in Canada.

3 Royal Commission on Bilingualism and Biculturalism, *Report of the Royal Commission on Bilingualism and Biculturalism*, 49.

4 Ibid., 128.

5 Ibid.

6 Ibid., xxvi.

7 Ibid., xxvii.

8 Ibid., 151.

9 Ibid., 22.

10 Minister of Indian Affairs and Northern Development, *Statement of the Government of Canada on Indian Policy* (Ottawa: Queen's Printer, 1969, cat. no. R32-2469).

11 Indian Chiefs of Alberta, "Foundational Document: Citizens Plus," *Aboriginal Policy Studies* 1, no. 2 (2011), accessed July 2016, https://ejournals.library.ualberta.ca/index.php/aps/article/view/11690/8926.

12 Manitoba Indian Brotherhood, *Wahbung: Our Tomorrows* (Winnipeg: Manitoba Indian Brotherhood, 1971), 109.

13 National Indian Brotherhood, *Indian Control of Indian Education* (Ottawa: National Indian Brotherhood, 1972), iii. Many members of the distinguished committee that produced the report continued to promote Aboriginal languages long after the release of the report. The members consisted of John Knockwood and Peter Christmas, Union of Nova Scotia Indians; Bary Nichols, Union of New Brunswick Indians; Larry Bisonnette, Indians of Quebec Association; Louis Debassige and Roland Chrisjohn, Union of Ontario Indians; Verna Kirkness, Manitoba Indian Brotherhood; Rodney Soonias, Federation of Saskatchewan Indians; Clive Linklater, Indian Association of Alberta; David Joe, Yukon Native Brotherhood; James Wah-shee, Indian Brotherhood of the Northwest Territories; and Dr. Jacqueline Weitz, National Indian Brotherhood. George Manuel was the president of the National Indian Brotherhood at the time.

14 Ibid., 15.

15 Ibid.

16 Ibid., 16.

17 John Sheridan Milloy, *A National Crime: The Canadian Government and the Residential School System, 1879 to 1986* (Winnipeg: University of Manitoba Press, 1999), 198–99; citing: Indigenous and Northern Affairs Canada File 4745-1 vol. 1, *Indian Education Program* (1972), 12: "The Department realized that 'the most formidable handicap that faces the Indian child entering [the provincial] school' was the requirement of being able to function in the English language, or in Quebec, French. To that end, it laid the greatest emphasis on the development of a 'language arts' program for day and residential schools. It also employed regional language supervisors who were to help children 'overcome any language difficulties' in the belief that 'much of the progress in Indian education' was to be realized by these 'improved methods of language instruction.'"

18 Milloy, *A National Crime*, 199.

19 Ibid.

20 Enacted by MCR # 65/1999–2000 on 20 Tsothóhrha/December 1999; amended by MCR#1/2006-2007 on 28 Enniskó:wa/March 2007. Michael L. Hoover, "The Revival of the Mohawk Language in Kahnawake," *Canadian Journal of Native Studies* 12, no. 2 (1992).

21 *Canada's Aboriginal Languages: An Overview of Current Activities in Language Retention* (Department of the Secretary of State, Ottawa, 1985).

22 Roderic P. Beaujot and Barbara Burnaby, *The Use of Aboriginal Languages in Canada: An Analysis of 1981 Census Data*, Social Trends Analysis Directorate and Canada Native Citizens Directorate (Ottawa: Department of the Secretary of State, 1987).

23 Mary E. Jamieson, *The Aboriginal Languages Policy Study: Phase II: Implementation Mechanism, September 1988*, ed. Assembly of First Nations (Ottawa: Assembly of First Nations, 1988), 3.

24 Ibid., 3.

25 Ibid., 14.

26 Ibid., 18.

27 Ibid., 20.

28 Assembly of First Nations, *Towards Linguistic Justice for First Nations* (Ottawa: Assembly of First Nations, 1990); Assembly of First Nations, *Towards Rebirth of First Nations Languages* (Ottawa: Assembly of First Nations, 1992); Assembly of First Nations, *National First Nations Language Strategy: A Time to Listen and the Time to Act,* Adopted by resolution of the Chiefs in Assembly, July 2000 (Ottawa: Assembly of First Nations, 2000).

29 Scott Haldane, George E. Lafond, and Caroline Krause, *Nurturing the Learning Spirit of First Nation Students: Report of the National Panel on First Nation Elementary and Secondary Education for Students on Reserve* (Ottawa: National Panel on First Nation Elementary and Secondary Education for Students on Reserve, 2012), vi.

30 Ibid., 1.

31 Ibid., 4.

32 H.B. Hawthorn, *A Survey of the Contemporary Indians of Canada: A Report on Economic, Political, Educational Needs and Policies* (Ottawa: Indian Affairs Branch, 1966), 37.

> Language is an integral part of any culture, in the anthropological sense of "culture." According to linguists, the structure of a language determines the mental categories and thought processes of those who have inherited the language. Few would dispute the fact that the spoken and written word is an essential instrument in the process of transmitting and absorbing (cultural) knowledge. In the field of education, there is a direct relationship between mastery of the language and success in learning. For all these reasons, the question of language of instruction in schools attended by Indians is thus of capital importance. Indian children who are forced to take courses in a language that is not their mother tongue find school more difficult than other children, during the first few years in particular.

33 Milloy, *A National Crime,* 185.

34 Truth and Reconciliation Commission of Canada, *Canada's Residential Schools: The Legacy,* vol. 5 of *The Final Report of the Truth and Reconciliation Commission of Canada* (Montreal: McGill-Queen's University Press, 2016).

35 House of Commons Standing Committee on Indian Affairs and Northern Development, *Minutes of Proceedings and Evidence of the Standing Committee on Indian Affairs and Northern Development: Respecting the Annual Reports of the Department of Indian Affairs and Northern Development (1967–68 and 1968–69), including Fifth Report to the House* (Ottawa: Queen's Printer, 1971), 763.

36 House of Commons and Senate, *Minutes of Proceedings and Evidence of the Special Joint Committee of the Senate and the House of Commons on the Constitution of Canada, Senate of the House of Commons, Issue No. 14,* 32nd Parl. 1st sess. (27 November 1980).

37 The federal government implemented a Special Joint Committee of the House of Commons and the Senate in 1980 to hear submissions from the public on constitutional amendments. The committee was composed of twenty-five members (ten from the Senate and fifteen from the House of Commons, including fifteen Liberals, eight Progressive Conservatives, and two New Democrats). The consultation process was originally organized as a thirty-day session of hearings but ended up as a three-month consultation process involving 914 individuals and groups submitting briefs, in addition to 214 oral presentations.

38 House of Commons and Senate, *Minutes of Proceedings and Evidence of the Senate and the House of Commons on the Constitution of Canada*, No. 6 (17 November 1980), at 30.
39 Ibid., No. 12 (25 November 1980), at 60.
40 Ibid., No. 12, at 82.
41 Ibid.
42 Ibid., No. 26 (15 December 1980), at 32.
43 Ibid., No. 26, at 33.
44 Ibid., No. 27 (16 December 1980), at 149–50.
45 Ibid., No. 27, at 150.
46 Ibid., No. 21 (8 December 1980), at 19.
47 Ibid., No 28 (17 December 1980), at 18.
48 National Indian Brotherhood, Submission to the Special Joint Committee on the Constitution, 1980–81, letter to Senator Harry Hays from Dilbert Riley, President of the National Indian Brotherhood, 11 November 1980, accessed 31 March 2017, http://historyofrights.ca/wp-content/uploads/committee/nib.pdf.
49 Federal-Provincial Meeting of Ministers on Aboriginal Constitutional Matters, *Public Documents*, prepared by Canadian Intergovernmental Conference Secretariat (Ottawa: Canadian Intergovernmental Conference Secretariat, Intergovernmental Document Centre, 1985).
50 Ibid.
51 Ibid.
52 Ibid.
53 Ibid.
54 Ibid.
55 Canadian Heritage and Indian and Northern Affairs, *Comprehensive Review of Federal Programing for Aboriginal Languages and Cultures Final Report* (May 2006, CH4-98/2005E-PDF 0-662-41412-8).
56 Ibid., 12–13.
57 Ibid., 13.
58 Ibid., 29.
59 Ibid.
60 Ibid.
61 House of Commons Standing Committee on Aboriginal Affairs, *You Took My Talk: Aboriginal Literacy and Empowerment* (Ottawa: Queen's Printer, 1990), 5.
62 Ibid., 14.
63 Ibid., 5.
64 Ibid., 14.
65 Ibid., 17.
66 Charlottetown Accord, Draft Legal Text, 1992, 37–38, accessed 2 November 2024, http://www.efc.ca/pages/law/cons/Constitutions/Canada/English/Proposals/CharlottetownLegalDraft.html.
67 Peter W. Hogg, *Constitutional Law of Canada*, 2nd ed. (Agincourt: Carswell, 1985), 184.
68 Ibid., 181.

69 Government of Canada, "Part 17.8: Powers of the Nunatsiavut Government in Relation to Culture and Language," in *Land Claims Agreement Between the Inuit of Labrador and Her Majesty the Queen in Right of Newfoundland and Labrador and Her Majesty the Queen in Right of Canada* (2005), 255–56, accessed 23 October 2024, https://www.rcaanc-cirnac.gc.ca/eng/1293647179208/1542904949105.

70 Examples: The Labrador Inuit Final Agreement, 2005, established the Nunatsiavut Government, which can make laws in relation to Inuit culture and language in Labrador Inuit communities. A division of the Nunatsiavut Government's Department of Culture, Recreation and Tourism is mandated to establish and administer policies, programs, and services for the use, development, and preservation of Inuktitut, among other matters.

71 Royal Commission on Aboriginal Peoples, *Report of the Royal Commission on Aboriginal Peoples*, vol. 3, *Gathering Strength* (Ottawa: Indian and Northern Affairs Canada and and Canadian Electronic Library, 1996), 577.

72 Ibid., Recommendation 3.6.10, 579.

73 Ibid., 578.

74 Ibid., Recommendation 3.5.9(g), 442.

75 Ibid., Recommendation 3.6.8, 577.

76 Task Force on Aboriginal Languages and Cultures, *Towards a New Beginning: A Foundational Report for a Strategy to Revitalize Indian, Inuit and Métis Languages and Cultures*, Report to the Minister of Canadian Heritage (Ottawa: Task Force on Aboriginal Languages and Cultures, June 2005), Part IX: "Thematic Summary of Recommendations and Concluding Comments," Recommendation 4, 113.

77 Task Force on Aboriginal Languages and Cultures, *Towards a New Beginning*.

78 Government of Canada, Statement of Apology to Former Students of Indian Residential Schools, delivered by Prime Minister of Canada Stephen Harper, 11 June 2008.

79 Québec (Province), Bill 101: Charter of the French Language. [Quebec]: C.-H. Dubé. 1977, chapter C-11, section 88.

> Notwithstanding sections 72 to 86, in the schools under the jurisdiction of the Cree School Board or the Kativik School Board, according to the Education Act for Cree, Inuit and Naskapi Native Persons (chapter I-14), the languages of instruction shall be Cree and Inuktitut, respectively, and the other languages of instruction in use in the Cree and Inuit communities in Québec on the date of the signing of the Agreement indicated in Section 1 of the Act approving the Agreement concerning James Bay and Northern Québec (chapter C-67), namely, 11 November 1975. The Cree School Board and the Kativik School Board shall pursue as an objective the use of French as a language of instruction so that pupils graduating from their schools will in future be capable of continuing their studies in a French school, college or university elsewhere in Québec, if they so desire. After consultation with the school committees, in the case of the Crees, and with the parents' committees, in the case of the Inuit, the commissioners shall determine the rate of introduction of French and English as languages of instruction. With the assistance of the Ministère de l'Éducation, the Cree School Board and the Kativik School Board shall take the necessary measures to have Sections 72 to 86 apply to children whose parents are not Crees or Inuit. For the purposes of the second paragraph of Section 79, a reference to the Education

Act is a reference to Section 450 of the Education Act for Cree, Inuit, and Naskapi Native Persons. This section, with the necessary changes, applies to the Naskapi of Schefferville.

80 Section 95 requires the introduction of "French in their administrations, both to communicate in French with the rest of Quebec and with those persons under their administration who are not contemplated in subparagraph (a) of that section, and to provide their services in French to those persons."

81 Michel Bastarache, *Language Rights in Canada*, 2nd ed. (Cowansville: Éditions Y. Blais, 2004), 223.

82 *R. v. St. Jean*, Unreported Territorial Court of the Yukon, 30 June 1983.

83 Steven Smyth, "Colonialism and Language in Canada's North: A Yukon Case Study," *Arctic* 49, no. 2 (June 1996): 157.

84 Languages Act, RSY 2002, c .133.

85 Yukon Act S.C. 2002, c. 7.

86 Barbara McMillan, "Educating for Cultural Survival in Nunavut: Why Haven't We Learned from the Past?" *Paideusis* 22, no. 2 (2015); Steven Nitah, "One Land—Many Voices: Report of the NWT Special Committee on the Review of the Official Languages Act," *Canadian Parliamentary Review* 25, no. 3 (2002).

87 Laurie Sarkadi, "N.W.T. Wants 8 Official Tongues," *Edmonton Journal*, 6 April 1990.

88 Ibid.

89 Official Languages Act, Revised Statutes of the Northwest Territories 1988, c. 0-1. Northwest Territories, *Official Languages Act*, R.S.N.W.T. 1988, c. 0-1, s. 11(2).

90 Ibid.

91 Nitah, "One Land—Many Voices"; Standing Committee on Government Operations and 16th Legislative Assembly of the Northwest Territories, *Final Report on the Review of the Official Languages Act 2008–2009, Reality Check: Securing a Future for the Official Languages of the Northwest Territories* (2009).

92 Province of Manitoba, Aboriginal Languages Recognition Act C.C.S.M. c. A1.5, accessed 1 June 2017, https://web2.gov.mb.ca/laws/statutes/ccsm/_pdf.php?cap=a1.5.

93 Terry Fenge and Paul Quassa, "Negotiation and Implementing the Nunavut Land Claims Agreement," *Policy Options*, 1 July 2009, accessed 2 November 2024, https://policyoptions.irpp.org/magazines/canadas-water-challenges/negotiating-and-implementing-the-nunavut-land-claims-agreement/.

94 S. Tulloch and V. Hust, "An Analysis of Language Provisions in the Nunavut Act and the Nunavut Land Claims Agreement," in G. Duhaime and N. Bernard, eds., *Arctic Economic Development and Self-Government* (Quebec: GETIC, Université Laval, 2003), 283–96; Katherine J. Wilson, Andrew Arreak, Jamesie Itulu, Sikumiut Community Management Committee, Gita J. Ljubicic, and Trevor Bell, "'When We're on the Ice, All We Have Is Our Inuit Qaujimajatuqangit': Mobilizing Inuit Knowledge as a Sea Ice Safety Adaptation Strategy in Mittimatalik, Nunavut," *Arctic* 74, no. 4 (2021): 525–49.

95 Nunavut Constitutional Forum, *Building Nunavut: A Working Document with a Proposal for an Arctic Constitution* (Northwest Territories: Department of Aboriginal Rights and Constitutional Development, 1983).

96 Ibid.; Ian Martin, "Inuit Language Loss in Nunavut: Analysis, Forecast, and Recommendations" (unpublished report, 2017).

97 Nunavut Constitutional Forum, *Building Nunavut*; Martin, "Inuit Language Loss in Nunavut."

98 Nunavut Tunngavik Incorporated, "Inuit Are Maintaining Inuktut Despite Mulroney Cabinet Secret Instructions to Block Its Use," news release, 5 December 2019, https://www.tunngavik.com/news/inuit-are-maintaining-inuktut-despite-mulroney-cabinet-secret-instructions-to-block-its-use/.

99 Ibid.

100 Ibid. Thomas R. Berger, *The Nunavut Project Conciliator's Final Report: Nunavut Land Claims Agreement: Implementation Contract Negotiations for The Second Planning Period*, 2003–2013 (Vancouver: Bull, Housser and Tupper, 2006), v.

101 Nunavut, Legislative Assembly, *Nunavut Hansard*, 4th Session 2nd Assembly (16 September 2008), 4948.

102 Ibid., 4949.

103 Nunavut Official Languages Act, S.Nu. 2008, c.10.

104 Nunavut Education Act, S.Nu. 2008, c.13.

105 Inuit Language Protection Act, S.Nu. 2008, c. 17.

106 Ibid.

107 Office of the Auditor General of Canada, *Report of the Auditor General of Canada to the Legislative Assembly of Nunavut—2013: Education in Nunavut* (Auditor General of Canada, 2013), 2.

108 Auditor General's Report, 3.

109 Special Committee to Review the Education Act, *Final Report*, Third Session, Fourth Legislative Assembly of Nunavut, 2015.

110 Ibid., 7.

111 Sandra Inutiq, "Indigenous Languages: Preservation and Revitalization: Articles 13, 14 and 16 of the United Nations Declaration on the Rights of Indigenous Peoples," paper prepared for International Expert Group Meeting, United Nations Department of Economic and Social Affairs, Division for Social Policy and Development, Secretariat of the Permanent Forum on Indigenous Issues, January 2016 (PFII/2016/EGM), 7.

112 Ibid.

113 Ibid.

114 Bob Weber, "Why Have Nunavut? Battle over Education Bill Goes to the Heart of Territory," *National Observer* online, 19 March 2017, https://www.nationalobserver.com/2017/03/19/news/why-have-nunavut-battle-over-education-bill-goes-heart-territory.

115 Ibid.

116 Peter Varga, "Nunavut Officials Say Bill 37 Will Strengthen DEAs," *Nunatsiaq News* online, 13 March 2017.

117 Weber, "Why Have Nunavut?"

118 Aluki Kotierk, Remarks to the United Nations Permanent Forum on Indigenous Issues, 16 April 2018.

119 Ibid.

120 Ian Martin, "Inuit Language Loss in Nunavut," 10. Unpublished report Inuit Language Loss in Nunavut: Analysis, Forecast, and Recommendations, 2017.

121 Aluki Kotierk, Presentation to the Senate Standing Committee on Aboriginal Peoples on Bill C-91 Indigenous Languages Act, 2 April 2019.

122 This is up from previous censuses (71.7 percent in 2001). Jean-François Lepage and Stéphanie Langlois, with Martin Turcotte, "Evolution of the Language Situation in Nunavut, 2001 to 2016," Statistics Canada, 9 July 2019; also reported in the *2018–2019 Annual Report of the Official Languages Commissioner of Nunavut*. See Office of the Languages Commissioner of Nunavut, *2018–2019 Annual Report* (Iqaluit: Office of the Languages Commissioner of Nunavut, 2019).

123 Tove Skutnabb-Kangas, Robert Phillipson, and Robert Dunbar, "Is Nunavut Education Criminally Inadequate? An Analysis of Current Policies for Inuktut and English in Education, International and National Law, Linguistic and Cultural Genocide and Crimes against Humanity," 26, https://www.tunngavik.com/files/2019/04/NuLinguicideReportFINAL.pdf.

124 Letter to Mr. Marc Garneau, Minister of Foreign Affairs from Fernand de Varennes, Special Rapporteur on Minority Issues, Koumbou Boly Barry, the Special Rapporteur on the Right to Education, Tlaleng Mofokeng, Special Rapporteur on the Right of Everyone to the Enjoyment of the Highest Standard of Physical and Mental Health, and José Francisco Calí Tzay, Special Rapporteur on the Rights of Indigenous Peoples, 3 August 2021. Reference AL CAN 3/2021.

125 Letter from Leslie Norton, Permanent Mission of Canada, to the Office of the United Nations and World Trade Organization to the Office of the High Commissioner for Human Rights, 7 June 2022, note no. GENEV-8164.

126 Ibid.

127 *Nunavut Tunngavik Incorporated, Bernice Tujjaaqtuqaq Clarke, and Lily Anne Maniapik v. the Commissioner of Nunavut as represented by the Government of Nunavut and the Government of Nunavut as represented by the Attorney General*, Court File 08-21-463-CVC, https://equality-rights-claim.tunngavik.com/files/2021/10/2021-10-13-Filed-NTIvAG-s.15-Charter-Inuit-Language-Rights-eng.pdf.

128 Derek Neary, "NTI Taking Territorial Government to Court over Language Education," *Nunavut News,* 12 October 2021, https://www.nunavutnews.com/news/nti-taking-territorial-government-to-court-over-inuit-language-education-7281036; Aluki Kotierk cited in Nunavut Tunngavik Incorporated, *NTI Files Lawsuit Against GN for Violating Equality Rights of Inuit Children and Youth*, 2021. https://www.tunngavik.com/files/2021/10/2021-10-13-Press-Release-and-Backgrounder-final.pdf.

129 Kira Wronska Dorward, "Judge's Ruling a Blow to the GN in Inuktitut Instruction Lawsuit," *Nunavut News* (online), 24 May 2024, https://www.nunavutnews.com/home/strike-against-the-gn-in-inuktitut-lawsuit-7361183#:~:text=Nunavut%20Court%20of%20Appeal%20finds,language%20rights%20lawsuit%20to%20proceed.

130 Statistics Canada, *Aboriginal People: Inuit: Fact Sheet for Nunavut. Catalogue 89-656-X2016017. 2016,* Statistics Canada, 2016, accessed 7 October 2024, https://www150.statcan.gc.ca/n1/pub/89-656-x/89-656-x2016017-eng.pdf.

131 Weber, "Why Have Nunavut?"

Chapter 4. International Law

1 International Covenant on Civil and Political Rights, 999 U.N.T.S., 171, 19 December 1966 (entered into force 23 March 1976).

2 International Covenant on Economic, Social and Cultural Rights, 993 U.N.T.S. 3, ATS 5, 6 ILM 360, 16 December 1966 (entered into force 3 January 1976).

3 International Convention on the Elimination of All Forms of Racial Discrimination, 660 U.N.T.S 195, [1975] ATS 40, 5 ILM 32, 7 March 1966 (entered into force 4 January 1969).

4 United Nations Convention on the Rights of the Child, UN Doc. A/Res/44/25, 20 November 1989.

5 Ibid.

6 UN Committee on the Rights of the Child (CRC), *General comment No. 11 (2009): Indigenous children and their rights under the Convention [on the Rights of the Child]*, CRC/C/GC/11, 12 February 2009, accessed 9 October 2024, https://www.refworld.org/legal/general/crc/2009/en/102812.

7 UN Human Rights Committee (HRC), *UN Human Rights Committee: Concluding Observations, Canada*, CCPR/C/CAN/CO/5, 20 April 2006, accessed 9 October 2024, para. 10. https://www.refworld.org/policy/polrec/hrc/2006/en/38904; Task Force on Aboriginal Languages and Cultures, *Towards a New Beginning: A Foundational Report for a Strategy to Revitalize Indian, Inuit and Métis Languages and Cultures*, Report to the Minister of Canadian Heritage (Ottawa: Department of Canadian Heritage, June 2005), available online at www.aboriginallanguagestaskforce.ca. The Task Force report recommended constitutional recognition of Aboriginal languages and guaranteed federal funding.

8 UN Committee on Economic, Social and Cultural Rights (CESCR), *UN Committee on Economic, Social and Cultural Rights: Concluding Observations, Canada*, E/C.12/CAN/CO/4; E/C.12/CAN/CO/5, 22 May 2006, accessed 9 October 2024 para. 33 and 67. https://www.refworld.org/policy/polrec/cescr/2006/en/23888.

9 Concluding Observations of The Human Rights Committee, 20 April 2006 (CCPR/C/CAN/CO/5), at para. 10.

10 UN Committee on Economic, Social and Cultural Rights (CESCR), *General Comment no. 21, Right of Everyone to Take Part in Cultural Life (art. 15, para. 1a of the Covenant on Economic, Social and Cultural Rights)*, E/C.12/GC/21, 21 December 2009, accessed 9 October 2024, https://www.refworld.org/legal/general/cescr/2009/en/83710.

11 Gerald Heckman, "International Human Rights Norms and Administrative Law," in *Administrative Law in Context*, ed. Colleen Flood and Lorne Sossin, 3d ed. (Toronto: Emond Publishing, 2018), 580.

12 Ibid.; S. James Anaya, "Indigenous Rights Norms in Contemporary International Law," *Arizona Journal of International and Comparative Law* 8, no. 2 (1991): 6, http://hdl.handle.net/10150/659463.

13 *Saskatchewan Federation of Labour v. Saskatchewan* [2015] 1 S.C.R. 245.

14 Although section 35 falls outside the parameters of the Charter of Rights and Freedoms, an analogous argument can be made to interpret section 35 in accordance with the international consensus on language rights and the principles that protect and advance language rights in international treaties that Canada has ratified. See *Saskatchewan Federation of Labour v. Saskatchewan* [2015] 1 S.C.R. 245 at para. 64, which states that "the Court has sought to ensure consistency between its interpretation of the *Charter*, on the one hand, and Canada's international obligations and the relevant principles of international law, on the other," and that "there is an emerging consensus" that has to be applied at para. 71.

15 In *Baker v. Canada (Minister of Citizenship and Immigration)*, [1999] 2 SCR 817, the Supreme Court of Canada considered whether Canada's obligations under the

International Convention on the Rights of the Child could influence interpretation of the Immigration Act. Justice L'Heureux-Dubé for the majority quoted Professor Ruth Sullivan: "[T]he legislature is presumed to respect the values and principles enshrined in international law, both customary and conventional. These constitute a part of the legal context in which legislation is enacted and read. In so far as possible, therefore, interpretations that reflect these values and principles are preferred." *Baker v. Canada*, 70. In *R. v. Hape*, 2007 SCC 26 the Supreme Court of Canada stated, "Every principle of customary international law is binding on all states unless superseded by another custom or by a rule set out in a international treaty.... These principles must also be drawn upon in [interpreting] the Charter." *R. v. Hape*, 46; and "In interpreting the scope of application of the Charter, the courts should seek to ensure compliance with Canada's binding obligations under international law where the express words are capable of supporting such a construction."

16 See UN General Assembly, *Permanent Forum on Indigenous Issues*, E/2000/22, UN General Assembly, 28 July 2000, accessed 9 October 2024, para. 2. https://www.un.org/esa/socdev/unpfii/documents/about-us/E-RES-2000-22.pdf: "Also decides that the Permanent Forum on Indigenous Issues shall serve as an advisory body to the Council with a mandate to discuss indigenous issues within the mandate of the Council relating to economic and social development, culture, the environment, education, health and human rights; in so doing the Permanent Forum shall: (a) Provide expert advice and recommendations on indigenous issues to the Council, as well as to programmes, funds and agencies of the United Nations, through the Council; (b) Raise awareness and promote the integration and coordination of activities relating to indigenous issues within the United Nations system."

17 Organization of American States, American Declaration on the Rights of Indigenous Peoples, Res. AG/doc.5537, adopted without vote by Organization of American States, General Assembly, 46th session, Santo Domingo, Dominican Republic, 15 June 2016, AG/RES. 2888 (XLVI-O/16).

18 Ibid.

19 Jody Wilson-Raybould, "Special Statement at the Opening Ceremonies of the United Nations Permanent Forum on Indigenous Issues, 15th Session," 9 May 2016, accessed 2 November 2024, https://www.canada.ca/en/department-justice/news/2016/05/special-statement-at-the-opening-ceremonies-of-the-united-nations-permanent-forum-on-indigenous-issues-15th-session.html.

20 Canada, United Nations Declaration on the Rights of Indigenous Peoples Act, S.C. 2021, c. 15.

21 United Nations Permanent Forum on Indigenous Issues, "Indigenous Languages: Preservation and Revitalization (Articles 13, 14 and 16 of the United Nations Declaration on the Rights of Indigenous Peoples)," Economic and Social Council, February 2016 (E/C.19/2016/10).

22 Ibid., para. 14.

23 Ibid., para. 22.

24 United Nations Permanent Forum on Indigenous Issues, "Report of the International Expert Group Meeting on Indigenous Languages," Economic and Social Council, 8 January 2008 (E/C.19/2008/3).

25 Ibid., para. 28.

26 United Nations Economic and Social Council, Permanent Forum on Indigenous Issues, 7th Sess., "Report of the International Expert group Meeting on Indigenous Languages," 21 January 2008 (E/C.19/2008/3), para. 44(d).

27 Ibid., para. 30.
28 Ibid., para. 42(a).
29 Ibid., para. 60.
30 Ibid., pars. 66, 67, 68, 69, and 75.
31 Expert Mechanism on the Rights of Indigenous Peoples, "Role of Language and Culture in the Promotion and Protection of the Rights and Identity of Indigenous Peoples," Human Rights Council, 16 August 2012, A/HRC/21/53.
32 See Ibid., Summary.
33 Expert Mechanism on the Rights of Indigenous Peoples, "Role of Language and Culture in the Promotion and Protection of the Rights and Identity of Indigenous Peoples," Human Rights Council, 16 August 2012, A/HRC/21/53.
34 Ibid., para 7.
35 Permanent Forum on Indigenous Issues, "Indigenous Languages: Preservation and Revitalization," para. 42.
36 Ibid., para. 58.
37 Ibid., para. 60.
38 United Nations Economic and Social Council, Permanent Forum on Indigenous Issues, 7th Session, "Report of the International Expert Group Meeting on Indigenous Languages," 21 January 2008 (E/C.19/2008/3).
39 United Nations Economic and Social Council, Permanent Forum on Indigenous Issues, "Report on the Seventh Session," 21 April–2 May 2008 (E/20080/43 E/C.19/2008/13), para. 96.
40 United Nations Economic and Social Council, Permanent Forum on Indigenous Issues, 7th Sess., "Report of the International Expert Group Meeting on Indigenous Languages," 21 January 2008 (E/C.19/2008/3).
41 United Nations Permanent Forum on Indigenous Issues, "Report of the International Expert Group Meeting on Indigenous Languages," Economic and Social Council, 8 January 2008 (E/C.19/2008/).
42 "Launch of International Year of Indigenous Languages 2019," UNESCO, 25 January 2019, last modified 20 April 2023, https://www.unesco.org/en/articles/launch-international-year-indigenous-languages-2019.
43 Irmgarda Kasinskaite-Buddeberg, Knowledge Societies Division, Communication and Information Sector, UNESCO, 17th Session of the United Nations Permanent Forum on Indigenous Issues, 16 April 2018, https://papersmart.unmeetings.org/media2/18558956/unesco.pdf.
44 Larisa Warhol, "Native American Language Education as Policy-in-Practice: An Interpretative Policy Analysis of the Native American Languages Act of 1990/1992," *International Journal of Bilingual Education and Bilingualism* 14, no. 3 (2011); Larisa Warhol, "Legacies of NALA: The Esther Martinez Native American Languages Preservation Act and Implications for Language Revitalization Policy and Practice," *Journal of American Indian Education* 51, no. 3 (2012), http://www.jstor.org/stable/43608638; Nāmaka Rawlins, William Pila Wilson, and Keiki Kawaiʻaeʻa, "Bill Demmert, Native American Language Revitalization, and His Hawai'i Connection," *Journal of American Indian Education* 50, no. 1 (2011), http://www.jstor.org/stable/43608603; Dorothy Aguilera and Margaret D. LeCompte, "Resiliency in Native Languages: The Tale of Three Indigenous Communities' Experiences with Language Immersion," *Journal of American Indian Education* 46, no. 3 (2007), http://www.jstor.org/stable/24398541; Jeston Morris, "Native American Languages

Summit 2014: Self-Determination as a Strategy for Language Revitalization and Maintenance," *Journal of American Indian Education* 54, no. 3 (2015), http://www.jstor.org/stable/10.5749/jamerindieduc.54.3.0125; Teresa Winstead, Adrea Lawrence, Edward J. Brantmeier, and Christopher J. Frey, "Language, Sovereignty, Cultural Contestation, and American Indian Schools: No Child Left Behind and a Navajo Test Case," *Journal of American Indian Education* 47, no. 1 (2008), http://www.jstor.org/stable/24398505; "Public Law 101-477: Native American Languages Act," *Journal of American Indian Education* 51, no. 3 (2012), http://www.jstor.org/stable/43608633; "Public Law 102-524: Native American Languages Act of 1992," *Journal of American Indian Education* 51, no. 3 (2012), http://www.jstor.org/stable/43608634.

45 Public Law 104 104 STAT. 1152 P.L. 101-477 (30 October 1990).

46 *Hearing Before the Committee on Indian Affairs on S. 575 to Amend the Native American Languages Act to Provide for the Support of Native American Language Survival Schools, United States Senate,* 108th Cong. 1st sess., 24 (2003).

47 Ibid., 25.

48 Ibid., 26.

49 Ibid., 27.

50 Ibid., 28.

51 Ibid.

52 Ibid., 31.

53 Ibid., 38. Unconventional spellings in this and the following extract reflect the original source.

54 Ibid., 45. Unconventional spellings in this and the following extract reflect the original source.

55 Ibid., 37.

56 Ibid., 43.

57 Ibid., 44.

58 Ibid., 37.

59 Ibid., 48.

60 Romain Chuffart, "Speaking of Rights: Indigenous Linguistic Rights in the Arctic," *Yearbook of Polar Law* 9 (2017): 7.

61 Hanna Helander, Pigga Keskitalo, and Tuija Turunen, "Saami Language Online Education Outside the Saami Homeland—New Pathways to Social Justice," in *Finland's Famous Education System*, ed. Martin Thrupp, Piia Seppänen, Jaakko Kauko, and Sonja Kosunen (Singapore: Springer, 2023), 304.

62 Ari Pál Kristinsson and Amanda Hilmarsson-Dunn, "Unequal Language Rights in the Nordic Language Community," *Language Problems and Language Planning* 36, no. 3 (2012); Otso Kortekangas, *Language, Citizenship, and Sámi Education in the Nordic North, 1900–1940* (Montreal and Kingston: McGill-Queen's University Press, 2021); Helander, Keskitalo, and Turunen, "Saami Language Online Education Outside the Saami Homeland"; Marja-Liisa Olthuis, Suvi Kivelä, and Tove Skutnabb-Kangas, *Revitalising Indigenous Languages: How to Recreate a Lost Generation* (Bristol: Multilingual Matters, 2013); Tanja Joona, "Safeguarding Cultural Rights of Sami Children and Youth in Finland, with Special Emphasis on the Linguistic Part of Cultural Identity: Current Challenges," *Yearbook of Polar Law* 9 (2017); Susan D. Penfield and Ari Sherris, eds. *Rejecting the*

Marginalized Status of Minority Languages: Educational Projects Pushing Back Against Language Endangerment (Blue Ridge Summit, PA: Multilingual Matters, 2019); David Kroik, "Language Teacher Identity and Language Acquisition in a South Saami Preschool: A Narrative Inquiry," *Australian Journal of Indigenous Education* 51, no. 2 (2022).

63 Helander, Keskitalo, and Turunen, "Saami Language Online Education Outside the Saami Homeland"; Finnish Sámi Parliament, "Land Rights, Linguistic Rights, and Cultural Autonomy for the Finnish Sami People," *Indigenous Affairs* 33 no. 4 (July–December 1997); Ulla Aikio-Puoskari, *The Education of the Sámi in the Comprehensive Schooling of Three Nordic Countries: Norway, Finland and Sweden* (Resource Centre for the Rights of Indigenous Peoples, 2005).

64 David Corson, "Norway's 'Sámi Language Act': Emancipatory Implications for the World's Aboriginal Peoples," *Language in Society* 24, no. 4 (1995); Asta Balto and Jon Todal, "Saami Bilingual Education in Norway," in *Encyclopedia of Language and Education*, vol. 5, *Bilingual Education*, ed. Jim Cummins and David Corson (Dordrecht: Kluwer Academic, 1997).

65 Finland in 1973, Norway in 1987, and Sweden in 1992.

66 Olthuis, Kivelä, and Skutnabb-Kangas, *Revitalising Indigenous Languages*.

67 Torvald Falch, Per Selle, and Kristin Strømsnes, "The Sámi: 25 Years of Indigenous Authority in Norway," *Ethnopolitics* 15, no. 1 (2016).

68 Norway, Act of 17 July 1998 no. 61 relating to Primary and Secondary Education and Training (the Education Act), https://www.regjeringen.no/contentassets/b3b9e92cce6742c39581b661a019e504/education-act-norway-with-amendments-entered-2014-2.pdf.

69 Ibid.

70 Joona, "Safeguarding Cultural Rights of Sami Children and Youth," 120.

71 Chuffart, "Speaking of Rights," 11.

72 Joona, "Safeguarding Cultural Rights of Sami Children and Youth," 118.

73 Ibid., 113.

74 Helander, Keskitalo, and Turunen, "Saami Language Online Education Outside the Saami Homeland," 304.

75 Ibid., 305.

76 Joona, "Safeguarding Cultural Rights of Sami Children and Youth," 118.

77 Anika Lloyd-Smith, Fabian Bergmann, Laura Hund, and Tanja Kupisch, "Can Policies Improve Language Vitality? The Sámi Languages in Sweden and Norway," *Frontiers in Psychology* 14 (2023): 4.

78 Eva Josefsen, *The Saami and the National Parliaments: Channels for Political Influence* (Mexico: Inter-Parliamentary Union and United Nations Development Programme, 2010).

79 Birger Winsa, "Language Planning in Sweden," *Journal of Multilingual and Multicultural Development* 20, no. 4–5 (1999).

80 Anika Lloyd–Smith, Fabian Bergmann, Laura Hund, and Tanja Kupisch, "Can Policies Improve Language Vitality? The Sámi Languages in Sweden and Norway," *Frontiers in Psychology* 14 (2023): 6.

81 Chuffart, "Speaking of Rights"; Ayo Næsborg-Andersen and Bassah Khalaf, "The Right of Indigenous Peoples to Education in Their Own Language—Greenlanders in Denmark and in Greenland," *Yearbook of Polar Law* 9, no. 1 (2018).

82 The Greenland Home Rule Act No. 577 of 29 November 1978.

83 Lars S. Vikor, *The Nordic Languages: Their Status and Interrelations* (Oslo: Novus Press, 1993), 110.

84 Tiina Saaresranta, "Education in Pursuit of the Development Dream? Effects of Schooling on Indigenous Development and Rights in Bolivia," *Nordic Journal of Human Rights* 32, no. 4 (2014); Sonia Comboni Salinas and José M. Juárez Núñez, "Education, Culture and Indigenous Rights: The Case of Educational Reform in Bolivia," *Prospects (Paris)* 30, no. 1 (2000); Rosaleen Howard, "Education Reform, Indigenous Politics, and Decolonisation in the Bolivia of Evo Morales," *International Journal of Educational Development* 29, no. 6 (2009).

85 Comboni Salinas and Juárez Núñez, "Education, Culture and Indigenous Rights," 110.

86 Bolivia, *Constitution of the Plurinational State of Bolivia*, translated by Max Planck Institute (Oxford: Oxford University Press, 2017), 5.I.

87 Ibid., 5.II.

88 Comboni Salinas and Juárez Núñez, "Education, Culture and Indigenous Rights," 108.

89 Saaresranta, "Education in Pursuit of the Development Dream?" 360.

90 Ibid.

91 Ibid., 371.

92 Ibid., 363.

93 Ibid.

94 Ibid., 364.

95 Ibid., 363.

96 Paul Moon, *Ka Ngaro Te Reo: Māori Language under Siege in the Nineteenth Century* (Dunedin: Otago University Press, 2016); Winifred Bauer, "Is the Health of Te Reo Māori Improving?," *Reo, Te* 51 (2008): 33–73; Donna Starks, Ray Harlow, and Allan Bell, "Who Speaks What Language in New Zealand," *Languages of New Zealand* (2005): 13–29; Rawinia Higgins, Poia Rewi, and Vincent Olsen-Reeder, eds., *The Value of the Māori Language: Te Hua o te Reo Māori* (Wellington: Huia Publishers, 2014).

97 Linda Johnson, "Maori Activism Across Borders 1950s–1980s" (PhD diss., Massey University, 2015), 154.

98 Waitangi Tribunal, "Report of the Waitangi Tribunal on the te reo Maori claim (Wai11)," Waitangi Tribunal Department of Justice, Wellington, New Zealand, 1986. (1986); Rodolfo Stavenhagen, "Taonga, Rights and Interests: Some Observations on the Framework of Protections for Māori Language," *Victoria University of Wellington Law Review* 42, no. 2 (2001).

99 *Māori Language Act*, 1987 (1987 No 176) (NZ). In contrast, the Māori Language Act 2016 gives Māori language recognition in circumstances beyond official ceremonies, but it does not clearly specify the extent of Māori language rights in New Zealand. In courts of law, commissions of inquiry, and tribunals, it confers the right to speak Māori to any member of the court, any party, witness, or counsel. It establishes Te Taura Whiri i te Reo Māori (Māori Language Commission). See *Te Ture mō Te Reo Māori 2016 Māori Language Act 2016* (2016 No 17) (NZ).

100 Rawinia Higgins, Poia Rewi, and Vincent Olsen-Reeder, eds., *The Value of the Māori Language: Te Hua o te Reo Māori* (Wellington, NZ: Huia Publishers, 2014).

101 *Te Heuheu Tukino v. Aotea District Maori Land Board* [1941] 2 NZLR 188, 210.

102 Katharina Ruckstuhl, "Public Policy and Indigenous Language Rights: Aotearoa New Zealand's Māori Language Act 2016," *Current Issues in Language Planning* 19, no. 3 (2018): 316–29.

103 *Māori Language Act* 2016, s.6 (2) and 5.

104 Julia De Bres, "The Hierarchy of Minority Languages in New Zealand," *Journal of Multilingual Development* 36, no. 7 (2015).

105 Mere Skerrett and Jenny Ritchie, "Te Rangatiratanga o Te Reo: Sovereignty in Indigenous Languages in Early Childhood Education in Aotearoa," *Kōtuitui* 16, no. 2 (2021); Roger Boshier, "Learning from the Moa: The Challenge of Māori Language Revitalization in Aotearoa/New Zealand," in *Indigenous Education*, ed. W. James Jacob, Sheng Yao Cheng, and Maureen K. Porter (Dordrecht: Springer, 2015), https://link.springer.com/book/10.1007/978-94-017-9355-1; Arohia Durie, "Emancipatory Maori Education: Speaking from the Heart," *Language, Culture, and Curriculum* 11, no. 3 (1998); Katharina Ruckstuhl, "Public Policy and Indigenous Language Rights: Aotearoa New Zealand's Māori Language Act 2016," *Current Issues in Language Planning* 19, no. 3 (2018); Richard A. Benton, "Perfecting the Partnership: Revitalising the Māori Language in New Zealand Education and Society 1987–2014," *Language, Culture, and Curriculum* 28, no. 2 (2015).

106 S. James Anaya, *Indigenous Peoples in International Law* (New York: Oxford University Press, 2004).

107 Fernand de Varennes, *Language Minorities and Human Rights* (The Hague: Martinus Nijhoff, 1996), 269. See also John P. McEvoy, "Language Rights: Aboriginal Peoples (New Brunswick, Canada)," *Canadian Law Libraries* 22, no. 4 (1997): 156; Rodolfo Stavenhagen, "Linguistic Minorities and Language Policy in Latin America: The Case of Mexico," in *Linguistic Minorities and Literacy: Language Policy Issue in Developing Countries*, ed. Florian Coulmas (Berlin: De Gruyter Mouton), 60–61; and de Varennes, *Language Minorities and Human Rights*, 257: "Mexico was the scene of serious discussions during the 1950's suggesting that it was inappropriate to teach in Spanish in an environment where the mother tongue was an Indigenous language. By the (mid) 1960's . . . literacy . . . in the native language and teaching Spanish as a second language became the official policy of the Mexican government. In the 1970's, a growing demand appeared for the whole educational programme in larger indigenous communities to be truly bilingual and bicultural."

Chapter 5. Indigenous Languages Act

1 Bill S-212, An Act for the Advancement of the Aboriginal Languages of Canada and to Recognize and Respect Aboriginal Language Rights, First Session, Forty-second Parliament, 64 Elizabeth II, 2015, Senate of Canada, First Reading, 9 December 2015.

2 Bill C-91, An Act Respecting Indigenous Languages, First Session, Forty-second Parliament, 64-65-66-67 Elizabeth II, 2015-2016-2017-2018-2019.

3 Indigenous Languages Act (S.C. 2019, c. 23).

4 Debates of the Senate, 1st Session, 42nd Parliament, Volume 150, Number 37, Official Report (Hansard), Tuesday, 17 May 2016, 1441.

5 Standing Committee on Procedure and House Affairs, *Evidence*, Number 95, 1st Session, 42nd Parliament, Tuesday, 27 March 2018, 1119.

6 Debates of the Senate, 1st Session, 42nd Parliament, Volume 150, Number 37, Official Report (Hansard), Tuesday, 17 May 2016, 1440.

7 Standing Committee on Procedure and House Affairs, *Evidence*, Number 95, 1st Session, 42nd Parliament, Tuesday, 27 March 2018, 1235.

8 Ibid.

9 Ibid., 1211.

10 1st Session, 42nd Parliament, Volume 150, Issue 73, 1550.

11 Standing Committee on Procedure and House Affairs, *Evidence*, Number 95, 1st Session, 42nd Parliament, Tuesday, 27 March 2018, 1211.

12 Ibid., 1215.

13 Debates of the Senate, 1st Session, 42nd Parliament, Volume 150, Number 73, Official Report (Hansard), Thursday, 17 November 2016, 1530.

14 Ibid., 1530.

15 Ibid., 1450.

16 Ibid., 1520.

17 Prime Minister Justin Trudeau, Mandate Letter to Department of Canadian Heritage, 12 November 2015.

18 Prime Minister Justin Trudeau, Speech to the Assembly of First Nations Special Chiefs Assembly, 6 December 2016, Gatineau, Quebec, https://www.pm.gc.ca/en/news/speeches/2016/12/06/prime-minister-justin-trudeaus-speech-assembly-first-nations-special.

19 Ibid.

20 Ibid.

21 *The Glendon Truth and Reconciliation Declaration on Indigenous Language Policy* (October 2016), 4, www. glendon.yorku.ca/crlcc/wp-content/uploads/sites/106/Glendon-declaration-Final-Draft-Oct-2016-public.pdf.

22 The report was circulated across Canada and an official launch of Glendon Declaration was held in November 2016.

23 First Peoples' Cultural Council, *Indigenous Languages Recognition, Preservation and Revitalization: A Report on the National Dialogue Session on Indigenous Languages*, prepared by Valerie Galley, Suzanne Gessner, Tracey Herbert, Karihwakeron Tim Thompson, and Lorna Wanosts'a7 Williams (Brentwood Bay: First Peoples' Cultural Council, 30 September 2016), 5–6. The report focused on four areas: language rights, legislation, and policy; community-based revitalization; education; and urban strategies. It was submitted to the Department of Canadian Heritage and to the Assembly of First Nations.

24 Canadian Heritage, "Important Step Taken Toward Co-Development of Indigenous Languages Legislation in Meeting between Government of Canada, Métis, Inuit and First Nations Leaders," Government of Canada, 15 June 2017, accessed 21 January 2023, https://www.newswire.ca/news-releases/important-step-taken-toward-co-development-of-indigenous-languages-legislation-in-meeting-between-government-of-canada-metis-inuit-and-first-nations-leaders-628682473.html.

25 Ibid.

26 Assembly of First Nations, Special Chiefs Assembly, *Co-developing an Indigenous Languages Act*, 4–6 December 2018, https://www.afn.ca/uploads/sca-2018/Documents/Dialogue%20Sessions/Day%201%20-%20December%204%2C%202018/01%20Languages/01%29%20Languages%20Powerpoint.pdf.

27 Canadian Heritage, "Important Step Taken," accessed 13 May 2018, https://www.canada.ca/en/canadian-heritage/news/2017/06/important_step_takentowardco-

developmentofindigenouslanguagesleg.html: "Today marks another step in the right direction in building the nation-to-nation relationship between Canada and the Métis Nation, and demonstrates that this government is serious about its partnerships with Indigenous Peoples. Notwithstanding that Métis residential schools are excluded from the federal government's settlement and apology to former Indian residential school students, the mandate of the TRC and its Calls to Action, we will engage fully in this legislative initiative which promises to have a significant impact on a true and lasting reconciliation between Canada and the Métis Nation once our outstanding issues are resolved."

28 Ibid.: "Inuit are pleased today to formally begin the distinctions-based process of co-developing First Nations, Inuit, and Métis languages legislation in partnership with the federal government. In the coming months, ITK will lead targeted engagement in Inuit Nunangat in order to gather input about desired content for federal legislation. Inuit insist that legislation be transformative and help facilitate Inuktut revitalization, maintenance, and promotion in our communities such that it is spoken in every sector of Inuit society."

29 Ibid.: "Revitalizing First Nations languages is a vital part of self-determination. Language is culture and central to our songs, stories, and ceremonies. The recognition, promotion, and recovery of First Nations languages—the original languages of these lands—will not only strengthen our Nations but enrich the whole country. We look forward to the First Nation engagement process supporting First Nations jurisdiction, and will ensure language rights are recognized as inherent rights. This vital work will be a lasting legacy for our children."

30 Canadian Heritage, *What We Heard Report: Consultations on the Implementation of the* Indigenous Languages Act, *Consultations on the Office of the Commissioner of Indigenous Languages and the Indigenous Languages Funding Model*, accessed 21 January 2023, https://www.canada.ca/en/canadian-heritage/campaigns/what-we-heard-ila.html.

31 Government of Canada, "Early Engagement Sessions: Indigenous Languages Legislation 2017–2018: Summary of Findings" (2018), 4.

32 Ibid., 5–6.

33 Ibid., 7.

34 Assembly of First Nations Engagement Sessions, Indigenous Languages Initiative, *National Engagement Sessions Report*, 5 December 2017, 3, https://www.afn.ca/wp-content/uploads/2018/04/17-12-12_Languages_AFN-ILI-Report_FINAL.pdf.

35 Joshua A. Fishman, *Reversing Language Shift: Theoretical and Empirical Foundations of Assistance to Threatened Languages* (Clevedon, UK: Multilingual Matters, 1991); Naa Huiying Lee and John Van Way, "Assessing Levels of Endangerment in the Catalogue of Endangered Languages (ELCat) Using the Language Endangerment Index (LEI)," *Language in Society* 45 (2016), doi:10.1017/S0047404515000962; Suzanne Romaine, "Language Endangerment and Language Death," in *The Routledge Handbook of Ecolinguistics*, eds. Alwin F. Fill and Hermine Penz (London: Routledge, 2017), https://www.routledgehandbooks.com/doi/10.4324/9781315687391.ch3 (accessed 26 December 2023); UNESCO Ad Hoc Expert Group on Endangered Languages, *Language Vitality and Endangerment*, adopted by the International Expert Meeting on UNESCO Programme Safeguarding of Endangered Languages (Paris, 10–12 March 2003), https://ich.unesco.org/doc/src/00120-EN.pdf (accessed 26 December 2023); Canadian Heritage and Indian and Northern Affairs Canada, *Comprehensive Review of Federal*

Programming for Aboriginal Languages and Cultures: Final Report (May 2006, CH4-98/2005E-PDF 0-662-41412-8), 12–13.

36 Chiefs of Ontario. Brief submitted to the House of Commons Standing Committee on Canadian Heritage, 42nd Parliament, 1st Session, 27 March 2019.

37 Indigenous Languages Act (S.C. 2019, c. 23).

38 *R v. Beaulac*, [1999] 1 SCR 718 at para. 20.

39 Assembly of First Nations, National Chief Perry Bellegarde Presentation to the Standing Committee on Aboriginal Peoples, 42nd Parliament, 1st Session, 20 March 2019.

40 Ibid.

41 Canadian Bar Association, Aboriginal Law Section, Brief submitted by Gaylene Schellenberg to the Senate Standing Committee on Aboriginal Peoples, Bill C-91 Indigenous Languages Act, 42nd Parliament, 1st Session, 31 May 2019.

42 Ellen Gabriel, Kontinónhstats—The Mohawk Language Custodian Association from Kanehsatà:ke. Presentation to the Standing Committee on Aboriginal Peoples on Bill C-91, An Act Respecting Indigenous Languages. 42nd Parliament, 1st Session. 2 April 2019.

43 Robert Matthew, T'selcéwtqen Clleq'mel'ten/Chief Atahm School, Presentation to the Senate Standing Committee on Aboriginal Peoples on Bill C-91, An Act Respecting Indigenous Languages, 42nd Parliament, 1st Session, 3 April 2019.

44 Canadian Heritage, Evaluation Services Directorate, "Evaluation of the Aboriginal Languages Initiative 2009–10 to 2013–14," 8 June 2015.

45 Department of Finance Canada, "Building a Strong Middle Class," Budget 2017, 22 March 2017, 167.

46 Government of Canada, *Action Plan for Official Languages 2023–2028: Protection, Promotion, Collaboration* (Canadian Heritage, 2023), https://www.canada.ca/en/canadian-heritage/services/official-languages-bilingualism/official-languages-action-plan/2023-2028.html#.

47 Pablo Rodriguez, Minister of Canadian Heritage and Multiculturalism Proceedings of the Standing Senate Committee on Aboriginal Peoples, *Evidence*, Number 55, 42nd Parliament, 1st Session, 28 May 2019.

48 Ibid., 55:20.

49 Ibid., 55:22.

50 United Nations Declaration on the Rights of Indigenous Peoples (2007), article 14.

51 Truth and Reconciliation Commission of Canada, *Calls to Action* (Truth and Reconciliation Commission of Canada, 2012), Call 48: "We call upon the church parties to the Settlement Agreement, and all other faith groups and interfaith social justice groups in Canada who have not already done so, to formally adopt and comply with the principles, norms, and standards of the *United Nations Declaration on the Rights of Indigenous Peoples* as a framework for reconciliation. This would include, but not be limited to, the following commitments: i) Ensuring that their institutions, policies, programs, and practices comply with the *United Nations Declaration on the Rights of Indigenous Peoples.*"

52 One of the main purposes of the Indigenous Languages Act is identified in section 5(g): to "contribute to the implementation of the United Nations Declaration on the Rights of Indigenous Peoples as it relates to Indigenous languages."

53 United Nations Declaration on the Rights of Indigenous Peoples Act Implementation Secretariat, *United Nations Declaration on the Rights of Indigenous Peoples Act Action Plan* (Department of Justice Canada, 2023), https://www.justice.gc.ca/eng/declaration/ap-pa/index.html.

54 Ibid., 54. Action 19 states that the Government of Canada will "Support First Nations control of First Nation education and self-determined education approaches at many levels, including the conclusion of Regional Education Agreements, as sustainable models (underpinned by funding comparable to provincial education systems), to close the education gap, leading to better outcomes. Ensuring robust and responsive education systems paves the way for access to higher education opportunities, all of which foster more prosperous communities (Indigenous Services Canada)." Ibid., 53.

55 Report of the Standing Committee on Indigenous and Northern Affairs, *Reclaiming, Revitalizing, Maintaining and Strengthening Indigenous Languages in Canada*, 44th Parliament, 1st Session, 23 June 2023, 25–26. Also referenced Andrea Bear Nicholas, Lorena Fontaine, David Leitch, and Fernand de Varennes, *What Canada's New Indigenous Languages Law Needs to Say and Say Urgently*. The brief was presentd by Lorena Sekwan Fontaine to the Senate Standing Committee on Indigenous Peoples. 42nd Parliament, 1st Session, 23 April 2019.

56 Senator Murray Sinclair, Proceedings of the Standing Senate Committee on Aboriginal Peoples, *Evidence*, Number 55, 42nd Parliament, 1st Session, 28 May 2019.

57 Indigenous Languages Act, S.C. 2019, c. 23 (Canada).

58 Ibid., s 49.1. As soon as feasible after the third anniversary of the day on which this section comes into force and after each subsequent third anniversary, a review of this Act and of its administration and operation is to be commenced by a committee of the Senate, of the House of Commons or of both Houses of Parliament that may be designated or established for that purpose.

59 Ibid., s. 49. Within five years after the day on which this section comes into force and every five years after that, the Minister must cause to be conducted an independent review of this Act, of its administration and operation, of any agreements or arrangements made under section 9 and of the activities of the Office. The review must be conducted by a person or body appointed by the Minister in consultation with the Office.

60 Letter from the Minister of Canadian Heritage, Honourable Pascale St-Onge to Mr. John Aldag, Chair, Standing Committee on Indigenous and Northern Affairs, 15 October 2023, in response to the Standing Committee on Indigenous and Northern Affairs' Ninth Report of the 44th Parliament, 13 June 2023, 9.

61 Marja-Liisa Olthuis, Suvi Kivelä, and Tove Skutnabb-Kangas, *Revitalising Indigenous Languages: How to Recreate a Lost Generation* (Bristol: Multilingual Matters, 2013); Tove Skutnabb-Kangas and Robert Dunbar, *Indigenous Children's Education as Linguistic Genocide and a Crime Against Humanity? A Global View* (Guovdageaidnu/Kautokeino: Gáldu, Resource Centre for the Rights of Indigenous Peoples, 2010); Andrea Bear Nicholas, "Linguicide: Submersion Education and the Killing of Languages in Canada," *Briarpatch*, 1 March 2011; Andrea Bear Nicholas, "Canada's Colonial Mission: The Great White Bird," in *Aboriginal Education in Canada: A Study in Decolonization*, ed. K.P. Binda and Sharilyn Calliou (Mississauga, ON: Canadian Educators' Press, 2011).

62 Louise Harding, Ryan DeCaire, Ursula Ellis, Karleen Delaurier-Lyle, Julia Schillo, and Mark Turin. "Language Improves Health and Wellbeing in Indigenous Communities: A Scoping Review," *Language and Health* 3, no. 1 (2025): 100047.

63 Peter Austin, *Language Vitality in a Globalized World* (Oxford: Oxford University Press, 2021); Suzanne Romaine, "Language Endangerment and Language Death," in *The Routledge Handbook of Ecolinguistics*, ed. Alwin F. Fill and Hermine Penz (London: Routledge, 2017), 40–55; UNESCO Ad Hoc Expert Group on Endangered Languages, *Language Vitality and Endangerment*, adopted by the International Expert Meeting on UNESCO Programme Safeguarding of Endangered Languages, Paris, 10–12 March 2003; Marja-Liisa Olthuis, Suvi Kivelä, and Tove Skutnabb-Kangas, *Revitalising Indigenous Languages: How to Recreate a Lost Generation. Linguistic Diversity and Language Rights* (Bristol: Multilingual Matters, 2013).

64 National Collaborating Centre for Aboriginal Health, *Culture and Language as Social Determinants of First Nations, Inuit and Metis Health*, Social Determinants of Health (Prince George, BC: National Collaborating Centre for Aboriginal Health, 2016).

65 Onowa McIvor, Art Napoleon, and Kerissa M. Dickie, "Language and Culture as Protective Factors for At-risk Communities," *Journal of Aboriginal Health* 5, no. 1 (2009); Onowa McIvor, "Protective Effects of Language Learning, Use and Culture on the Health and Well-being of Indigenous People in Canada," Paper presented at 17th FEL Conference on Endangered Languages Beyond Boundaries, Ottawa, ON, 2–4 October 2013; Richard T. Oster, Angela Grier, Rick Lightning, Maria J. Mayan, and Ellen L. Toth, "Cultural Continuity, Traditional Indigenous Language, and Diabetes in Alberta First Nations: A Mixed Methods Study," *International Journal for Equity in Health* 13 (2014); Michael J. Chandler and Christopher E. Lalonde, "Cultural Continuity as a Hedge Against Suicide in Canada's First Nations," *Transcultural Psychiatry* 35 (1998); Michael J. Chandler and Christopher E. Lalonde, "Cultural Continuity as a Protective Factor Against Suicide in First Nations Youth," in "Aboriginal Youth, Hope or Heartbreak: Aboriginal Youth and Canada's Future," special issue, *Horizons* 10 (2008); Serafín M. Coronel-Molina and Teresa L. McCarty, eds., *Indigenous Language Revitalization in the Americas* (New York: Routledge, 2016); Joseph P. Gone, "Redressing First Nations Historical Trauma: Theorizing Mechanisms for Indigenous Culture as Mental Health Treatment," *Transcultural Psychiatry* 50 (2023); Noriko Aikawa, *Conference Handbook on Endangered Languages of the Pacific Rim*, UNESCO's Programme on Languages (Osaka: Endangered Languages of the Pacific Rim Project, 2001); Fishman, *Reversing Language Shift*; Hague Recommendations Regarding the Education Rights of National Minorities, *International Journal on Minority and Group Rights*, special issue on the Education Rights of National Minorities (Organization for Security and Co-operation in Europe, 1996), http://www.osce.org/hcnm/; Ken Hale, "On Endangered Languages and the Importance of Linguistic Diversity," in *Endangered Languages: Language Loss and Community Response*, ed. Lenore A. Grenoble and Lindsay J. Whaley (Cambridge: Cambridge University Press, 1998).

66 Debates of the Senate 1st Session, 42nd Parliament, vol. 150, no. 73, Official Report (Hansard), Thursday, 17 November 2016, 1520.

67 David Crystal, *Language Death* (Cambridge: Cambridge University Press, 2000); Joseph Dupris, "Maqlaqsyalank hemyeega: Goals and Expectations of Klamath-Modoc Revitalization," *Language Documentation and Conversation* 13 (2019); Ken Hale, Michael Krauss, Lucille J. Watahomigie, Akira Y. Yamamoto, Collette Craig, Laverne Masayesva Jeanne, and Nora C. England, "Endangered Languages," *Language* 68, no. 1 (1992); Leanne Hinton, Leena Huss, and Gerald Roche, eds., *The Routledge Handbook of Language Revitalization* (New York: Routledge, 2018); Teresa L. McCarty, "Indigenous Language Revitalization," in *Encyclopedia of Bilingual*

Education, ed. J.M. González (Los Angeles: Sage, 2008); Daniel Nettle, and Suzanne Romaine, *Vanishing Voices: The Extinction of the World's Languages* (Oxford: Oxford University Press, 2000); Tove Skutnabb-Kangas, "Language Rights and Revitalization," in *The Routledge Handbook of Language Revitalization,* ed. Leanne Hinton, Leena Huss, and Gerald Roche (New York: Routledge, 2018).

68 Nadine Charron, "Exploring the Links Between Aboriginal-language-medium Instruction and Academic Performance: A Literature Review in Support of the PCH Aboriginal Languages Initiative" (Canada Heritage: Aboriginal Affairs Branch, Policy and Research Directorate, 2010).

69 Teresa L. McCarty, Mary Eunice Romero, and Ofelia Zepeda, "Reclaiming the Gift: Indigenous Youth Counter-Narratives on Native Language Loss and Revitalization," *American Indian Quarterly* 30, no. 1/2 (2006): 28–48; Teresa L. McCarty, *Ethnography and Language Policy* (New York, NY: Routledge, 2011).

70 UNESCO Ad Hoc Expert Group on Endangered Languages. *Language Vitality and Endangerment.* Adopted by the International Expert Meeting on UNESCO Programme Safeguarding of Endangered Languages, Paris, 10–12 March 2003.

71 Ibid.; Stéphanie Langlois and Annie Turner, *Aboriginal Languages and Selected Vitality Indicators in 2011* (Ottawa: Statistics Canada, 2014).

72 Fishman, *Reversing Language Shift*; Stéphanie Langlois and Annie Turner, *Aboriginal Languages and Selected Vitality Indicators in 2011* (Ottawa: Statistics Canada, 2014); Lee and Van Way, "Assessing Levels of Endangerment in the Catalogue of Endangered Languages (ELCat)"; Mary Jane Norris, "Aboriginal Languages in Canada: Trends and Perspectives on Maintenance and Revitalization," *Aboriginal Policy Research Consortium International (APRCi)* 122 (2006): 197–226; Mary Jane Norris, "Canada's Aboriginal Languages," *Canadian Social Trends* 51 (1998); Romaine, "Language Endangerment and Language Death"; UNESCO Ad Hoc Expert Group on Endangered Languages, *Language Vitality and Endangerment.*

73 Ibid., 428.

74 Leanne Hinton, Leena Huss, and Gerald Roche, "What Works in Language Revitalization," in *The Routledge Handbook of Language Revitalization*, ed. Leanne Hinton, Leena Huss, and Gerald Roche (New York, NY: Routledge, 2018), 495.

75 A. Seegerts, *The Gift of Language and Culture: Documenting the Success of the Onion Lake Cree Immersion Program and the Need for Ongoing Development, Expansion, and Committed Funding Resources* (Regina: Federation of Saskatchewan Indian Nations, 2002); Nadine Charron, "Exploring the Links Between Aboriginal Language-Medium Instruction and Academic Performance: A Literature Review in Support of the PCH Aboriginal Languages Initiatives," (unpublished policy paper for the Aboriginal Affairs Branch, Policy and Research, October 2010); Esther Usborne, Josephine Peck, Donna-Lee Smith, and Donald M. Taylor, "Learning Through an Aboriginal Language: The Impact on Students' English and Aboriginal Languages Skills," *Canadian Journal of Education* 34, no. 4 (2011); Jessica Murray, Erin Aupanekis, and Karen Rempel, "Cree Language Survey Results Opaskwayak Cree Nation" (The Pas: Opaskwayak Educational Authority, 2013).

76 Murray, Aupanekis, and Rempel, "Cree Language Survey Results Opaskwayak Cree Nation."

77 Louellyn White, *Free to Be Mohawk: Indigenous Education at the Akwesasne Freedom School* (Norman: University of Oklahoma Press, 2015).

78 Usborne, Peck, Smith, and Taylor, "Learning Through an Aboriginal Language."

79 The general purpose of section 23 of the Charter is clear: it is to preserve and promote the two official languages of Canada and the cultures represented by those languages, by ensuring that each language flourishes, as far as possible, in provinces where it is not spoken by the majority (*Mahe v. Alberta*, [1990] 1 S.C.R. 342) at para. 31). Section 23 means more than teachers who provide instruction in French to students who receive it in that language, and that educational institutions can objectively be considered as those of the linguistic minority (*Re Education Act of Ontario* (*Re Education Act of Ontario and Minority Language Education Rights*, 10 D.L.R. (4th) 491, (C.A. On.)) at paragraph 107).

Section 23 also seeks to preserve and promote the minority, by granting minority language educational rights to minority language parents throughout Canada. The guarantee cannot be separated from a concern for the culture associated with the language. Language is more than a mere means of communication, it is part and parcel of the identity and culture of the people speaking it (*Mahe v. Alberta* at paragraph 31). The right to minority language education in section 23 is designed to enhance our country's bilingualism and biculturalism, and maintain the unique partnership between language groups that sets our country apart among nations (*CSF de la C-B* (*Conseil scolaire francophone de la Colombie-Britannique) v. British Columbia*, 2016 BCSC 1764) at paragraph 123). Section 23(1)(b) and section 23(2) of the Charter have the same purpose and must be interpreted in the same way.

Section 23(2) has another specific purpose: to provide continuity minority language education rights, to ensure family unity, and to accommodate mobility (*Solski* (*Solski (Tutor of) v. Quebec (Attorney General)*, [2005] 1 S.C.R. 201) at paragraph 2).

80 Section 23 stipulates as a minimum a right to primary and secondary *instruction* in the minority language (paragraph 23(3)(a)). In addressing pedagogical requirements specifically, it is important to consider the value of linguistic minority education as part of the determination of the services appropriate for the number of students. The pedagogical requirements established to address the needs of the majority language students cannot be used to trump cultural and linguistic concerns appropriate for the minority language students (*Arsenault-Cameron v. Prince Edward Island,* [2000] *1 S.C.R. 3* at paragraph 38).

81 In *R v. Beaulac*, [1999] 1 SCR 768, Justice Bastarache reviews the Supreme Court's case law and observes, at para. 17, that "the new language cases are significant because they re-affirm the importance of language rights as supporting official language communities and their culture." In particular, he states, at para. 19: "Another reference, with regard to education this time, *Reference re Public Schools Act (Man.), s. 79(3), (4) and (7)*, [1993] 1 S.C.R. 839, reinforced the cultural purpose of language guarantees." At p. 850, the Court said: "Several interpretative guidelines are endorsed in *Mahe* for the purposes of defining s. 23 rights. Firstly, courts should take a purposive approach to interpreting the rights. Therefore, in accordance with the purpose of the right as defined in *Mahe*, the answers to the questions should ideally be guided by that which will most effectively encourage the flourishing and preservation of the French-language minority in the province. Secondly, the right should be construed remedially, in recognition of previous injustices that have gone unredressed and which have required the entrenchment of protection for minority language rights." These pronouncements are a reflection of the fact that there is no contradiction between protecting individual liberty and personal dignity and the wider objective of recognizing the rights of official language communities. The objective of protecting official language minorities, as set out in s. 2 of the Official

Languages Act, is realized by the possibility for all members of the minority to exercise independent, individual rights which are justified by the existence of the community.

"Language rights are not negative rights, or passive rights; they can only be enjoyed if the means are provided. This is consistent with the notion favoured in the area of international law that the freedom to choose is meaningless in the absence of a duty of the State to take positive steps to implement language guarantees." See J.E. Oestreich, "Liberal Theory and Minority Group Rights," *Human Rights Quarterly* 21 (1999): 112; Peter Jones, "Human Rights, Group Rights, and Peoples' Rights," *Human Rights Quarterly* 21 (1999): 83: "[A] right . . . is conceptually tied to a duty"; and R. Cholewinski, "State Duty Towards Ethnic Minorities: Positive or Negative?" *Human Rights Quaterly* 10 (1988): 344. He concludes, at para. 25, by holding that "Language rights must *in all cases* be interpreted purposively, in a manner consistent with the preservation and development of official language communities in Canada" (my emphasis).

The idea of positive obligations was also enshrined in 2005 in Part VII of the Official Languages Act, which states (see particularly s. 41(2)): "The Government of Canada is committed to (a) enhancing the vitality of the English and French linguistic minority communities in Canada and supporting and assisting their development; and (b) fostering the full recognition and use of both English and French in Canadian society."

Additionally, s. 41(5) states that "Every federal institution has the duty to ensure that positive measures are taken for the implementation of the commitments under subsection (1) to (3)" and at s 45.1(2) "For greater certainty, this implementation shall be carried out while respecting the jurisdiction and powers of the provinces and territories." Provinces have a positive duty to ensure that minority language educational facilities are provided out of public funds where the numbers so warrant. Those rights temper the Province's broad, plenary jurisdiction over education (*CSF de la C-B* at paragraph 373). The financial impact of the provision of specific facilities will vary from region to region. It follows that assessment of what will constitute appropriate facilities should only be undertaken on the basis of a distinct geographical unit within the province (*Reference re Public Schools Act (Man.)* at paragraph 29). Both a textual and purposive analysis of section 23(3) of the Charter indicate that instruction should take place in facilities located in the community where those children reside.

82 Section 23 of the Charter is also remedial in nature. History reveals that section 23 was designed to correct, on a national scale, the progressive erosion of minority official language groups and to give effect to the concept of the "equal partnership" of the two official language groups in the context of education and to actively encourage both languages to flourish (*Mahe v. Alberta* at paragraph 35; *Reference re Public Schools Act (Man.)* (*Reference re Public Schools Act (Man.)*, [1993] 1 S.C.R. 839) at page 79; *Arsenault-Cameron* (*Arsenault-Cameron v. Prince Edward Island*, [2000] 1 S.C.R. 3) at paragraphs 26–27; *Doucet-Boudreau* (*Doucet-Boudreau v. Nova Scotia (Minister of Education)*, [2003] 3 S.C.R. 3) at paragraph 28).

Section 23 guarantees the right to minority language education as a tool for combating assimilation. Schools must be built and have a duty to attempt to fight assimilation, even if they only exist to serve those students until they grow older, start their own homes and assimilate (*CSF de la C-B*, at paragraph 343). Section 23 requires prompt action to prevent assimilation and ensure that generations of rights holders do not lose their rights (*CSF de la C-B*, at paragraphs 419 and 6841).

83 Any broad guarantee of language rights, especially in the context of education, cannot be separated from a concern for the culture associated with the language. Minority schools themselves provide community centres where the vitality and preservation of minority language culture can occur. They provide needed locations where the minority community can meet and facilities which they can use to express their culture (*Mahe v. Alberta* at paragraph 33; *Solski (Solski (Tutor of) v. Quebec (Attorney General)* at paragraph 3). The school is the single most important institution for the survival of the official language community, which is itself a true beneficiary under Section 23 of the Charter (*Arsenault-Cameron v. Prince Edward Island* at paragraph 29; (*CSF de la C-B* 2016 at paragraph 367). Minority language schools provide a foundation for other institutions and community leadership, counterbalancing the influence of the majority language (*CSF de la C-B* 2016 at paragraph 368). They also serve as a primary site for socializing children into the French language and culture, and play an essential role ensuring children experience additive, rather than subtractive, bilingualism (*CSF de la C-B* 2016 at paragraph 368).

84 Minority language rights are recognized when there is a sufficient number of people within a region who need and will benefit from English or French language education.

85 *Mahe v. Alberta* at para. 369–80. In my view, it is essential, in order to further this purpose, that, where the numbers warrant, minority language parents possess a measure of management and control over the educational facilities in which their children are taught. Such management and control is vital to ensure that their language and culture flourish. It is necessary because a variety of management issues in education, e.g., curricula, hiring, expenditures, can affect linguistic and cultural concerns. I think it incontrovertible that the health and survival of the minority language and culture can be affected in subtle but important ways by decisions relating to these issues. To give but one example, most decisions pertaining to curricula clearly have an influence on the language and culture of the minority students.

Furthermore, as the historical context in which s. 23 was enacted suggests, minority language groups cannot always rely upon the majority to take account of all of their linguistic and cultural concerns. Such neglect is not necessarily intentional: the majority cannot be expected to understand and appreciate all of the diverse ways in which educational practices may influence the language and culture of the minority. In commenting on various setbacks experienced by the francophone minority in Ontario, the Court of Appeal of that province noted that "[l]ack of meaningful participation in management and control of local school boards by the Francophone minority made these events possible" (*Reference Re Education Act of Ontario*, *supra*, at p. 531). A similar observation was made by the Prince Edward Island Court of Appeal in *Reference Re Minority Language Educational Rights (P.E.I.)*, *supra*, at p. 259: "It would be foolhardy to assume that Parliament intended to . . . leave the sole control of the program development and delivery with the English majority. If such were the case, a majority language group could soon wreak havoc upon the rights of the minority and could soon render such a right worthless." I agree with the sentiments expressed in these statements. If section 23 is to remedy past injustices and ensure that they are not repeated in the future, it is important that minority language groups have a measure of control over the minority language facilities and instruction.

86 *Reference Re Secession of Quebec* [1998] 2 *S.C.R.* 217, para. 82. Consistent with this long tradition of respect for minorities, which is at least as old as Canada itself, the framers of the Constitution Act, 1982, included in s. 35 explicit protection for existing aboriginal and treaty rights. . . . The "promise" of s. 35, as it was termed in *R. v. Sparrow*, [1990] 1 S.C.R. 1075, at p. 1083, recognized not only the ancient occupation of land by aboriginal peoples, but their contribution to the building of Canada, and the special commitments made to them by successive governments. The protection of these rights, so recently and arduously achieved, whether looked at in their own right or as part of the larger concern with minorities, reflects an important underlying constitutional value.

87 Truth and Reconciliation Commission of Canada, *Honouring the Truth, Reconciling for the Future: Summary of the Final Report of the Truth and Reconciliation Commission of Canada*, 155.

Appendix

1 *Hudson's Bay Miscellany, 1670–1870*, The Hudson's Bay Record Society, vol. 30, (Winnipeg: Hudson's Bay Record Society, 1975), B.239/f/12, fos. 1–9.

BIBLIOGRAPHY

Government Sources

An Act to Amend the Indian Act, Public Law c. 50 (10-11 Geo. V.), S.c. (1919–20).

An Act to Amend the Indian Act, S.C. 1919–20, c. 50 (10-11 Geo. V).

Act Approving the Agreement Concerning James Bay and Northern Québec. c C-67.

Bill C-91, *An Act Respecting Indigenous Languages*. First Session, Forty-second Parliament, 64-65-66-67 Elizabeth II, 2015–2016–2017–2018–2019.

Bill S-212, *An Act for the Advancement of the Aboriginal Languages of Canada and to Recognize and Respect Aboriginal Language Rights*. 1st Session, 42nd Parliament, 64 Elizabeth II, 2015.

Bolivia (Plurinational State of)'s Constitution of 2009. Oxford University Press, 2017. Accessed 31 March 2017. https://www.constituteproject.org/constitution/Bolivia_2009.pdf.

British House of Commons. *Report from the Committee Appointed to Inquire into the State and Condition of the Countries Adjoining to Hudson's Bay, and of the Trade Carried on There*. London: House of Commons, 1749. Accessed 3 October 2024. https://www.canadiana.ca/view/oocihm.9_02954/2.

Canada. Indigenous Languages Act S.C. 2019, c. 23.

Canadian Charter of Rights and Freedoms. Part I of the Constitution Act, 1982, being Schedule B to the Canada Act 1982 (UK), 1982, c 11.

Canadian Heritage, Evaluation Services Directorate, "Evaluation of the Aboriginal Langauges Initiatve 2009–10 to 2013–14," 8 June 2015.

Canadian Heritage. "Important Step Taken toward Co-Development of Indigenous Languages Legislation in Meeting between Government of Canada, Metis, Inuit and First Nations Leaders." News release, 15 June 2017. Accessed 21 January 2023. https://www.newswire.ca/news-releases/important-step-taken-toward-co-development-of-indigenous-languages-legislation-in-meeting-between-government-of-canada-metis-inuit-and-first-nations-leaders-628682473.html.

———. *What We Heard Report: Consultations on the Implementation of the* Indigenous Languages Act. *Consultations on the Office of the Commissioner of Indigenous Languages and the Indigenous Languages Funding Model*. Accessed 21 January 2023. https://www.canada.ca/en/canadian-heritage/campaigns/what-we-heard-ila.html.

Canadian Heritage and Indian and Northern Affairs Canada. *Comprehensive Review of Federal Programming for Aboriginal Languages and Cultures, Final Report*. CH4-98/2005E-PDF 0-662-41412-8. May 2006.

Charlottetown Accord. Draft Legal Text, 9 October 1992.

Constitution Act, 1982: Amended by Constitution Amendment Proclamation, 1983 (S1/84-102).

Debates of the Senate 1st Session, 42nd Parliament, Volume 150, Number 73, Official Report (Hansard). Thursday, 17 November 2016.

Department of Finance Canada, "Building a Strong Middle Class." Budget 2017, 22 March 2017, 167.

Education Act, SNu 2008, c. 15.

Federal-Provincial Meeting of Ministers on Aboriginal Constitutional Matters. Public Documents. Prepared by Canadian Intergovernmental Conference Secretariat. Ottawa: Canadian Intergovernmental Conference Secretariat, Intergovernmental Document Centre, 1985.

Finnish Sámi Parliament. "Land Rights, Linguistic Rights, and Cultural Autonomy for the Finnish Sami People," *Indigenous Affairs* 33 no. 4 (July–December 1997).

Government of Canada. *Action Plan for Official Languages 2023–2028: Protection, Promotion, Collaboration*. Canadian Heritage, 2023.

———. "Early Engagement Sessions: Indigenous Languages Legislation 2017–2018: Summary of Findings." 2018.

———. *Indian Residential Schools Settlement Agreement, Schedule "N" Mandate for the Truth and Reconciliation Commission*. Ottawa, 2006.

———. *The Indian Residential Schools Settlement Agreement, Official Court Website for the Settlement of the Indian Residential Schools Class Action Litigation*. Ottawa, 2006.

———. *Land claims agreement between the Inuit of Labrador and her majesty the queen in right of Newfoundland and Labrador and her majesty the queen in right of Canada* (2005). Accessed 23 October 2024. https://www.rcaanc-cirnac.gc.ca/eng/1293647179208/1542904949105.

———. Statement of Apology to Former Students of Indian Residential Schools. Delivered by Prime Minister of Canada, Stephen Harper, 11 June 2008. Accessed 23 October 2024. https://www.rcaanc-cirnac.gc.ca/eng/1100100015644/1571589171655.

Government of Nunavut. *Inuit Qaujimajatuqangit: Education Framework for Nunavut Curriculum*. Nunavut Department of Education, 2007.

Government of Yukon. *Report on Implementation of French Language Services*. 1990, Phase I–Identification of services.

Greenland Home Rule Act No. 577 of 29 November 1978.

House of Commons and Senate 32nd 1st Session. Minutes of Proceedings and Evidence of the Special Joint Committee of the Senate and the House of Commons on the Constitution of Canada.

House of Commons Standing Committee on Aboriginal Affairs. *You Took My Talk: Aboriginal Literacy and Empowerment*. Ottawa: Queen's Printer, 1990.

House of Commons Standing Committee on Indian Affairs and Northern Development. *Minutes of Proceedings and Evidence of the Standing Committee on Indian Affairs and Northern Development: Respecting the Annual Reports of the Department of Indian Affairs and Northern Development (1967–68 and 1968–69), Including Fifth Report to the House.* Ottawa: Queen's Printer, 1971.

Indian Residential Schools Settlement Agreement. 8 May 2006. Residential Schools Settlement Official Court Notice.

Inuit Language Protection Act, Statutes of Nunavut 2008, c. 17.

Legislative Assembly of Nunavut. Hansard. 4th Session. 2nd Assembly. 16 September 2008. Iqaluit: Queen's Printer. 4912–79.

Letter from Leslie Norton, Permanent Mission of Canada to the Office of the United Nations and World Trade Organization to the Office of the High Commissioner for Human Rights, 7 June 2022, note no. GENEV-8164.

Letter to Mr. Marc Garneau, Minister of Foreign Affairs from Fernand de Varennes, Special Rapporteur on Minority Issues, Koumbou Boly Barry, the Special Rapporteur on the Right to Education, Tlaleng Mofokeng, Special Rapporteur on the Right of Everyone to the Enjoyment of the Highest Standard of Physical and Mental Health, and José Francisco Calí Tzay, Special Rapporteur on the Rights of Indigenous Peoples, 3 August 2021. Reference AL CAN 3/2021.

Letter from the Minister of Canadian Heritage, Honourable Pascale St-Onge to Mr. John Aldag, Chair, Standing Committee on Indigenous and Northern Affairs, 15 October 2023, in response to the Standing Committee on Indigenous and Northern Affairs' Ninth Report of the 44th Parliament, 13 June 2023.

Manitoba. *Aboriginal Languages Recognition Act* C.C.S.M. c. A1.5.

Minister of Indian Affairs and Northern Development. *Statement of the Government of Canada on Indian Policy.* Ottawa: Queen's Printer, 1969.

Northwest Territories, Education, Culture and Employment. *Inuuqatigiit: The Curriculum from the Inuit Perspective.* Government of Northwest Territories, 1996.

Norway. Act of 17 July 1998 no. 61 relating to Primary and Secondary Education and Training (the Education Act). Accessed 2 November 2024. https://www.regjeringen.no/contentassets/b3b9e92cce6742c39581b661a019e504/education-act-norway-with-amendments-entered-2014-2.pdf.

Nunavut Education Act, S.Nu. 2008, c.13.

Nunavut Constitutional Forum, *Building Nunavut: A Working Document with a Proposal for an Arctic Constitution*. Nunavut Constitutional Forum, 1983.

Nunavut Tunngavik Incorporated. *2009/10 Annual Report on the State of Inuit Culture and Society—Our Primary Concern: Inuit language in Nunavut.* Iqaluit, NU: Nunavut Tunngavik Incorporated, 2011.

Nunavut Tunngavik Incorporated, Bernice Tujjaaqtuqaq Clarke, and Lily Anne Maniapik v. the Commissioner of Nunavut as represented by the Government of Nunavut and the Government of Nunavut as represented by the Attorney General, Court File 08-21-463-CVC. Accessed 7 October 2024. https://equality-rights-claim.tunngavik.com/files/2021/10/2021-10-13-Filed-NTIvAG-s.15-Charter-Inuit-Language-Rights-eng.pdf.

Nunavut Tunngavik Incorporated. *NTI Files Lawsuit Against GN for Violating Equality Rights of Inuit Children and Youth,* 2021. Accessed 7 October 2024. https://www.tunngavik.com/files/2021/10/2021-10-13-Press-Release-and-Backgrounder-final.pdf.

Nunavut Legislative Assembly, *Nunavut Hansard*, 4th Session 2nd Assembly, 16 September 2008 Office of the Auditor General of Canada. *Report of the Auditor General of Canada to* the Legislative Assembly of Nunavut—2013: Education in Nunavut. Auditor General of Canada, 2013.

Office of the Auditor General of Canada. *Report of the Auditor General of Canada to the Legislative Assembly of Nunavut—2013: Education in Nunavut*. Ottawa: Auditor General of Canada, 2013.

Office of the Independent Special Interlocutor for Missing Children and Unmarked Graves and Burial Sites associated with Indian Residential Schools, *Sites of Truth, Sites of Conscience Unmarked Burials and Mass Graves of Missing and Disappeared Indigenous Children in Canada*. Ohsweken, ON: Independent Special Interlocutor, 2024.

Office of the Languages Commissioner of Nunavut. "Recommendations Regarding Changes to the Official Languages Act." Submitted to the Special Committee of the Legislative Assembly Reviewing the *Official Languages Act*. 18 January 2002.

Office of the Languages Commissioner of Nunavut. *2018–2019 Annual Report*. Iqaluit: Office of the Languages Commissioner of Nunavut, 2019.

Official Languages Act, Revised Statutes of the Northwest Territories 1988, c. 0-1.

Official Languages Act, Statutes of Nunavut 2008, c. 10.

Official Report of the Debates of the House of Commons of the Dominion of Canada. 1st Session, 5th Parliament, February 8th–April 19th, 1883. Ottawa: MacLean, Roger, 1883.

Parliament Special Joint Committee on the Constitution of Canada. Minutes of Proceedings and Evidence of the Special Joint Committee of the Senate and of the House of Commons on the Constitution of Canada. 1980.

Prime Minister Justin Trudeau. Mandate Letter to Department of Canadian Heritage, 12 November 2015.

———. Speech to the Assembly of First Nations Special Chiefs Assembly. Gatineau, Quebec, 6 December 2016.

Privy Council. Order in Council. 3327, 10 November 1894.

———. Order in Council. 1658, 6 October 1908.

Public Documents. Federal-Provincial Meeting of Ministers on Aboriginal Constitutional Matters. Canadian Intergovernmental Conference Secretariat. Ottawa, ON, 1985.

Public Law 104 104 STAT. 1152 P.L. 101-477. 30 October 1990.

Québec (Province). Bill 101: Charter of the French Language. [Quebec]: C.-H. Dubé. 1977.

Royal Commission on Aboriginal Peoples. *Report of the Royal Commission on Aboriginal Peoples*. Vol. 3, *Gathering Strength*. Ottawa: Canadian Communicaitions, 1996.

Royal Commission on Bilingualism and Biculturalism. *Preliminary Report*. Ottawa: Queen's Printer, 1965.

Royal Commission on Bilingualism and Biculturalism. *Report of the Royal Commission on Bilingualism and Biculturalism*. Vol. 1. Ottawa: Queen's Printer, 1967.

Special Committee to Review the Education Act Final Report. Third Session. Fourth Legislative Assembly of Nunavut. 2015.

Special Joint Committee on the Constitution of Canada. *Minutes of Proceedings and Evidence of the Special Joint Committee of the Senate and of the House of Commons on the Constitution of Canada.* 1980.

Standing Committee on Government Operations and 16th Legislative Assembly of the Northwest Territories. *Final Report on the Review of the Official Languages Act 2008-2009, Reality Check: Securing a Future for the Official Languages of the Northwest Territories,* 2009.

Standing Committee on Indigenous and Northern Affairs, 44th Parliament. *Reclaiming, Revitalizing, Maintaining and Strengthening Indigenous Languages in Canada.* 44th Parliament, 1st Session, 23 June 2023.

Standing Committee on Procedure and House Affairs, *Evidence*, Number 95, 1st Session, 42nd Parliament, 27 March 2018.

Statistics Canada. Aboriginal People: Inuit: Fact Sheet for Nunavut. Catalogue 89-656-X2016017. 2016.

———. *Census in Brief: Indigenous Languages Across Canada: Census of Population, 2021.* Statistics Canada and Minister of Industry, 2023.

———. *National Household Survey. Aboriginal People and Languages.* 2011. Catalogue no. 99-011-X2011003.

United States Senate, Committee on Indian Affairs. "Hearing on S. 575 to Amend the Native American Languages Act to Provide for the Support of Native American Language Survival Schools." 108th Congress 1st session, 15 May 2003. Washington, DC.

Waitangi Tribunal. "Report of the Waitangi Tribunal on the Te Reo Maori Claim." 1986. https://forms.justice.govt.nz/search/Documents/WT/wt_DOC_68482156/Report%20on%20the%20Te%20Reo%20Maori%20Claim%20W.pdf.

Court Cases

Arsenault-Cameron v. Prince Edward Island, [2000] 1 S.C.R. 3.

Baker v. Canada (Minister of Citizenship and Immigration), [1999] 2 SCR 817.

Broadcasting (Assets No. 1) (unreported, High Court of New Zealand, Wellington, McGechean J. 3 May 1991, CP 942/88, 20).

Broadcasting (Assets No. 2) [1992] 2 NZLR.

Calder et al. v. Attorney-General of British Columbia, [1973] S.C.R. 313.

CA Yellowknife (*Northwest Territories (A.G.) v. Association des parents ayants droit de Yellowknife*, 2015 NWTCA 2.

Cree-Naskapi (of Quebec) Act (S.C. 1984, c. 18).

CSF de la C-B (*Conseil scolaire francophone de la Colombie-Britannique) v. British Columbia*, 2016 BCSC 1764.

Doucet-Boudreau v. Nova Scotia (Minister of Education), [2003] 3 S.C.R. 3.

Guerin et al. v. The Queen (1984), 2 SCR.

Lalonde v. Ontario (2001) 56 O.R. (3d) 505.

Mahe v. Alberta, [1990] 1 S.C.R. 342.

Maori Affairs Act, 1953 (1953 No 94) (NZ).

Māori Language Act, 1987 (1987 No 176) (NZ).

Quebec Session Reference [1998] 2 S.C.R. 217.

R. v. Beaulac [1999] 1 *S.C.R.*

R v. Hape [2007] SCC 26.

R. v. Powley [2003] 2 S.C.R. 207.

R. v. St. Jean Unreported Territorial Court of the Yukon, 30 June 1983.

R. v. Van der Peet [1996] 2 S.C.R. 507.

Re Education Act of Ontario (*Re Education Act of Ontario and Minority Language Education Rights*, 10 D.L.R. (4th) 491, (C.A. On.).

Re Minority Language Educational Rights (*Re Minority Language Educational Rights* (1988), 49 D.L.R. (4th) 499 (C.A. P.E.I.).

Reference Re Manitoba Language Rights [1985] 1 S.C.R. 721.

Reference Re Bill 30, An Act to Amend the Education Act (Ont.)[1987] 1 SCR 1148.

Reference Re Minority Language Educational Rights (P.E.I.) (1988), 69 Nfld. and P.E.I.R. 236 (PEICA).

Reference Re Public Schools Act (Man.) [1993] 1 S.C.R. 839.

Reference Re Secession of Quebec [1998] 2 *S.C.R.* 217.

Saskatchewan Federation of Labour v. Saskatchewan [2015] 1 S.C.R. 245.

SOE Case [1987] 1 NZLR 641.

Solski (*Solski (Tutor of) v. Quebec (Attorney General)*, [2005] 1 S.C.R. 201.

Te Heuheu Tukino v. Aotea District Maori Land Board [1941] 2 NZLR.

Te Reo Māori Claim (WAI 11 1986).

Te Ture mō Te Reo Māori 2016 Māori Language Act 2016 (2016 No 17) (NZ).

Te Weehi [1986] 1 NZLR.

Waitangi Tribunal. "Report of the Waitangi Tribunal on the Te Reo Maori Claim." Wai 11, Department of Justice: Wellington: New Zealand, 1986.

Yukon Act S.C. 2002.

International Treaties and Documents

International Convention on the Elimination of All Forms of Racial Discrimination, (entered into force 4 January 1969) 660 UNTS 195, [1975] ATS 40, 5 ILM 32, 7 March 1966.

International Covenant on Civil and Political Rights, (adopted 19 December 1966, entered into force 23 March 1976) 999 U.N.T.S. 171.

International Covenant on Economic, Social, and Cultural Rights, (opened for signature 16 December 1966 entered into force 3 January 1976) 993 U.N.T.S. 3.

Organization of American States. American Declaration on the Rights of Indigenous Peoples, Adopted without vote by Organization of American States, General Assembly, 46th session. Santo Domingo, Dominican Republic, 15 June 2016. AG/RES. 2888 (XLVI-O/16).

UNESCO Ad Hoc Expert Group on Endangered Languages. *Language Vitality and Endangerment.* Adopted by the International Expert Meeting on UNESCO

Programme Safeguarding of Endangered Languages. Paris, 10–12 March 2003. Accessed 26 December 2023. https://ich.unesco.org/doc/src/00120-EN.pdf.

UNESCO International Decade of Indigenous Languages 2022–2032. https://en.unesco.org/idil2022-2032.

"UNESCO New York," UNESCO. Accessed 28 April 2025. Last modified 20 April 2023. https://www.unesco.org/en/articles/launch-international-year-indigenous-languages-2019.

United Nations Charter. 1945. 1 UNTS XVI. Accessed 13 June 2017. http://www.un.org/en/charter-united-nations/.

United Nations Committee on Economic, Social and Cultural Rights (CESCR). *UN Committee on Economic, Social and Cultural Rights: Concluding Observations, Canada*, E/C.12/CAN/CO/4; E/C.12/CAN/CO/5. 22 May 2006. https://www.refworld.org/policy/polrec/cescr/2006/en/23888.

United Nations Committee on Economic, Social and Cultural Rights. *General comment no. 21, Right of everyone to take part in cultural life (art. 15, para. 1a of the Covenant on Economic, Social and Cultural Rights)*, E/C.12/GC/21. 21 December 2009. https://www.refworld.org/legal/general/cescr/2009/en/83710.

United Nations Committee on the Rights of the Child. (CRC). *General comment No. 11 (2009): Indigenous children and their rights under the Convention [on the Rights of the Child]*, CRC/C/GC/11. 12 February 2009.

United Nations Convention on the Rights of the Child. 20 November 1989. UN Doc. A/Res/44/25.

United Nations Declaration on the Rights of Indigenous Peoples Act, S.C. 2021, c. 15.

United Nations Declaration on the Rights of Indigenous Peoples Act Implementation Secretariat. *United Nations Declaration on the Rights of Indigenous Peoples Act Action Plan*. Department of Justice Canada, 2023.

United Nations Economic and Social Council, Permanent Forum on Indigenous Issues. "Report on the Seventh Session." April–2 May 2008. E/20080/43 E/C.19/2008/13. 21.

United Nations General Assembly. *Declaration on the Rights of Indigenous Peoples: resolution / adopted by the General Assembly*, A/RES/61/295. 2 October 2007. Accessed 3 October 2024. https://www.un.org/development/desa/indigenouspeoples/declaration-on-the-rights-of-indigenous-peoples.html.

———. International Covenant on Civil and Political Rights. Treaty Series, 999, 171. 1966.

———. *Permanent Forum on Indigenous Issues*, E/2000/22, UN General Assembly. 28 July 2000. https://www.un.org/esa/socdev/unpfii/documents/about-us/E-RES-2000-22.pdf.

United Nations Human Rights Committee. *UN Human Rights Committee: Concluding Observations, Canada*, CCPR/C/CAN/CO/5. 20 April 2006. https://www.refworld.org/policy/polrec/hrc/2006/en/38904.

United Nations Human Rights Council. *Expert Mechanism on the Rights of Indigenous Peoples : resolution / adopted by the Human Rights Council on 30 September 2016*, A/HRC/RES/33/25. https://www.refworld.org/legal/resolution/unhrc/2016/en/114967.

United Nations Permanent Forum on Indigenous Issues. "Expert Group Meeting on the Theme Indigenous Languages: Preservation and Revitalization (Articles 13, 14 and 16 of the United Nations Declaration on the Rights of Indigenous Peoples)." Economic and Social Council. February 2016. E/C.19/2016/10.

———. "Report of the International Expert Group Meeting on Indigenous Languages. Economic and Social Council." 8 January 2008. E/C.19/2008/3.

———. "Study on International Criminal Law and the Judicial Defence of Indigenous Peoples' Rights. (submitted by the Special Rapporteur Bartlomé Clavero. 8 January 2008. E/C.19/2011/4.

United Nations Permanent Forum on Indigenous Issues, 7th Session, "Report of the International Expert Group Meeting on Indigenous Languages." 21 January 2008. Economic and Social Council. E/C.19/2008/3.

United Nations Special Rapporteur on Minority Issues. *Language Rights of Linguistic Minorities, A Practical Guide for Implementation*, March 2017. Accessed April 2017. http://www.ohchr.org/Documents/Issues/Minorities/SR/LanguageRightsLinguisticMinorities_EN.pdf.

United Nations, *Who are indigenous peoples?*, 15th Session of the United Nations Permanent Forum on Indigenous Issues. Fact Sheet 1 (Secretariat of the Permanent Forum on Indigenous Issues, 2015). Accessed 3 October 2024. https://www.un.org/esa/socdev/unpfii/documents/5session_factsheet1.pdf.

Secondary Sources

A Collection of Psalms and Hymns, in the Language of the Cree Indians of North-West America. [London?]: Printed for the Society for Promoting Christian Knowledge, 1874.

Absolon, Kathleen E. *Kaandosswin: How We Come to Know*. Winnipeg: Fernwood Publishing, 2011.

Aguilera, Dorothy, and Margaret D. LeCompte. "Resiliency in Native Languages: The Tale of Three Indigenous Communities' Experiences with Language Immersion." *Journal of American Indian Education* 46, no. 3 (2007): 11–36.

Ahenakew, Edward. *Voices of the Plains Cree*, edited by Ruth Matheson Buck. Regina: Canadian Plains Research Center, University of Regina, 1995.

Aikawa, Noriko. *Conference Handbook on Endangered Languages of the Pacific Rim*. UNESCO's Programme on Languages. Osaka: Endangered Languages of the Pacific Rim Project, 2001.

Aikio-Puoskari, Ulla. *The Education of the Sámi in the Comprehensive Schooling of Three Nordic Countries: Norway, Finland and Sweden*. Resource Centre for the Rights of Indigenous Peoples, 2005. Accessed 3 December 2017. http://arcticcircle.uconn.edu/SEEJ/sami1.html.

———. "Sámi Language in Finnish Schools." In *Bicultural Education in the North: Ways of Preserving and Enhancing Indigenous Peoples' Languages and Traditional Knowledge*, edited by Erich Kasten. Münster: Waxmann, 1998.

Allan, B., and J. Smylie. *First Peoples, Second Class Treatment: The Role of Racism in the Health and Well-Being of Indigenous Peoples in Canada*. Toronto: Wellesley Institute, 2015.

Anaya, S. James. *Indigenous Peoples in International Law*. New York: Oxford University Press, 2004.

———. "Indigenous Rights Norms in Contemporary International Law." *Arizona Journal of International and Comparative Law* 8, no. 2 (1991): 1–39.

Archibald, Jo-Ann. *Indigenous Storywork.* Vancouver: UBC Press, 2008.

Arthurson, Virgina. *First Nation Languages: Why We Need Them.* Winnipeg: Manitoba First Nations Education Resource Centre, 2012.

Assembly of First Nations. *National First Nations Language Strategy: A Time to Listen and the Time to Act.* Ottawa: Assembly of First Nations, 2000.

———. *Towards Linguistic Justice for First Nations.* Ottawa: Assembly of First Nations, 1990.

———. *Towards Rebirth of First Nations Languages.* Ottawa: Assembly of First Nations, 1992.

Assembly of First Nations Engagement Sessions, Indigenous Languages Initiative. *National Engagement Sessions Report.* 5 December 2017. https://www.afn.ca/wp-content/uploads/2018/04/17-12-12_Languages_AFN-ILI-Report_FINAL.pdf.

Assembly of First Nations, Special Chiefs Assembly. *Co-developing an Indigenous Languages Act.* 4–6 December 2018. https://www.afn.ca/uploads/sca-2018/Documents/Dialogue%20Sessions/Day%201%20-%20December%204%2C%202018/01%20Languages/01%29%20Languages%20Powerpoint.pdf.

Austin, Peter. *Language Vitality in a Globalized World.* Oxford: Oxford University Press, 2021.

Baer, Lars-Anders, with Ole Henrik Magga, Robert Dunbar, Tove Skutnabb. "Forms of Education of Indigenous Children as Crimes against Humanity?" Expert paper submitted to United Nations Permanent Forum on Indigenous Issues, 8 February 2008. UN Doc E/C.19/2008/7.

Baker, Howard Robert, II. "Law Transplanted, Justice Invented: Sources of Law for the Hudson's Bay Company in Rupert's Land, 1670–1870." MA thesis, University of Manitoba, 1996.

Balto, Asta, and Jon Todal. "Saami Bilingual Education in Norway." In *Encyclopedia of Language and Education,* Vol. 5, *Bilingual Education*, edited by Jim Cummins and David Corson. Dordrecht: Kluwer Academic, 1997.

Barsh, Russel Lawrence, and James Youngblood Henderson. "The Supreme Court's Van der Peet Trilogy: Naive Imperialism and Ropes of Sand." *McGill Law Journal* 42 (1997): 993–1011.

Bastarache, Michel. *Language Rights in Canada.* 2nd ed. Cowansville: Éditions Y. Blais, 2004.

Batibo, Herman M. *Language Decline and Death in Africa: Causes, Consequences and Challenges.* Clevedon: Multilingual Matters, 2005.

Bauer, Winifred. "Is the health of te reo Maori improving?" *Reo, Te* 51 (2008): 33–73.

Bear Nicholas, Andrea. "Canada's Colonial Mission: The Great White Bird." In *Aboriginal Education in Canada: A Study in Decolonization*, edited by K.P. Binda and Sharilyn Calliou. Mississauga: Canadian Educators' Press, 2011.

———. "Linguicide: Submersion Education and the Killing of Languages in Canada." *Briarpatch* 40, no. 2 (2011): 4–8.

———. "Linguistic Decline and the Educational Gap: A Single Solution Is Possible in the Education of Indigenous Peoples." Fredericton: Assembly of First Nations, 2009.

Bear Nicholas, Andrea, Lorena Sekwan Fontaine, David Leitch, and Fernand de Varennes, *What Canada's New Indigenous Languages Law Needs to Say and Say Urgently*. Senate Standing Committee on Indigenous Peoples. 42nd Parliament,, 1st Session. 28 February 2019.

Beaujot, Roderic P., and Barbara Burnaby. *The Use of Aboriginal Languages in Canada: An Analysis of 1981 Census Data*. Social Trends Analysis Directorate and Canada Native Citizens Directorate. [Ottawa]: Department of the Secretary of State, 1987.

Bellgarde, Perry. National Chief, Assembly of First Nations, Presentation to the Senate Standing Committee on Aboriginal Peoples. 42nd Parliament, 1st Session. 20 March 2019.

Benton, Richard A. "Perfecting the Partnership: Revitalising the Māori Language in New Zealand Education and Society 1987–2014." *Language, Culture, and Curriculum* 28, no. 2 (2015): 99–112.

Berger, Thomas R. *The Nunavut Project Conciliator's Final Report: Nunavut Land Claims Agreement: Implementation Contract Negotiations for The Second Planning Period, 2003–2013*. Vancouver: Bull, Housser and Tupper, 2006.

Blondin-Perrin, Alice. *My Heart Shook Like a Drum: What I Learned at the Indian Mission Schools, Northwest Territories*. Ottawa: Borealis Press, 2009.

Boon, T.C.B. *The Anglican Church from the Bay to the Rockies: History of the Ecclesiastical Province of Rupert's Land and Its Dioceses from 1820 to 1955*. Toronto: Ryerson Press, 1962.

Borrows, John. *Canada's Indigenous Constitution*. Toronto: University of Toronto Press, 2010.

———. *Drawing Out Law: A Spirit's Guide*. Toronto: University of Toronto Press, 2010.

———. "Indigenous Love, Law, and Land in Canada's Constitution." In *Fragile Freedoms: The Global Struggle for Human Rights*, edited by Steven Lecce, Neil McArthur, and Arthur Schafer. Oxford: Oxford University Press, 2017.

Boshier, Roger. "Learning from the Moa: The Challenge of Māori Language Revitalization in Aotearoa/New Zealand." In *Indigenous Education*, edited by W. James Jacob, Sheng Yao Cheng, and Maureen K. Porter. Dordrecht: Springer, 2015.

Bradford, Tolly. *Prophetic Identities: Indigenous Missionaries on British Colonial Frontiers, 1850–75*. Vancouver: UBC Press, 2012.

Brass, Eleanor. *I Walk in Two Worlds*. Calgary: Glenbow Museum, 1987.

Brenzinger, Matthias, Akira Yamamoto, Noriko Aikawa, Dmitri Koundiouba, Anahit Minasyan, Arienne Dwyer, Colette Grinevald, Michael Krauss, Osahito Miyaoka, Osamu Sakiyama, Rieks Smeets, and Ofelia Zepeda. *Language Vitality and Endangerment*. International Expert Meeting on Safeguarding of Endangered Languages. Paris: UNESCO, 2003.

Bringing Them Home: Report of the National Inquiry into the Separation of Aboriginal and Torres Strait Islander Children from Their Families. Sydney, N.S.W: Human Rights and Equal Protection Commission, 1997.

Bryce, Peter. *The Story of a National Crime: An Appeal for Justice to the Indians of Canada; the Wards of the Nation, Our Allies in the Revolutionary War, Our Borthers-in-Arms in the Great War.* Ottawa: James Hope and Sons, 1922.

———. *The Story of a National Crime: Being a Record of the Health Conditions of the Indians of Canada from 1904 to 1921.* Report. Ottawa: James Hope and Sons, 1922.

Burpee, Lawrence J. *The Search for the Western Sea: The Story of the Exploration of North-Western America.* Toronto: Musson, 1908.

Burwash, Rev. Nathanael. "The Gift to a Nation of Written Language." *Proceedings and Transactions of the Royal Society of Canada* 5 (1911): 3–21.

Campbell, Maria. *Halfbreed.* Lincoln: University of Nebraska Press, 1982.

Canadian Bar Association, Aboriginal Law Section, Brief submitted to the Senate Standing Committee on Aboriginal Peoples on Bill C-91, An Act Respecting Indigenous Languages, 42nd Parliament, 1st Session, 31 May 2019.

Canadien, Albert. *From Lishamie.* Penticton: Theytus Books, 2010.

Cantoni, Gina, ed. *Stabilizing Indigenous Languages.* Northern Arizona University Center for Excellence in Education. Flagstaff: Northern Arizona University Press, 1996.

Cardinal, Harold. *Treaty Elders of Saskatchewan: Our Dream Is That Our Peoples Will One Day Be Clearly Recognized as Nations.* Calgary: University of Calgary Press, 2000.

———. *The Unjust Society.* Madeira Park: Douglas and McIntyre, 1999.

Chandler, Michael J., and Christopher E. Lalonde. "Cultural Continuity as a Hedge against Suicide in Canada's First Nations." *Transcultural Psychiatry* 35 (1998): 191–219.

———. "Cultural Continuity as a Protective Factor against Suicide in First Nations Youth." In "Aboriginal Youth, Hope or Heartbreak: Aboriginal Youth and Canada's Future." Special issue, *Horizons* 10 (2008): 68–72.

Charron, Nadine. "Exploring the Links Between Aboriginal Language-Medium Instruction and Academic Performance: A Literature Review in Support of the PCH Aboriginal Languages Initiatives." Canadian Heritage: Aboriginal Affairs Branch, Policy and Research, October, 2010.

Chiefs of Ontario. Brief submitted to the House of Commons Standing Committee on Canadian Heritage. 42nd Parliament, 1st Session. 27 March 2019.

Cholewinski, R. "State Duty Towards Ethnic Minorities: Positive or Negative?" *Human Rights Quarterly* 10 (1988): 344–71.

Chrisjohn, Roland David, Sherri Lynn Young, and Michael Maraun. *The Circle Game: Shadows and Substance in the Indian Residential School Experience in Canada.* Penticton: Theytus Books, 1997.

Chuffart, Romain. "Speaking of Rights: Indigenous Linguistic Rights in the Arctic." *Yearbook of Polar Law* 9 (2017): 3–23.

Comboni Salinas, Sonia, and José M. Juárez Núñez. "Education, Culture and Indigenous Rights: The Case of Educational Reform in Bolivia." *Prospects (Paris)* 30, no. 1 (2000): 105–24.

Coronel-Molina, Serafín M., and Teresa L. McCarty, eds. *Indigenous Language Revitalization in the Americas.* New York: Routledge, 2016.

Corson, David. "Norway's 'Sámi Language Act': Emancipatory Implications for the World's Aboriginal People." *Language in Society* 24, no. 4 (1995): 493–514.

Craft, Aimée. *Breathing Life into the Stone Fort Treaty: An Anishnabe Understanding of Treaty One*. Saskatoon: Purich, 2013.

Crystal, David. *Language Death*. Cambridge: Cambridge University Press, 2000.

De Bres, Julia. "The Hierarchy of Minority Languages in New Zealand." *Journal of Multilingual Development* 36, no. 7 (2015): 677–93.

Deiter, Constance. *From Our Mothers' Arms: The Intergenerational Impact of Residential Schools in Saskatchewan*. Toronto: United Church Publishing House, 1999.

Deloria, Vine, and James Treat. *For This Land: Writings on Religion in America*. New York: Routledge, 1999.

Del Valle, Sandra. *Language Rights and the Law in the United States: Finding Our Voices*. Clevedon: Multilingual Matters, 2003.

Dempsey, James. "Effects on Aboriginal Cultures Due to Contact with Henry Kelsey." In *Three Hundred Prairie Years: Henry Kelsey's "Inland Country of Good Report,"* edited by Henry Epp. Regina: Canadian Plains Research Center, University of Regina, 1993.

Department of the Secretary of State, *Canada's Aboriginal Languages: An Overview of Current Activities in Language Retention*. Ottawa, 1985.

De Varennes, Fernand. *Language Minorities and Human Rights*. The Hague: Martinus Nijhoff, 1996.

De Varennes, Fernand, Koumbou Boly Barry, Tlaleng Mofokeng, and José Francisco Calí Tzay to Marc Garneau, 3 August 2021. AL CAN 3/2021.

Dion, Joseph F., and Hugh Aylmer Dempsey. *My Tribe, the Crees*. Calgary: Glenbow Museum, 1979.

Dorward, Kira Wronska. "Judge's Ruling a Blow to the GN in Inuktitut Instruction Lawsuit." *Nunavut News*, 24 May 2024.

Doughty, Arthur G., Chester Martin, and Arthur Dobbs. *The Kelsey Papers*. Ottawa: Public Archives of Canada and Northern Ireland Public Record Office; F.A. Acland, printer, 1929.

Dupris, Joseph. "Maqlaqsyalank hemyeega: Goals and Expectations of Klamath-Modoc Revitalization." *Language Documentation and Conversation* 13 (2019): 155–96.

Durie, Arohia. "Emancipatory Maori Education: Speaking from the Heart." *Language, Culture, and Curriculum* 11, no. 3 (1998): 297–308.

Epp, Henry T., ed. *Three Hundred Prairie Years: Henry Kelsey's "Inland Country of Good Report."* Regina: Canadian Plains Research Center, University of Regina, 1993.

Evans, James. *The Speller and Interpreter, in Indian and English: For the Use of the Mission Schools, and Such as May Desire to Obtain a Knowledge of the Ojibway Tongue*. New York: D. Fanshaw, 1837.

Evans, Mary, Augusta Tappage, and Jean E. Speare. *The Days of Augusta*. Vancouver: J.J. Douglas, 1973.

Eyford, Ryan. *White Settler Reserve: New Iceland and the Colonization of the Canadian West*. Vancouver: University of British Columbia Press, 2016.

Falch, Torvald, Per Selle, and Kristin Strømsnes. “The Sámi: 25 Years of Indigenous Authority in Norway.” *Ethnopolitics* 15, no. 1 (2016): 125–43.

Fenge, Terry and Paul Quassa, “Negotiation and implementing the Nunavut Land Claims Agreement.” Policy Options. 1 July 2009. Accessed 2 November 2024, https://policyoptions.irpp.org/magazines/canadas-water-challenges/negotiating-and-implementing-the-nunavut-land-claims-agreement/.

First Peoples' Cultural Council. *Indigenous Languages Recognition, Preservation and Revitalization: A Report on the National Dialogue Session on Indigenous Languages.* Prepared by Valerie Galley, Suzanne Gessner, Tracey Herbert, Karihwakeron Tim Thompson, and Lorna Wanosts'a7 Williams. Brentwood Bay, BC: First Peoples' Cultural Council. Accessed 30 September 2016, www.fpcc.ca/files/PDF/General/FPCC__National_Dialogue_Session_Report_Final.pdf.

Fishman, Joshua A. “Maintaining Languages: What Works and What Doesn't.” In *Stabilizing Indigenous Languages,* edited by Gina Cantoni, Northern Arizona University Center for Excellence in Education. Flagstaff, AZ: Northern Arizona University, 1996.

———. *Reversing Language Shift: Theoretical and Empirical Foundations of Assistance to Threatened Languages.* Clevedon: Multilingual Matters, 1991.

Fontaine, Lorena Sekwan. Brief submiited to the Standing Committee on Canadian Heritage on Bill C-91, An Act Respecting Indigenous Languages, 42nd Parliament, 1st Session. 28 February 2019.

Fontaine, Theodore. *Broken Circle: The Dark Legacy of Indian Residential Schools: A Memoir*. Surrey: Heritage House, 2010.

French, Alice. *My Name Is Masak.* Winnipeg: Peguis, 1997.

Friesen, Jean. “Magnificent Gifts: The Treaties of Canada with the Indians of the Northwest 1869–1876.” *Transactions of the Royal Society of Canada* 1 (1986): 41–51.

Gabrielle, Ellen, Kontinónhstats—The Mohawk Language Custodian Association from Kanehsatà:ke. Presentation the Senate Standing Committee on Indigenous Peoples. on Bill C-91, An Act Respecting Indigenous Languages, 42nd Parlialment, 1st Session. 2 April 2019.

George, Earl Maquinna. *Living on the Edge: Nuu-chah-nulth History from an Ahousaht Chief's Perspective.* Winlaw: Sono Nis Press, 2003.

Glendon Truth and Reconciliation Declaration on Indigenous Language Policy. October 2016. www. glendon.yorku.ca/crlcc/wp-content/uploads/sites/106/Glendon-declaration-Final-Draft-Oct-2016-public.pdf.

Gone, Joseph P. “Redressing First Nations Historical Trauma: Theorizing Mechanisms for Indigenous Culture as Mental Health Treatment.” *Transcultural Psychiatry* 50 (2013): 683–706.

Governor and Committee to George Simpson, 11 March 1823. Hudson's Bay Company Archives, A.6/21, folder 50.

Graham, Elizabeth. *The Mush Hole: Life at Two Indian Residential Schools.* Waterloo: Heffle Publishing, 1997.

Grant, Agnes. *Finding My Talk: How Fourteen Native Women Reclaimed Their Lives After Residential School.* Calgary: Fifth House, 2004.

Grant, John Webster. *Moon of Wintertime: Missionaries and the Indians of Canada in Encounter since 1534.* Toronto: University of Toronto Press, 1984.

Green, Leslie. "Are Language Rights Fundamental?" *Osgoode Hall Law Journal* 25, no. 4 (1987): 639–69.

Green, Leslie, and Denise Réaume. "Education and Linguistic Security in the Charter." *McGill Law Journal* 34, no. 4 (1989): 777–816.

Hagedorn, Nancy L. "'A Friend to Go Between Them': The Interpreter as Cultural Broker During Anglo-Iroquois Councils, 1740–70." *Ethnohistory* 35, no. 1 (1988): 60–80.

Hague Recommendations Regarding the Education Rights of National Minorities. *International Journal on Minority and Group Rights.* Special Issue on the Education Rights of National Minorities (Organization for Security and Co-operation in Europe, 1996.

Haldane, Scott, George E. Lafond, and Caroline Krause. *Nurturing the Learning Spirit of First Nation Students: Report of the National Panel on First Nation Elementary and Secondary Education for Students on Reserve.* Ottawa: National Panel on First Nation Elementary and Secondary Education for Students on Reserve, 2012.

Hale, Ken. "On Endangered Languages and the Importance of Linguistic Diversity." In *Endangered Languages; Language Loss and Community Response*, edited by Lenore A. Grenoble and Lindsay J. Whaley. Cambridge: Cambridge University Press, 1998.

Hale, Ken, Michael Krauss, Lucille J. Watahomigie, Akira Y. Yamamoto, Collette Craig, Laverne Masayesva Jeanne, and Nora C. England. "Endangered Languages." *Language* 68, no. 1 (1992): 1–42.

Hallett, Darcy, Michael J. Chandler, and Christopher E. Lalonde. "Aboriginal Language Knowledge and Youth Suicide." *Cognitive Development* 22, no. 3 (2007): 392–99.

Harding, Louise, Ryan DeCaire, Ursula Ellis, Karleen Delaurier-Lyle, Julia Schillo, and Mark Turin. "Language Improves Health and Wellbeing in Indigenous Communities: A Scoping Review." *Language and Health* 3, no. 1 (2025): 1–19. doi:10.1016/j.laheal.2025.100047.

Harrowitz, Jason. "Francis Calls Abuse of Indigenous People in Canada a 'Genocide,'" *New York Times*, 30 July 2022, https://www.nytimes.com/2022/07/30/world/americas/pope-francis-canada-genocide.html.

Harvey, Sean P. *Native Tongues: Colonialism and Race from Encounter to the Reservation.* Cambridge: Harvard University Press, 2015.

Hawthorn, H.B. *A Survey of the Contemporary Indians of Canada: A Report on Economic, Political, Educational Needs and Policies.* Ottawa: Indian Affairs Branch, 1966.

Hearne, Samuel, and Joseph Burr Tyrrell. *A Journey from Prince of Wales's Fort in Hudson's Bay to the Northern Ocean.* London: Printed for A. Strahan and T. Cadell, 1795.

Heckman, Gerald. "International Human Rights Norms and Administrative Law." In *Administrative Law in Context*, edited by Colleen Flood and Lorne Sossin, 3rd ed. Toronto: Emond Publishing, 2018.

Helander, Hanna, Pigga Keskitalo, and Tuija Turunen. "Saami Language Online Education Outside the Saami Homeland—New Pathways to Social Justice." In *Finland's Famous Education System*, edited by Martin Thrupp, Piia Seppänen, Jaakko Kauko, and Sonja Kosunen. Singapore: Springer, 2023.

Henderson, James Sakej Youngblood. "Treaties and Indian Education." In *First Nations Education in Canada: The Circle Unfolds*, edited by Marie Ann Battiste and Jean Barman. Vancouver: UBC Press, 1995.

Higgins, Rawinia, Poia Rewi, and Vincent Olsen-Reeder, eds. *The Value of the Māori Language: Te Hua o te Reo Māori*. Wellington: Huia Publishers, 2014.

Hinton, Leanne, and Kenneth L. Hale. *The Green Book of Language Revitalization in Practice*. San Diego: Academic Press, 2001.

Hinton, Leanne, Leena Huss, and Gerald Roche, eds. *The Routledge Handbook of Language Revitalization*. New York: Routledge, 2018.

Hogg, Peter W. *Constitutional Law of Canada*. 2nd ed. Agincourt: Carswell, 1985.

Hoover, Michael L. "The Revival of the Mohawk Language in Kahnawake." *Canadian Journal of Native Studies* 12, no. 2 (1992): 269–87.

Horden, John. *The New Testament, Translated into the Cree Language*. London: Printed for the British and Foreign Bible Society, 1980.

Horden, Reverend, and E.A. Watkins. Letters, 1865–1866, Church Mission Society Archives. University of Birmingham. GY C1 F1 1, 1865.

Hornberger, Nancy H. *Can Schools Save Indigenous Languages?: Policy Practices on Four Contents*. Basingstoke: Palgrave MacMillan, 2008.

Howard, Rosaleen. "Education Reform, Indigenous Politics, and Decolonisation in the Bolivia of Evo Morales." *International Journal of Educational Development* 29, no. 6 (2009): 583–93.

Hudson's Bay Miscellany, 1670–1870. The Hudson's Bay Record Society, vol. 30, Winnipeg: Hudson's Bay Record Society, 1975. B.239/f/12, fos., 1975.

Hyde, J. Keith. *St John's College Assembly Minutes*, St. John's College, University of Manitoba, Winnipeg. May 2019. Accessed 3 October 2024. https://umanitoba.ca/st-johns-college/sites/st-johns-college/files/2021-04/Assembly%20Agenda%20September%2017%202019.pdf.

Ignace, Marianne B. *Handbook for Aboriginal Languages Programming in British Columbia*. Report prepared for the First Nations Education Steering Committee, Aboriginal Languages Sub-committee. North Vancouver, BC: First Nations Education Steering Committee, April 1998.

Indian Chiefs of Alberta. "Foundational Document: Citizens Plus." *Aboriginal Policy Studies* 1, no. 2 (2011): 188–281.

Inutiq, Sandra. Paper prepared for International Expert Group Meeting, United Nations Department of Economic and Social Affairs, Division for Social Policy and Development, Secretariat of the Permanent Forum on Indigenous Issues "Indigenous Languages: Preservation and Revitalization: Articles 13, 14 and 16 of the United Nations Declaration on the Rights of Indigenous Peoples." January 2016. PFII/2016/EGM.

Isham, James, Edwin Ernest Rich, and A.M. Johnson. *James Isham's Observations on Hudsons Bay, 1743*. Toronto: published by the Champlain Society for the Hudson's Bay Record Society, 1949.

Jamieson, Mary E. *The Aboriginal Languages Policy Study: Phase II: Implementation Mechanism, September 1988*. Edited by Assembly of First Nations. Ottawa: Assembly of First Nations, 1988.

Joe, Rita. "Four Poems." *Canadian Women Studies/Les cahiers de la femme* 10, nos. 2/3 (Summer/Fall 1989): 28–29.

Johnson, Linda. "Maori Activism Across borders 1950s-1980s." PhD diss., Massey University, 2015.

Johnston, Basil. *Indian School Days*. Toronto: Key Porter Books, 1988.

Jones, Peter. "Human Rights, Group Rights, and Peoples' Rights." *Human Rights Quarterly* 21 (1999): 80–107.

Joona, Tanja. "Safeguarding Cultural Rights of Sami Children and Youth in Finland, with Special Emphasis on the Linguistic Part of Cultural Identity: Current Challenges." *Yearbook of Polar Law* 9 (2017): 109–32.

Josefsen, Eva. *The Saami and the national parliaments: Channels for political influence*. Mexico: Inter-Parliamentary Union and United Nations Development Programme, 2010.

Kasinskaite-Buddeberg, Irmgarda. *Knowledge Societies Division, Communication and Information Sector*. UNESCO, 17th Session of the United Nations Permanent Forum on Indigenous Issues, 16 April 2018. Accessed 20 May 2024. https://papersmart.unmeetings.org/media2/18558956/unesco.pdf.

Kelsey, Henry. *A Dictionary of the Hudson's-Bay Indian Language*. London, 1710.

King, David Paul. "The History of the Federal Residential School for the Inuit Located in Chesterfield Inlet, Yellowknife, Inuvik and Churchill, 1955–1970." MA thesis, Trent University, 1999.

Knockwood, Isabelle, and Gillian Thomas. *Out of the Depths: The Experiences of Mi'kmaw Children at the Indian Residential School at Shubenacadie, Nova Scotia*. Lockeport: Roseway, 1992.

Kontinónhstats, Ellen Gabriel. *The Mohawk Language Custodian Association from Kanehsatà:ke*. Presentation the Standing Committee on Aboriginal Peoples on Bill C-91, An Act Respecting Indigenous Languages. 42nd Parliament, 1st Session. 2 April 2019.

Kortekangas, Otso. *Language, Citizenship, and Sámi Education in the Nordic North, 1900–1940*. Montreal and Kingston: McGill-Queen's University Press, 2021.

Kotierk, Aluki. Presentation to the Senate Standing Committee on Aboriginal Peoples on Bill C-91 Indigenous Languages Act, 2 April 2019.

———. Remarks to the United Nations Permanent Forum on Indigenous Issues, 16 April 2018.

Kristinsson, Ari Pál, and Amanda Hilmarsson-Dunn. "Unequal Language Rights in the Nordic Language Community." *Language Problems and Language Planning* 36, no. 3 (2012): 222–36.

Kroik, David. "Language Teacher Identity and Language Acquisition in a South Saami Preschool: A Narrative Inquiry." *Australian Journal of Indigenous Education* 51, no. 2 (2022): 1–16.

Kulchyski, Peter. *Aboriginal Rights Are Not Human Rights: In Defence of Indigenous Struggles*. Winnipeg: ARP Books, 2013.

Langlois, Stéphanie, and Annie Turner. *Aboriginal Languages and Selected Vitality Indicators in 2011*. Ottawa: Statistics Canada, 2014.

Lavell-Harvard, Dawn Memee, and Jeannette Corbiere Lavell, eds. *"Until Our Hearts Are on the Ground": Aboriginal Mothering, Oppression, Resistance and Rebirth*. Coe Hill: Demeter Press, 2006.

Lee, Naa Huiying, and John Van Way. "Assessing Levels of Endangerment in the Catalogue of Endangered Languages (ELCat) Using the Language Endangerment Index (LEI)." *Language in Society* 45 (2016): 271–92.

Lemkin, Raphael. *Axis Rule in Occupied Europe: Laws of Occupation, Analysis of Government, Proposal of Redress*. Washington: Carnegie Endowment for International Peace, 1944.

Lepage, Jean-François and Stéphanie Langlois, with Martin Turcotte. "Evolution of the Language Situation in Nunavut, 2001 to 2016." Statistics Canada, Catalogue no. 89-657-X2019010. 9 July 2019.

LeRat, Harold, and Linda Ungar. *Treaty Promises, Indian Reality: Life on a Reserve*. Saskatoon: Purich, 2005.

Lloyd-Smith, Anika, Fabian Bergmann, Laura Hund, and Tanja Kupisch. "Can Policies Improve Language Vitality? The Sámi Languages in Sweden and Norway." *Frontiers in Psychology* 14 (2023) 1059696–1059696. doi:10.3389/fpsyg.2023.1059696.

López, Luis Enrique. Paper commissioned for the Education for all Global Monitoring Report 2010. "Reaching the Unreached: Indigenous Intercultural Bilingual Education in Latin America." 2009. UNESCO, 2010/ED/EFA/MRT/PI/29.

Loppie Reading, C., and F. Wien. "Health Inequalities and Social Determinants of Aboriginal Peoples' Health." Prince George: National Collaborating Centre for Aboriginal Health, 2009.

Mabindisa, Isaac Kholisile. "The Praying Man: The Life and Times of Henry Bird Steinhauer." PhD diss., University of Alberta, 1984.

MacLean, John. *James Evans, Inventor of the Syllabic System of the Cree Language*. Toronto: W. Briggs. 1890.

Malksoo, Lauri. "Language Rights in International Law: Why the Phoenix Is Still in the Ashes." *Florida Journal of International Law* 12, no. 3 (1999): 431–65.

Manitoba Indian Brotherhood. *Wahbung: Our Tomorrows*. Winnipeg: Manitoba Indian Brotherhood, 1971.

Martin, Ian. "Inuit Language Loss in Nunavut: Analysis, Forecast, and Recommendations." Unpublished report, 2017.

Mason, William. Letter from Hudson's Bay Territories to the Church Missionary Society, Church Mission Society Archives. University of Birmingham. GY C1 042 3, 1854.

Matthew, Robert. T'selcéwtqen Clleq'mel'ten/Chief Atahm School. Presentation the Standing Committee onAboriginal Peoples on Bill C-91, An Act Respecting Indigenous Languages, 42nd Parliament, 1st Session. 3 April 2019.

McCarty, Teresa L. "Indigenous Language Revitalization." In *Encyclopedia of Bilingual Education*, edited by Josué M. González. Los Angeles: Sage, 2008. 389-90.

———. *Ethnography and Language Policy*. New York: Routledge, 2011.

McCarty, Teresa L., Mary Eunice Romero, and Ofelia Zepeda. "Reclaiming the Gift: Indigenous Youth Counter-Narratives on Native Language Loss and Revitalization." *American Indian Quarterly* 30, no. 1/2 (2006): 28–48.

McEvoy, John P. "Language Rights: Aboriginal People (New Brunswick, Canada)." *Canadian Law Libraries* 22, no. 4. (1997): 156–58.

McInnes, Brian D. *Sounding Thunder: The Stories of Francis Pegahmagabow.* Winnipeg: University of Manitoba Press, 2016.

McIvor, Onowa. Paper presented at 17th FEL Conference on Endangered Languages Beyond Boundaries."Protective Effects of Language Learning, Use and Culture on the Health and Well-being of Indigenous People in Canada." Ottawa, ON, 2–4 October 2013.

McIvor, Onowa, Art Napoleon, and Kerissa M. Dickie. "Language and Culture as Protective Factors for At-risk Communities." *Journal of Aboriginal Health* 5, no. 1 (2009): 6–25.

McLachlin, Beverley. "Reconciling Unity and Diversity in the Modern Era: Tolerance and Intolerance." The Global Centre for Pluralism, Aga Khan Museum, Toronto, ON, 28 May 2015.

McLeod, Neal. *Cree Narrative Memory: From Treaties to Contemporary Times.* Saskatoon: Purich, 2007.

McMillan, Barbara. "Educating for Cultural Survival in Nunavut: Why Haven't We Learned from the Past?" *Paideusis* 22, no. 2 (2015): 24–37.

McNab, David. "Herman Merivale and the Native Question, 1837–1861." *Albion: A Quarterly Journal Concerned with British Studies* 9, no. 4 (1977): 359–84.

Miller, J.R. *Shingwauk's Vision: A History of Native Residential Schools.* Toronto: University of Toronto Press, 1996.

Milloy, John Sheridan. *A National Crime: The Canadian Government and the Residential School System, 1879 to 1986.* Winnipeg: University of Manitoba Press, 1999.

Minutes of a Conference by the Revs. J. Horden and E.A. Watkins on the Subject of the Syllabrium in use for the Cree and Esquimaux Languages, November 24. Church Mission Society Archives. University of Birmingham. GY C1 6a, 1865.

Miscellaneous Papers from the Diocese of Moosonee. Correspondence overseas with General Secretary. Church Mission Society Archives. University of Birmingham. GY C1 6a, 1865.

Moon, Paul. *Ka Ngaro Te Reo: Māori Language under Siege in the Nineteenth Century.* Dunedin: Otago University Press, 2016.

Morris, Alexander. *The Treaties of Canada with the Indians of Manitoba and the North-West Territories, Including the Negotiations on Which They Were Based, and Other Information Relating Thereto.* Belfords, Clarke, 1880 repr. Saskatoon: Fifth House Publishers, 1991.

Morris, Jeston. "Native American Languages Summit 2014: Self-Determination as a Strategy for Language Revitalization and Maintenance." *Journal of American Indian Education* 54, no. 3 (2015): 125–44.

Morton, Arthur Silver, and Lewis Gwynne Thomas. *A History of the Canadian West to 1870–71: Being a History of Rupert's Land (the Hudson's Bay Company's Territory) and of the North-West Territory (including the Pacific Slope).* 2nd ed. Toronto: University of Toronto Press, 1973; published in cooperation with University of Saskatchewan.

Murdoch, John. "Syllabics: A Successful Educational Innovation." MA thesis, University of Manitoba, 1981.

Murray, Jessica, Erin Aupanekis, and Karen Rempel. "Cree Language Survey Results Opaskwayak Cree Nation." The Pas: Opaskwayak Educational Authority, 2013.

Naesborg-Andersen, Ayo, and Bassah Khalaf. "The Right of Indigenous Peoples to Education in Their Own Language—Greenlanders in Denmark and in Greenland." *Yearbook of Polar Law* 9, no. 1 (2018): 79–108.

National Collaborating Centre for Aboriginal Health. *Culture and Language as Social Determinants of First Nations, Inuit and Métis Health*. Social Determinants of Health. Prince George, BC: National Collaborating Centre for Aboriginal Health, 2016. https://www.ccnsa-nccah.ca/docs/determinants/FS-CultureLanguage-SDOH-FNMI-EN.pdf.

National Indian Brotherhood. *Indian Control of Indian Education*. Ottawa: National Indian Brotherhood, 1972.

———. Submission to the Special Joint Committee on the Constitution, 1980–81. Letter to Senator Harry Hays from Dilbert Riley, President of the National Indian Brotherhood, 11 November 1980. Accessed 31 March 2017. http://historyofrights.ca/wp-content/uploads/committee/nib.pdf.

National Inquiry into Missing and Murdered Indigenous Women and Girls. *Reclaiming Power and Place*. Vol. 1a. Gatineau: National Inquiry into Missing and Murdered Indigenous Women and Girls, 2019.

———. *Supplementary Report—A Legal Analysis of Genocide*. Ottawa, 2019.

Nettle, Daniel, and Suzanne Romaine. *Vanishing Voices: The Extinction of the World's Languages*. Oxford: Oxford University Press, 2000.

Nitah, Steven. "One Land—Many Voices: Report of the NWT Special Committee on the Review of the Official Languages Act." *Canadian Parliamentary Review* 25, no. 3 (2002): 4–8.

Nock, David A. *A Victorian Missionary and Canadian Indian Policy: Cultural Synthesis vs Cultural Placement*. Waterloo: Wilfrid Laurier University Press, 1988.

Norris, Mary Jane. "Aboriginal Languages in Canada: Trends and Perspectives on Maintenance and Revitalization." *Aboriginal Policy Research Consortium International (APRCi)* 122 (2006): 197–226.

———. "Canada and Greenland." In *UNESCO Atlas of the World's Languages in Danger*, 3rd ed., edited by Chris Moseley. Paris: UNESCO Publishing, 2010.

———. "Canada's Aboriginal Languages." *Canadian Social Trends* 51 (1998): 8–16.

———. Report and Reference Manual on Documentation and Classification of Aboriginal Languages in Canada, 3rd ed. Unpublished report originally prepared for Aboriginal Affairs Directorate, Department of Canadian Heritage. Norris Research Inc, 2016.

Norris Research. Demographic, Socio-Economic, and Language Research on Indigenous Peoples in Canada, 2016.

Northern Public Affairs. "Canada and UNDRIP: Indigenous Leaders Respond to the Announcement." 11 May 2016. www.northernpublicaffairs.ca/index/canada-undrip-indigenous-leaders-respond-to-announcement/.

Norton, Ruth. "Aboriginal Languages: Multiplicity and Insufficiencies." In *Les droits linguistiques au Canada: collusions ou collisions?*, edited by Sylvie Léger, Proceedings of the First Conference, University of Ottawa, 4–6 November 1993. Ottawa: Centre canadien des droits linguistiques, University of Ottawa, 1995.

Nunavut Tunngavik Incorporated. "Inuit Are Maintaining Inuktut Despite Mulroney Cabinet Secret Instructions to Block Its Use." News release, 5 December 2019.

Oestreich, J.E. "Liberal Theory and Minority Group Rights." *Human Rights Quarterly* 21 (1999): 108–32.

Office of the Independent Special Interlocutor for Missing Children and Unmarked Graves and Burial Sites associated with Indian Residential Schools, "Sites of Truth, Sites of Conscience: Unmarked Burials and Mass Graves of Missing and Disappeared Indigenous Children in Canada," 2024.

Olthuis, Marja-Liisa, Suvi Kivelä, and Tove Skutnabb-Kangas. *Revitalising Indigenous Languages: How to Recreate a Lost Generation*. Linguistic Diversity and Language Rights. Bristol: Multilingual Matters, 2013.

Origins of Cree Syllabics conference. Centre for Race and Culture. Edmonton, Alberta, 4–5 June 2013.

Oster, Richard T., Angela Grier, Rick Lightning, Maria J. Mayan, and Ellen L. Toth. "Cultural Continuity, Traditional Indigenous Language, and Diabetes in Alberta First Nations: A Mixed Methods Study." *International Journal for Equity in Health* 13 (2014): 1–11.

Parkinson, Phil. "'Strangers in the House': The Maori Language in Government and the Maori Language in Parliament 1865–1900." *Victoria University of Wellington Law Review* 32, no. 3 (2001): 856–914.

Pasanen, Annika. "Becoming a New Speaker of Saami Languages through Intensive Adult Education." In *Rejecting the Marginalized Status of Minority Languages: Educational Projects Pushing Back Against Language Endangerment*, edited by Susan D. Penfield and Ari Sherris. Blue Ridge Summit: Multilingual Matters, 2019.

Pettipas, Katherine. *The Diary of the Reverend Henry Budd, 1870–1875*. Winnipeg: Manitoba Record Society, 1974.

Phillipson, Robert. "Indigenous Children's Education as Linguistic Genocide and a Crime against Humanity? A Global View." *Journal of Contemporary European Studies* 20, no. 3 (2012): 377–81.

Ponting, J. Rick. *Arduous Journey: Canadian Indians and Decolonization*. Toronto: McClelland and Stewart, 1988.

"Public Law 101-477: Native American Languages Act." *Journal of American Indian Education* 51, no. 3 (2012): 9–11.

"Public Law 102-524: Native American Languages Act of 1992." *Journal of American Indian Education* 51, no. 3 (2012): 12–14.

Rawlins, Nāmaka, William Pila Wilson, and Keiki Kawaiʻaeʻa. "Bill Demmert, Native American Language Revitalization, and His Hawai'i Connection." *Journal of American Indian Education* 50, no. 1 (2011): 74–85.

Ray, Arthur J. *Indians in the Fur Trade: Their Role as Trappers, Hunters, and Middlemen in the Lands Southwest of Hudson Bay, 1660–1870; With a New Introduction*. Toronto: University of Toronto Press, 1998.

Reardon, James Michael. *George Anthony Belcourt: Pioneer Catholic Missionary of the Northwest, 1803–1874; His Life and Times*. St. Paul: North Central Publishing, 1955.

Réaume, Denise G. "The Demise of the Political Compromise Doctrine: Have Official Language Use Rights Been Revived?" *McGill Law Journal* 47, no. 3 (2002): 593–624.

Réaume, Denise, and Leslie Green. "Education and Linguistic Security in the Charter." *McGill Law Journal* 34, no. 4 (1989): 777–816.

Robson, Joseph. *An Account of Six Years Residence in Hudson's-Bay: From 1733 to 1736, and 1744 to 1747 : Containing a Variety of Facts, Observations and Discoveries, Tending to Shew, I. the Vast Importance of the Countries about Hudson's-Bay to Great Britain . . . II. the Interested View of the Hudson's-Bay Company . . . : To Which Is Added an Appendix, Containing, I. a Short History of the Discovery of Hudson's-Bay . . . the Whole Illustrated by a Draught of Churchill-River, and Plans of York-Fort, and Prince of Wales's Fort*. Printed for T. Jeffreys, 1759.

Rodriguez, Pablo. Minister of Canadian Heritage and Multiculturalism Proceedings of the Standing Senate Committee on Aboriginal Peoples Issue 55—Evidence, 28 May 2019. 42nd Parliament, 1st Session.

Romaine, Suzanne. "Language Endangerment and Language Death." In *The Routledge Handbook of Ecolinguistics*, edited by Alwin F. Fill and Hermine Penz. Accessed 26 December 2023. London: Routledge, 2017. https://www.routledgehandbooks.com/doi/10.4324/9781315687391.ch3.

Rosenberg, Sheri P. "Genocide Is a Process, Not an Event." *Genocide Studies and Prevention* 7, no. 1 (2012): 16–23.

Ross, Alexander. *The Red River Settlement: Its Rise, Progress, and Present State with Some Account of the Native Races and Its General History to the Present Day.* 1856. Reprint, Edmonton: Hurtig, 1972.

Ruckstuhl, Katharina. "Public Policy and Indigenous Language Rights: Aotearoa New Zealand's Māori Language Act 2016." *Current Issues in Language Planning* 19, no. 3 (2018): 316–29.

Russell, Dale R. *Eighteenth-Century Western Cree and Their Neighbours*. Hull: Canadian Museum of Civilization, 1991.

Saaresranta, Tiina. "Education in Pursuit of the Development Dream? Effects of Schooling on Indigenous Development and Rights in Bolivia." *Nordic Journal of Human Rights* 32, no. 4 (2014): 352–71.

Saddleback, Jerry. "Cree Syllabics." Paper presented at Origins of Cree Syllabics conference, Edmonton, Alberta, 4–5 June 2013.

Sarkadi, Laurie. "N.W.T. Wants 8 Official Tongues." *Edmonton Journal*, 6 April 1990.

Seegerts, A. *The Gift of Language and Culture: Documenting the Success of the Onion Lake Cree Immersion Program and the Need for Ongoing Development, Expansion, and Committed Funding Resources*. Regina: Federation of Saskatchewan Indian Nations, 2002.

Shkilnyk, Anastasia M. *Canada's Aboriginal Languages: An Overview of Current Activities in Language Retention*. Ottawa: Department of the Secretary of State, 1985.

Sinclair, Murray, Mazina Giizhik. Proceedings of the Standing Senate Committee on Aboriginal Peoples Issue 55—Evidence, 28 May 2019. 42nd Parliament, 1st Session.

Sinclair, Murray, Mazina Giizhik, Sara Sinclair, and Niigaan Sinclair. *Who We Are: Four Questions for a Life and a Nation.* New York: McClelland and Stewart, 2024.

Skerrett, Mere, and Jenny Ritchie. "Te Rangatiratanga o Te Reo: Sovereignty in Indigenous Languages in Early Childhood Education in Aotearoa." *Kōtuitui* 16, no. 2 (2021): 250–64.

Skutnabb-Kangas, Tove. "Language Rights and Revitalization." In *The Routledge Handbook of Language Revitalization*, edited by Leanne Hinton, Leena Huss, and Gerald Roche. New York: Routledge, 2018.

———. *Linguistic Genocide in Education—or Worldwide Diversity and Human Rights?* Mahwah: Lawrence Erlbaum Associates, 2000.

———. "Marvellous Human Rights Rhetoric and Grim Realities—Language Rights in Education." *Journal of Language, Identity, and Education* 1, no. 3 (2002): 179–205.

Skutnabb-Kangas, Tove, and Robert Dunbar. *Indigenous Children's Education as Linguistic Genocide and a Crime Against Humanity? A Global View.* Guovdageaidnu/Kautokeino: Gáldu, Resource Centre for the Rights of Indigenous Peoples, 2010.

Skutnabb-Kangas, Tove, Robert Phillipson, and Robert Dunbar. *Is Nunavut Education Criminally Inadequate? An Analysis of Current Policies for Inuktut and English in Education, International and National Law, Linguistic and Cultural Genocide and Crimes Against Humanity*. n.d. Accessed 20 May 2024. https://www.tunngavik.com/files/2019/04/NuLinguicideReportFINAL.pdf.

Skutnabb-Kangas, Tove, and Robert Phillipson. "Linguicide." In *Concise Encyclopedia of Sociolinguistics*, Rajend Mesthrie and R.E. Asher. Elsevier Science and Technology, 2001.

———. eds. *Linguistic Human Rights: Overcoming Linguistic Discrimination.* Berlin: Mouton de Gruyter, 1995.

Slattery, Brian. "Aboriginal Language Rights." In *Language and the State: The Law and Politics of Identity: Proceedings of the Second National Conference on Constitutional Affairs,* edited by David Schneiderman. Centre for Constitutional Studies. Montreal and Cowansville: Éditions Yvon Blais, 1991.

———. "The Generative Structure of Aboriginal Rights." *Supreme Court Law Review* (2d) 38 (2007): 595–628.

———. "The Legal Basis of Aboriginal Title." In *Aboriginal Title in British Columbia: Delgamuukw v. The Queen*, edited by Frank Cassidy. Montreal: Institute for Research on Public Policy, 1992.

———. "The Organic Constitution: Aboriginal People and the Evolution of Canada." *Osgoode Hall Law Journal* 34, no. 1 (1996): 101–112.

———. "A Taxonomy of Aboriginal Rights." In *Let Right Be Done: Aboriginal Title, the Calder Case, and the Future of Aboriginal Rights*, edited by Hamar Foster, Heather Raven, and Jeremy Webber. Vancouver: UBC Press, 2007.

———. "Understanding Aboriginal Rights." *The Canadian Bar Review* 66 (1987): 727–83.

Sluman, Norma, and Jean Goodwill. *John Tootoosis.* Winnipeg: Pemmican Publications, 1984.

Smith, Donald B. *Sacred Feathers: The Reverend Peter Jones (Kahkewaquonaby) and the Mississauga Indians.* Lincoln: University of Nebraska Press, 1987.

Smith, Linda Tuhiwai. *Decolonizing Methodologies: Research and Indigenous Peoples.* 3rd Ed. London: Zed Books, 2011.

Smyth, Steven. "Colonialism and Language in Canada's North: A Yukon Case Study," *Arctic* 49, no. 2 (June 1996): 155–61.

Starks, Donna, Ray Harlow, and Allan Bell. "Who speaks what language in New Zealand." *Languages of New Zealand* (2005): 13–29.

Stavenhagen, Rodolfo. "Linguistic Minorities and Language Policy in Latin America: The Case of Mexico." In *Linguistic Minorities and Literacy: Language Policy Issues in Developing Countries*, edited by Florian Coulmas. Berlin: De Gruyter Mouton, 1984.

———. *Report of the Special Rapporteur on the Situation of Human Rights and Fundamental Freedoms of Indigenous People, Rodolfo Stavenhagen.* 6 January 2005. United Nations Commission on Human Rights, Economic and Social Council. UN Doc E/CN.4/2005/88.

———. "Taonga, Rights and Interests: Some Observations on the Framework of Protections for Māori Language." *Victoria University of Wellington Law Review* 42, no. 2 (2001): 241–58.

Stevenson, Winona L. "The Church Missionary Society Red River Mission and the Emergence of a Native Ministry 1820–1860, with a Case Study of Charles Pratt of Touchwood Hills." MA thesis, University of British Columbia, 1988.

St-Onge, Pascale. Pascale St-Onge, Minister of Canadian Heritage to Mr. John Aldag, Chair, Standing Committee on Indigenous and Northern Affairs. 15 October 2023.

Syllabrium Adapted to the Cree, Saulteaux and to the Esquimaux Languages, Church Mission Society Archives. University of Birmingham. GY C1 1F, 1865.

Syllabrium for the Cree Language and Syllabrium Prepared for the Esquimaux Language. Church Missionary Society Records, Church Mission Society Archives. University of Birmingham. GY C1 1F, 1865.

Task Force on Aboriginal Languages and Cultures. *Towards a New Beginning: A Foundational Report for a Strategy to Revitalize First Nation, Inuit and Métis Languages and Cultures.* Report to the Minister of Canadian Heritage. Ottawa: Task Force on Aboriginal Languages and Cultures, June 2005.

Terry Teegee, British Columbia, Assembly of First Nations. National Chief Perry Bellegarde Brief presnted to the Standing Committee on Indigenous Peoples. 42nd Parlialment, 1st Session, 20 March 2019.

Translated Letter from Cree Syllabics to English. Church Missionary Society Records, Church Mission Society Archives. University of Birmingham. C1 0 33 117, 1865.

Truth and Reconciliation Commission of Canada. *Calls to Action.* Truth and Reconciliation Commission of Canada, 2012.

———. *Canada's Residential Schools: The History, Part 1, Origins to 1939.* Vol. 1 of *The Final Report of the Truth and Reconciliation Commission of Canada* Montreal and Kingston: McGill-Queen's University Press, 2015.

———. *Canada's Residential Schools: The Legacy*. Vol. 5 of *The Final Report of the Truth and Reconciliation Commission of Canada*. Montreal and Kingston: McGill-Queen's University Press, 2016.

———. *Final Report of the Truth and Reconciliation Commission of Canada. Volume One, Summary : Honouring the Truth, Reconciling for the Future*. Toronto: James Lorimer and Company, 2015.

Timpson, Annis May. "Reconciling Indigenous and Settler Language Interests: Language Policy Initiatives in Nunavut." *Journal of Canadian Studies* 43, no. 2 (2009): 159–80.

Titley, Brian E. *A Narrow Vision: Duncan Campbell Scott and the Administration of Indian Affairs*. Vancouver: University of British Columbia Press, 1986.

Treaty 7 Elders and Tribal Council, with Walter Hildebrandt, Sarah Carter, and Dorothy First Rider. *The True Spirit and Original Intent of Treaty 7*. Montreal and Kingston: McGill-Queen's University Press, 1997.

Tulloch, Shelley, and Victoria Hust. "An Analysis of Language Provisions in the Nunavut Act and the Nunavut Land Claims Agreement." In *Arctic Economic Development and Self-Government*, edited by G. Duhaime and N. Bernard. Quebec: GETIC, Université Laval, 2003.

Usborne, Esther, Josephine Peck, Donna-Lee Smith, and Donald M. Taylor. "Learning through an Aboriginal Language: The Impact on Students' English and Aboriginal Language Skills." *Canadian Journal of Education* 34, no. 4 (2011): 200–15.

Usher, Jean. "Apostles and Aborigines: The Social Theory of the Church Missionary Society." *Histoire Sociale/Social History* 7 (1971): 28–52.

Vargra, Peter. "Nunavut Officials Say Bill 37 Will Strengthen." *Nunatsiaq News* online, 13 March 2017. https://nunatsiaq.com/stories/article/65674nunavut_officials_say_bill_37_will_strengthen_deas/.

Vikor, Lars S. *The Nordic Languages: Their Status and Interrelations*. Oslo: Novus Press, 1993.

Voce, Antonio, Leyland Cecco, and Chris Michael. "'Cultural Genocide': The Shameful History of Canada's Residential Schools—Mapped." *The Guardian*. 6 September 2021.

Walters, Mark. "British Imperial Constitutional Law and Aboriginal Rights: A Comment on *Delgamuukw v. British Columbia*." *Queen's Law Journal* 17 (1992): 350–413.

Warhol, Larisa. "Legacies of NALA: The Esther Martinez Native American Languages Preservation Act and Implications for Language Revitalization Policy and Practice." *Journal of American Indian Education* 51, no. 3 (2012): 70–91.

———. "Native American Language Education as Policy-in-Practice: An Interpretative Policy Analysis of the Native American Languages Act of 1990/1992." *International Journal of Bilingual Education and Bilingualism* 14, no. 3 (2011): 279–99.

Warkentin, John, Arthur G. Doughty, and Chester Martin. *The Kelsey Papers*. Regina: Canadian Plains Research Center, University of Regina, 1994.

Watkins, E.A. *A Dictionary of the Cree Language: As Spoken by the Indians of the Hudson's Bay Company's Territories*. London: Society for Promoting Christian Knowledge, 1865.

———. E.A. Watkins to Church Mission Society Archives. University of Birmingham. GY C1 5, 10 February 1865.

Watkins, E.A., J.A. Mackay, R. Faries, Church of England in Canada General Synod. *A Dictionary of the Cree Language: As Spoken by the Indians in the Provinces of Quebec, Ontario, Manitoba, Saskatchewan and Alberta*. Toronto: Published under the direction of the General Synod of the Church of England in Canada, 1938.

Watts, Isaac, and John Horden. *Watts' First Catechism for Children*. Moose Factory: Printed by J. Horden, 1855.

Weber, Bob. "Why Have Nunavut? Battle Over Education Bill Goes to the Heart of Territory." *National Observer* online, 19 March 2017. https://www.nationalobserver.com/2017/03/19/news/why-have-nunavut-battle-over-education-bill-goes-heart-territory.

West, John. *Report to the Hudson's Bay Company and the Church Missionary Society*, 3 December 1823. Public Archives of Canada, Church Mission Society Archives, A. 98, 96.

Whillans, James W. *First in the West: The Story of Henry Kelsey, Discoverer of Canadian Prairies*. Edmonton: Applied Art Products, 1955.

White, Louellyn. *Free to Be Mohawk: Indigenous Education at the Akwesasne Freedom School*. Norman: University of Oklahoma Press, 2015.

Willis, Jane. *Geniesh: An Indian Girlhood*. Toronto: New Press, 1973.

Wilson, Katherine J., Andrew Arreak, Jamesie Itulu, Sikumiut Community Management Committee, Gita J. Ljubicic, and Trevor Bell. "'When We're on the Ice, All We Have Is Our Inuit Qaujimajatuqangit': Mobilizing Inuit Knowledge as a Sea Ice Safety Adaptation Strategy in Mittimatalik, Nunavut." *Arctic* 74, no. 4 (2021): 525–49.

Wilson-Raybould, Jody. "Special Statement at the Opening Ceremonies of the United Nations Permanent Forum on Indigenous Issues, 15th Session" 9 May 2016. Accessed 2 November 2024. https://www.canada.ca/en/department-justice/news/2016/05/special-statement-at-the-opening-ceremonies-of-the-united-nations-permanent-forum-on-indigenous-issues-15th-session.html.

Winsa, Birger. "Language Planning in Sweden." *Journal of Multilingual and Multicultural Development* 20, no. 4–5 (1999): 376–473.

Winstead, Teresa, Adrea Lawrence, Edward J. Brantmeier, and Christopher J. Frey. "Language, Sovereignty, Cultural Contestation, and American Indian Schools: No Child Left Behind and a Navajo Test Case." *Journal of American Indian Education* 47, no. 1 (2008): 46–64.

Woolford, Andrew John. *This Benevolent Experiment: Indigenous Boarding Schools, Genocide, and Redress in Canada and the United States*. Lincoln: University of Nebraska Press, 2015.

———. "Unsettling Genocide Studies at the Eleventh Conference of the International Association of Genocide Scholars, July 16–19, 2014, Winnipeg-Canada," *Genocide Studies and Prevention: An International Journal* 9, no. 2 (2015): 98–102. doi:10.5038/1911-9933.9.2.1321.

Young, Doris. Personal communication. September 2007.

INDEX